Enhancing the Auditor's Fraud Detection Ability

European University Studies

Europäische Hochschulschriften

Publications Universitaires Européennes

Series V

Economics and Management

Reihe V Série V

Volks- und Betriebswirtschaft

Sciences économiques, gestion d'entreprise

Vol./Bd. 2727

PETER LANG

Frankfurt am Main · Berlin · Bern · Bruxelles · New York · Oxford · Wien

Maria Krambia-Kapardis

Enhancing the Auditor's Fraud Detection Ability

An Interdisciplinary Approach

PETER LANG
Europäischer Verlag der Wissenschaften

Die Deutsche Bibliothek - CIP-Einheitsaufnahme

Maria Krambia-Kapardis:

Enhancing the Auditor's Fraud Detection Ability : An Interdisciplinary Approach / Maria Krambia-Kapardis. - Frankfurt am Main ; Berlin ; Bern ; Bruxelles ; New York ; Oxford ; Wien : Lang, 2001
(European university studies : Ser. 5, Economics and Management ; Vol. 2727)
Zugl.: Edith Cowan, Univ., Diss., 1999
ISBN 3-631-36972-7

ISSN 0531-7339
ISBN 3-631-36972-7
US-ISBN 0-8204-4807-9

To my children Elena and Kostandinos Raphael, my husband Andros and my parents.

Table of Contents

Preface and Acknowledgements

A contemporary issue of concern to both external auditors and financial statement users is fraud-detection by auditors. My own interest in fraud detection by auditors was aroused in the late 1980's while working as an auditor with a large accounting firm in Melbourne, Australia. The ability of auditors to detect material irregularities, including fraud, should be enhanced to enable them to apply "reasonable skill and care" in carrying out the audit. Such proficiency in fraud detection is needed if the profession is to avoid costly litigation, ever-increasing indemnity insurance and erosion of the profession's credibility. In the pages that follow it is argued that such enhancement can be achieved if auditors both utilise knowledge about the aetiology of fraud in psychology, sociology and criminology as well as synthesise a broad range of approaches to fraud detection.

In an attempt to fill a significant gap in our knowledge, following an outline of the background and motivation of the research reported, a multidisciplinary discussion of the aetiology of fraud enables the development of a three-component model which comprises: rationalisations (R), opportunity (O) and a crime-prone motivated person (P), hence the acronym ROP. Next, the book examines closely relevant auditing guidelines and a number of fraud detection models that have been proposed in order to develop an eclectic fraud detection model (with the ROP model as one of its components).

A study of 50 major fraud cases investigated and prosecuted by the Major Fraud Group (MFG) of the Victoria Police in Australia is then reported which tested the applicability of the ROP model. The study identified a number of inter-relationships between offence, offender and victim characteristics. The findings obtained also confirm the applicability of the model in the field and have yielded a two-level criminal profile of serious fraud offenders which includes a new taxonomy of such offenders. The taxonomy consists of twelve specific typologies. In addition, the MFG study findings cast doubt on Gottfredson and Hirschi's (1990) assertion in their *General Theory of Crime* that white-collar offenders are not significantly different from common offenders.

Findings are also reported from a postal survey of 108 auditors which investigated the experience of auditors with detecting six different types of material irregularities, including management fraud, employee fraud and error. The findings provide support for the applicability of the eclectic fraud detection model. The survey has also found that: it is rare for even experienced auditors to encounter material irregularities; that different types of irregularity (e.g., management fraud) occur more frequently in some industries (manufacturing and construction) than in others; the irregularity is likely to take one form (e.g., window dressing and misappropriation of funds) rather than another and finally that management review and tests of controls are more likely to alert an auditor to the existence of management fraud. In support of earlier research findings, data analysis reveals that the lack of an effective internal control system and the absence of a code of corporate conduct are statistically significant correlates of an irregularity having a material impact on the financial accounts of a company. In contrast to claims by earlier researchers, the survey findings show that fraud risk-assessment utilising red flags alone is not effective.

Both the ROP model and the eclectic fraud detection model are further refined in the light of the findings from the two empirical studies. Without ignoring limitations of the two surveys, the work reported in this book sheds new light on the aetiology of fraud, shows that neither audit experience nor red flags alone is sufficient to improve auditors' fraud detection performance and provides another dimension to fraud risk-assessment. The new knowledge should be added to the auditor's armoury to enhance the audit effectiveness and efficiency and to reduce the fraud detection component of the expectation gap.

This book is an adaptation of my doctoral dissertation thesis. The work reported in this book would not have been possible without the assistance received from a number of individuals, including: my doctoral supervisor Professor Gary S. Monroe; Commander Allen Bowles for permitting me access to Victoria Police files on major fraud that enabled me to carry out one of the two components of my empirical research and all the detectives who assisted in locating the files and discussed particular cases with me; all those accountants who responded to my questionnaire. In addition, the Departments of Accounting of Edith Cowan University and Victoria University of Technology provided financial support for the empirical part of the thesis. Publication of the book has been made possible with financial assistance from Mr. Vasos Galatariotis and the Latsia Municipality. I am grateful to both of them. Finally, the present work would not have been possible without the moral support, patience and understanding of my husband, children and parents. As this book goes to print a sense of gratitude goes to all of them. Of course, none of the individuals mentioned are responsible for any weaknesses, mistakes or opinions expressed in the pages that follow.

November, 2000

Maria Krambia-Kapardis
Associate Professor
Intercollege, Nicosia, Cyprus.

Abbreviations

AAERs	Securities and Exchange Commission and Auditing Enforcement Releases (U.S.)
AICPA	American Institute of Certified Public Accountants
APB	Auditing Practices Board (U.K)
ASC	Australian Securities Commission
ASCPA	Australian Society of Certified Practising Accountants
AUS	Auditing Standards (Australia)
AuSB	Auditing Standards Board (Australia)
COSO	Commission on Sponsoring Organisations of the Treadway Commission (U.S)
CICA	Canadian Institute of Chartered Accountants
DPP	Director of Public Prosecutions
ICAA	The Institute of Chartered Accountants in Australia
ICAEW	Institute of Chartered Accountants of England and Wales
IFAC	International Federation of Accountants
MFG	Major Fraud Group of the Victoria Police, Australia
NCA	National Crime Authority, Australia
NCSC	National Companies and Securities Commission, Australia
NZSA	New Zealand Society of Accountants
ROP	ROP Model of fraud aetiology

CHAPTER 1

INTRODUCTION

- Auditors' responsibilities for fraud detection
- Justifying research into fraud-detection by auditors

BACKGROUND AND MOTIVATION FOR THE RESEARCH

Auditor's responsibilities for fraud detection

Acts that result in a materially misstated financial report are of particular interest to auditors. Fraud for or against a company can take the form of fraudulent financial reporting, also known as management fraud (i.e., "intentional misstatements or omissions of amounts or disclosures in financial statements") and misappropriation of assets or employee fraud, also known as defalcation (i.e., "theft of an entity's assets"). The terms "fraud" (including management and employee fraud) and "irregularity" are used interchangeably.

The Australian Accounting Research Foundation AUS 210 (AARF) (1995a, para.05(a)), defines fraud "as any act which involves the use of deception to obtain an illegal advantage", i.e., the misappropriation of assets or intentional misstatements in the accounts by management, employees or third parties. Fraud may involve: manipulation, falsification or alteration of records or documents; suppression or omission of the effects of transactions from records or documents; and/or recording of transactions without substance; or misapplication of accounting policies (AUS 210, para.07). The key concept is deception intended to financially benefit the deceiver in one way or another.

Auditors have responsibilities for detecting and reporting fraud. Auditing Standards and rulings by the courts in English-speaking western common law countries such as the U.K, U.S, Canada, Australia and New Zealand provide guidance on this matter. As far as the common law is concerned, a close examination of the relevant judicial pronouncements in Australia and the U.K[1] shows that it has been a mixed blessing for the auditing profession (see Godsell, 1990 for a discussion). Over the years, it has clarified the auditor's responsibilities in carrying out an audit; it has cast doubt on the auditor's ability[2] to safeguard the investors' interests by ensuring that fraud and error are detected, and has defended the auditor who is deceived by management[3]. The relevant common law also demonstrates that

[1] Until 22 years ago, developments in the common law in Australia used to follow English precedent. Today, even though decisions by courts in England and Wales are not binding on Australian courts, they are considered relevant and are cited with approval.

[2] LJ Chelmsford in *Spackman v. Evans* (1868), 3 L.R. 171; Coleridge, LJ in *Arnold v. Armitage* 1885, 1 TLR 670.

[3] Lopes, LJ in *Re Kingston Cotton Mill* Ltd (No. 2) [1896]2 Ch. 279, at 290.

while auditors do not have a legal duty to detect fraud *per se* they have a legal duty to audit with due care and skill[4] and that includes considering the possibility of fraud[5], "if there is anything calculated to excite suspicion he should probe it to the bottom"[6], and reporting suspicions about fraud to the appropriate entity[7]. It should be noted that "what is reasonable skill, care and caution must depend on the circumstances of each case"[8].

Internationally[9], both the accounting profession as well as governments have invested heavily in the issue of the cost of fraud and fraud detection by auditors. The auditing profession in Australia, U.K., U.S., together with the International Federation of Accountants, state in their auditing standards[10] that the responsibility for the prevention and detection of irregularities rests with management and that auditors should plan and conduct the audit so as to have a reasonable expectation of detecting fraud and other irregularities. It is explained further that while the auditor does have a legal and professional duty to exercise reasonable skill and care in planning and conducting the audit, the auditor does not have a similar responsibility to detect irregularities that do not have a material financial impact[11].

---

[4] Lindley, LJ in *Re London and General Bank* (No.2) (1895), 2 Ch. 677, at 682-683; Lopes, LJ in *Re. Kingston Cotton Mill Ltd* (No. 2) 2 Ch. 279, at 284.

[5] LJ Denning in *Fomento (Stirling Area) Ltd v. Selsdon Fountain Pen Co Ltd.* [1958] 1 All E.R. 11; Moffit, J in *Pacific Acceptance v. Forsyth & Others* (1970) 92 W.N. (N.S.W.) 29.

[6] Lopes, LJ in *Re Kingston Cotton Mill Ltd* (No. 2) [1896] 2 Ch. 289; Alverstone, LJ in *Re City Equitable Fire Assurance Company* [1925] Ch. 406.

[7] Pidgeon J in *W.A. Chip and Pulp Pty Ltd v. Arthur Young & Co* (1987) 5 A.C.L.C. at 1004.

[8] Lopes LJ in *Re Kingston Cotton Mill* at. 288.

[9] For Australia see: the two Senate Commissions investigating the auditor's duties (Royal Commission of Inquiry into the Activities of the Nugan Hand Group, 1985; McCusker Report, 1990) and one working party commissioned by the ASCPA/ICAA which reported in 1994 (But see Monroe and Woodliff, 1994, for a critique). The two accounting bodies in Australia established a Financing Reporting and Audit Expectation Gap Taskforce to report on the working party's recommendations. The report was issued in 1996. For the U.S. see: Commission on Auditors' Responsibilities (CAR), [Cohen Commission], AICPA, 1978); National Commission on Fraudulent Financial Reporting [Treadway Commission] (AICPA, 1987); Public Oversight Board Report (1993); For Canada see the Macdonald Commission report (CICA, 1988). For the U.K. see: ICAEW (1985) and Cadbury (1992) but see, also, Humphrey et al. (1992) for a discussion.

[10] AUS 210, AARF (1955a, para.9); Auditing Practices Board SAS 110 (APB), (1995, para.10); SAS 82, AICPA (1997, para.2); and International Federation of Accountants ISA 240, IFAC (1995, para.5); IFAC (2000, par.16-19).

[11] Australian auditing standards do not define what is meant by "reasonable care and skill". However, Judge Rogers in *AWA v. Daniels, t/a Deloitte, Haskins & Sells & Ors* (1992) 10 ACLC 933 determined what is reasonable by asking auditors in a similar tier firm to the defendant to interpret or outline what they would have done under the same circumstances.

The ability of the external auditor to detect material irregularities, including fraud, is coming under increasing scrutiny and auditors are under considerable pressure to accept responsibility for detecting material fraud. A number of surveys in the 1990's have documented that audit beneficiaries want an expanded role for auditors as society's corporate watchdog and that this view contrasts with that of auditors themselves (Humphrey, Moizer and Turley, 1992, 1993; Monroe and Woodliff, 1994; Porter, 1988, 1993). The auditing profession has been trying to reconcile the public's expectation of auditors with the potential to safeguard the interest of investors with the fact that an audit cannot guarantee that if there is a material irregularity such as fraud it will necessarily be detected 100% of the time (Chandler, Edwards and Andersen, 1993). At the same time, the profession has endeavoured to minimise its legal liability and costly litigation when failing to detect fraud or error.

Accounting firms and auditors[12] have been facing a litigation crisis with outstanding claims running into billions of dollars and as much again in settled claims[13]. In such litigation, what is alleged against auditors is that they have breached their duty of care to their client and/or a third party in carrying out the audit and, consequently, failed to detect fraud that had been instrumental in causing significant financial loss if not the complete collapse of a corporation. Another financial impact is the fact that professional indemnity insurance is becoming "increasingly expensive and almost unacceptably high"[14] (Gill and Cosserat, 1996:97).

According to fraud victimisation studies, it appears that the cost of fraud is very high and indeed it seems to be on the increase (Ernst and Young, 2000, 1996 and KPMG, 1999, 1996, 1995a). A company fraud victimisation survey by Deakin University (1994) sampled 1,500 medium and large corporations in Victoria. Of the 628 (42%) business entities that responded to the questionnaire, 71% reported fraud within their organisation and the cost of fraud was estimated at $941 million. In addition to the cost incurred by the victims, the cost of fraud includes the financial

[12] The auditor of Rothwells, Louis Carter was personally charged and convicted with conspiracy to defraud the public by "deceitfully concealing and falsely portraying Rothwells' financial position in three annual reports, plus half-yearly consolidated statements in 1988" (Sykes, 1996:1; and "Rothwells officers", 1996:5). He was sentenced to 4 years' and 3 months' imprisonment and was released on parole in 17 months ("Rothwells fraud pair", 1996:3; Carter, L. (2000).)

[13] The level of litigation against auditors was one of the issues giving cause for concern in the United Kingdom's Auditing Practices Board discussion paper (APB, 1992).

[14] A submission of the National Joint Limitation of Liability Task Force of the Institute of Chartered Accountants in Australia and the Australian Society of Certified Practising Accountants to the Inquiry into the Law of Joint and Several Liability, established by the Federal Attorney-General and the NSW Attorney-General (1994:3), has quoted the figure of $60,000 per partner per annum for the [then] Big Six firms.

costs arising out of litigation against auditors who fail to detect fraud as well as damage to the accounting profession's credibility.

The prevention and detection of fraud is expected to continue to be an important issue. Criminologists such as Grabosky and Smith (1996) have argued that Australia, as indeed other countries, has been experiencing profound social, economic and technological changes which increase opportunities for fraud. The same authors have also argued that new forms of fraud may be expected in many areas of industry, commerce and public administration as a result of the globalisation of financial markets and improved technology. A survey by the Audit Faculty of the Institute of Chartered Accountants of England and Wales (ICAEW) found that most accountants expect fraud to increase substantially during the next five years. This is attributed to a lower standard of ethics, increased pressure on individuals to perform, the impact of down-sizing and increased reliance on computers and their sophistication ("Fraud Fears", 1997: 13).

Justifying research into fraud detection by auditors

A study of fraud commission and the auditor's ability to detect fraud is warranted for several reasons. First, there exists an expectation gap as far as the role of auditors in fraud detection is concerned. The courts have stated that auditors can be held negligent if they have breached their duty of care to their client by not applying "reasonable care and skill" in carrying out the audit. However, the auditing profession with its mandatory auditing standards indicates that the auditor is not responsible for detecting material irregularities and "has distanced itself from these responsibilities" (Monroe and Woodliff, 1994:49). A better understanding of how and why fraud is committed and who is likely to commit fraud should improve the fraud detection abilities of auditors, thus enabling them to better meet their legal and professional responsibilities and the expectations of financial report users.

Second, by its very nature, fraud is a complex subject and difficult to detect. Auditors are not very good at detecting fraud as they rarely encounter fraud and they are not usually experts at fraud detection[15]. This is partly because there is a void in the auditing literature as there appears to be no comprehensive model of the aetiology of commercial fraud and its detection by auditors. Although Cressey

---

[15] Auditing Standard SAS 82, AICPA (1997, para. 7) acknowledge that fraud, particularly when concealed through falsified documentation, is difficult for auditors to detect since auditors are not trained nor are they "experts in such authentication". It can also be argued that if auditors rely on experience alone to become experts at identifying irregularities, then they are unlikely to become experts in due course owing to the fact that irregularities are infrequent (Ashton, 1991; Loebbecke, et al., 1989). Support for the argument that auditors are not experts at fraud detection is found in Ashton's (1991) literature review which shows convincingly that audit experience alone cannot make auditors fraud-detection experts. However, KPMG developed a data-base of error frequencies for a population of international audits (Ashton, 1991).

(1986), Loebbecke, Einning and Willingham (1989) and Albrecht, Wernz and Williams (1995) have presented models of why people commit fraud, their models can be criticised for not doing so within a psychological, sociological or criminological framework, and for not dealing adequately with the notion of traits that render someone to be crime-prone. In other words, the existing models make no attempt to account for individual differences as far as the aetiology of fraud is concerned by considering the individual offender's personality traits which predispose him/her to commit fraud under particular circumstances. In addition, the three models have also failed to conceptualize the opportunity to commit fraud so as to include the broader socioeconomic context in which fraud takes place and to locate it within a theoretical framework such as Clarke's (1980) situational approach to criminal behaviour. Clarke's approach stresses the importance of opportunity, both in understanding the aetiology of crime and for crime prevention.

This book argues that because management and employee fraud is by its very nature complex and difficult to detect, auditors' fraud-detection abilities need to be enhanced to enable them to apply "reasonable care and skill" in carrying out an audit. Such enhancement can come about by utilising knowledge about the aetiology of fraud in such disciplines as psychology, sociology and criminology, and by synthesising different approaches to fraud detection. A close examination of a broad range of explanations put forward by psychologists, sociologists, and criminologists as to why people commit fraud allows the identification of a number of correlates of fraud and enables the construction of a descriptive model of the aetiology of fraud. A better understanding of why fraud occurs and the type of individual likely to commit fraud should enable auditors to be better at detecting fraud.

Finally, research into fraud is scarce. Very little is known about the types of crimes committed, the characteristics of those who commit such crimes and auditors' experiences with detecting fraud. Auditors' fraud detection abilities can also be enhanced by carrying out empirical research into fraud detection so that auditors learn through the experiences of others.

The research reported in this book is intended to encapsulate in a model available knowledge about the aetiology of fraud and fraud-detection by auditors. Research has been noticeably deficient in both of these areas. At a theoretical level, the critical evaluation of available perspectives and empirical findings relevant to both the issues mentioned is used to construct a descriptive aetiological model of fraud (ROP model) and an eclectic fraud detection model. The model of fraud developed in this volume incorporates and expands on ideas in the models presented by Cressey (1986), Loebbecke et al. (1989) and Albrecht et al. (1995) by utilizing research findings from the auditing, psychology, sociology and criminology literatures. The probability of fraud occurring is modeled as a function of the opportunity (O) for the crime to be committed, one or more motivated crime-prone persons (P) being in a position to commit the crime, and the use of rationalisations

(R) or justifications to enable the individual(s) concerned to commit the crime by overcoming any inhibitions imposed by one's conscience or perceptions of the risks involved. Thus, the ROP model includes the notions of rationalisations, crime-prone persons and situational factors which are found in the psychology, sociology and criminology literatures. The fraud detection model developed in this book incorporates the ROP model into its design.

The applicability of each model was examined empirically in two separate studies. In the first study, predictions pertinent to the aetiology of fraud generally, and fraud offenders' characteristics specifically, were examined in a study of 50 serious fraud cases prosecuted by the Major Fraud Group (MFG) of the Victoria Police. This study provided a partial test of the ROP model, including demographic, *modus operandi* and criminal justice characteristics of the offenders surveyed. The study furnished a two-component profile and a taxonomy of the major fraud offender.

The second study which involved a survey of auditors who had experience in detecting irregularities, including fraud, yielded findings about fraud detection and tested the applicability of the fraud detection model. Findings pertaining to the notion of crime-prone individuals, company fraud-victimisation proneness and fraud-detection by auditors are reported and discussed.

Both studies as well as the two models developed are original and enable comparisons to be made between Australian and U.S. auditors as far as fraud detection is concerned. By providing knowledge that can be used in practice to improve auditors' fraud-detection ability, this book reduces to some extent the fraud-detection component of the expectation gap.

OUTLINE OF THE BOOK

In view of the noticeable lack of knowledge by auditors as far as the aetiology of fraud is concerned, the next chapter draws on a number of perspectives within psychology, sociology, and criminology in order to identify correlates of fraud. A number of different theoretical perspectives in psychology, sociology and criminology are discussed and critically evaluated. Chapter 3 examines the usefulness of auditing guidelines as far as fraud detection is concerned and a number of approaches to fraud detection are also critiqued, including the Loebbecke et al. (1989) fraud assessment model.

On the basis of the theoretical discussion in Chapters 2 and 3, two models are developed in Chapter 4, one addressing the reasons why people commit fraud and one of fraud detection by auditors. Chapter 5 reports findings from a study of 50 major fraud offenders and provides case summaries of 11 illustrative cases. Chapter 6 describes a survey of 108 Australian auditors' experience of detecting irregularities, including management and employee fraud.

The final chapter discusses both the findings obtained and the conclusions that can be drawn from them, as well as policy implications. The two models discussed in Chapter 4 are revised in the light of the empirical findings in Chapters 5 and 6. Finally, Chapter 7 considers in what sense this book can be said to be making an original contribution to the knowledge about the aetiology of fraud and fraud detection by auditors.

CHAPTER 2

AN INTERDISCIPLINARY APPROACH TO THE AETIOLOGY OF FRAUD

- The aetiology of fraud.
- A critique of the *general theory of crime.*
- Psychological correlates of white-collar offending.
- Sociological correlates of white-collar offending.
- Situational correlates of white-collar offending.
- Conclusions.

INTRODUCTION: THE AETIOLOGY OF FRAUD

Deception offences such as fraud are examples of criminal behaviour. Therefore, accountants and auditors should look to the criminological literature for insights into the correlates of such behaviour. In the last century, psychiatrists, psychologists and sociologists have put forward general theories of criminal behaviour[1]. In most cases, the aim has been to provide a single theory that accounts for crime in general. However, given the variety of behaviours that can be assumed under "crime", the search has been largely unsuccessful. As Walker (1987) put it, the search for a single theory of crime can be compared to searching for one theory of disease. Disappointed with the search for a single theory, some criminologists have shifted their attention away from individual offenders and have, instead, concentrated on characteristics of situations which make it easier to commit an offence (Clarke, 1980). This chapter discusses a number of theories of crime. To put this discussion in context, the following questions are considered:

i. Are white-collar offenders in some significant way different from conventional offenders?
ii. Can existing theories of criminal behaviour provide an adequate explanation for white-collar crime in general and fraud in particular?
iii. If a specific explanation for white-collar offences like fraud is needed, should we look for causes within the individual offender, the situation in which the offence is committed or both?
iv. Can one legitimately talk about causes or correlates regarding the question of who, how, and why fraud is committed?

Following the discussion of the various theories of crime from a criminological perspective, auditing theories of fraud detection are considered in the next chapter.

---

[1] See Blackburn, 1993; Feldman, 1993; and Williams, 1991, Williams III, F.P and Mcshane, M.D. (2000) for reviews.

EXPLANATIONS FOR WHITE-COLLAR OFFENDERS

Can general theories of criminal behaviour provide an adequate explanation for white-collar crime in general and fraud in particular?

Theories of criminal behaviour in the twentieth century have been dominated by positivism. Positivism in criminology is based on the belief that human behaviour is determined, i.e., that there are causes of human behaviour which can be explained by natural laws. Another characteristic of positivism is that one should be concerned with "facts" rather than metaphysical issues. Finally, positivistic criminologists believe that the best way to discover the natural laws governing a particular behaviour is by means of the "scientific method" as used in the natural sciences (Blackburn, 1993:18). Deterministic explanations of criminal behaviour are found in psychiatry, psychology and sociology.

Positivist theories in criminology explaining crime in deterministic terms, have focused on the offender in their search for causes of criminal behaviour[2]. This practice is in contrast to the Classical School's emphasis on an offender's deeds as the result of the choices of rational agents who are therefore responsible for the behaviour in question. Positivistic criminologists have been criticised by critical criminologists such as Taylor, Walton, and Young (1973) for: (1) not questioning the concept of "causes"; (2) ignoring the fact that human behaviour is rational and people interact with their environment (including the criminal justice system) in a dynamic way; (3) not questioning the medical model; and (4) for treating people as passive rather than active decision makers. Positivism characterises most theories of crime in this century, including theories of white-collar crime.

In contrast, the Classical School of thought in criminology (see Beccaria, 1963) builds on the premise that offenders are agents with free will. Consequently, because criminal behaviour is conceived of as the result of rational decision making, i.e., is free willed, the Classical School focuses on the type of crime that has been committed and considers how serious it is in order to decide the degree of retribution the offender should be sentenced to. Unlike those interested in the rehabilitation of offenders, the Classical School is not interested in the individual offender and his/her personality, position in life, or needs, and thus conceives of retribution as commensurate to the severity of the crime alone.

It should be noted that theories of criminal behaviour have been mainly concerned with juvenile delinquents (rather than adult offenders) as well as with offenders known to authorities. With these limitations of general theories of criminal behaviour in mind, let us consider four well-known psychological and three sociological theories of criminal behaviour as well as the situational approach to crime.

---

[2] Positivistic criminologists also emphasise the need to rehabilitate, rather than punish, the offender.

Are white-collar offenders in some significant way different from conventional offenders?

Gottfredson and Hirschi (1990)[3] put forward a *general theory of crime* which attempts to synthesise both offender-based explanations (i.e., both psychological and sociological explanations that focus on attributes of the individual) as well as offence-based explanations within criminology (i.e., those that highlight the importance of opportunities for crimes to be committed). Drawing on Bottoms' (1993) critique of the theory, the following can be said about their general theory of crime: a number of explanatory elements are utilised to explain how crimes are possible, namely opportunity, a suitable target, a free-thinking but basically self-interested hedonistic individual lacking in self-control and making a free choice, and the absence of effective crime-prevention situational factors. Noting that committing crimes even in the case of persistent, career offenders takes up but a part of their time, the theory attempts to account for individual differences in how different people are likely to commit different offences or the same offences to a greater degree.

Gottfredson and Hirschi (1990) make use of the concept of *self-control.* According to these criminologists, low self-control is an enduring criminal predisposition which is the result of defective socialisation. For them, socialisation, whether effective or ineffective, takes shape primarily within the family and the school. They conceive of low self-control as a single, unidimensional, enduring trait which is made up of: (1) impulsivity, a preference for simple rather than complex tasks; (2) risk-seeking, a preference for physical rather than intellectual activities; (3) being self-centred; and (4) having an explosive temper (pp.89-91). Low self-control is also said to predispose people to engage in certain other kinds of irresponsible behaviour which are not necessarily criminal offences (pp.91-94). Gottfredson and Hirschi maintain that self-control is lacking in persons whose socialisation within the family was characterised by the absence of nurturance, discipline and training. More specifically, they argue that low self-control is established when parents: (1) do not monitor closely their children's behaviour; (2) do not recognise deviant behaviour when it takes place; and (3) fail to punish such behaviour (p.97). Furthermore, it is also argued that people with low self-control are not only more likely to commit offences but are also more likely to be unsuccessful at school, as employees, and in their marriages.

For Gottfredson and Hirschi, a primary cause of criminal behaviour is the combination or interaction of low self-control and opportunity to commit a crime. By itself, however, neither factor is a major cause of crime. The general theory of crime posits that the incidence of crime in society decreases as a person's self-control increases with age. Thus, the commission of crime is explained in terms of a situation providing an *opportunity* for an offence to be committed and without effective

---

[3] Their theory is an extension of Hirschi's (1969) control theory discussed below.

"*capable guardians*"[4] and the presence or not of a person with weak enough self-control (in turn, a function of his/her socialisation and age).

Finally, Gottfredson and Hirschi maintain that specialisation among offenders is a myth and that criminals are "*versatile*", i.e., they perpetrate "a wide variety of criminal acts, with no strong inclination to pursue a specific criminal act or a pattern of criminal acts to the exclusion of others" (p.91). However, as Bottoms (1993:70) states "the empirical world is more complex than Gottfredson and Hirschi allow for". Before discussing this and other serious criticisms levelled against the general theory of crime, let us first consider some empirical support for Gottfredson and Hirschi's basic premise that a combination of low self-control and opportunity is a (perhaps the) primary cause of crime.

Grasmick, Tittle, Bursik, and Arneklev (1993) reported a self-report study of offending that used a 24-item questionnaire measuring self-control and crime opportunity in face-to-face opportunities with a random sample of 389 adults in Oklahoma City. The questionnaire items developed by Grasmick et al. tap six components of the personality trait of self-control derived from Gottfredson and Hirschi's conceptualisation of the trait. Their results support the general theory of crime, namely that it is the combination of low self-control and crime opportunity which predicts both "fraud" (Gottfredson and Hirschi's term for property offences) and "force" (Gottfredson and Hirschi's term for violent personal crimes) that the respondents reported committing. However, contrary to what the general theory would have predicted, crime opportunity was a significant predictor of both fraud and force independent of its interaction with low self-control. Grasmick et al. also found that crime opportunity was a better predictor of whether those surveyed had committed fraud than low self-control. Grasmick et al. concluded that their findings provide promising support for certain aspects of the general theory and that the theory has identified one mechanism that affects crime. Their data, however, "seem to weaken the theory's structural challenge" and falls short of the expectations generated by the appearance of the theory (p.24). Piquero and Rosay (1998), however, have expressed concerns about the reliability and validity of Grasmick et al.'s self-control scale[5].

Regarding major criticisms levelled against Gottfredson and Hirschi's general theory of crime, Bottoms (1993:72) points out that two different schools of thought within criminology, positivism and classicism, are treated as potentially

---

[4] As termed in Cohen and Felson's (1979) routine activities/opportunity theory, a "capable guardian" in this context refers to the presence of one or more persons (e.g., police presence, neighbours looking on) or technology (e.g., security cameras) that discourages offending because it significantly increases the risk of apprehension. In the context of fraud, the existence of middle management and/or competent internal and/or external auditors who watch out for fraud constitute an example of a "capable guardian".

[5] See Longshore, Stein and Turner (1998) for a response to Piquero and Rosay (1998) and a defence of Grasmick et al.'s scale.

complementary. In fact, classicism and positivism are inherently contradictory. Other criticisms of the theory discussed by Bottoms (see pp.68-73) revolve around: (1) the absence of empirical support for their premise that the age-distribution of crime does not vary across social and cultural conditions; (2) a failure to show convincingly that their theory covers all crime as they claim; (3) available empirical literature contradicts their assertion that crimes basically "require little foresight, planning or effort" (p.69); (4) their treatment of the relationship between gender and victimisation is inadequate; and, finally (5) they completely ignore "the socialisation and social control potential of *communities*" (p.71).

Grasmick et al. (1993) criticise the theory for placing too little emphasis on criminal opportunity which most likely is linked to social structure. The same authors also point out that: Gottfredson and Hirschi's definition of low self-control includes risk seeking whereas (in an apparently logically inconsistent way) their definition of criminal opportunity includes little risk of detection. The validity of Gottfredson and Hirschi's assumption that everybody is equally motivated to commit offences and that individual differences in offending are attributable primarily to low self-control and/or crime opportunity is questioned by Grasmick et al. Finally, Grasmick et al. criticise Gottfredson and Hirschi's failure to elaborate on the situational circumstances and individual characteristics which might mute or counteract the effect of low self-control (p.25). Consequently, they conclude that the theory "needs expansion, refinement, and elaboration before it can explain crime to the degree Gottfredson and Hirschi imply" (p.26).

Benson and Moore (1992:252) argued that Gottfredson and Hirschi's theory "is inadequate in explaining white-collar crime; its rejection of motives as important causal forces is misguided". Evidence against Gottfredson and Hirschi comes from studies[6] showing that white-collar offenders are different from common criminals in terms of a number of demographic and criminal justice characteristics (Benson and Moore, 1992; Marshall, Albrecht and Cherrington, 1980; Thomas, 1992; Weisburd, Chayet and Waring, 1990, and Wheeler, Weisburd, Waring and Bode, 1988). It should be noted in this respect that a limitation of such studies is that they have been concerned with white-collar criminals reported to the police and processed by the courts. In view of the large volume of crimes and offenders that remain unknown to the authorities (Williams, 1991:51-60), findings reported by such studies cannot be readily generalised to white-collar criminals at large. Their findings are nevertheless useful in increasing our knowledge about white-collar offenders processed by the police, courts, and prisons. Another limitation of the empirical studies discussed below is that, with the exception of Virta (2000), the data upon which their findings are based is dated. Therefore, it is by no means clear whether one should expect, for example, today's fraud offenders to have the same demographic and criminal justice

[6] See Krambia-Kapardis, M. (2000). Enhancing the auditor's fraud-detection ability: an interdisciplinary approach. Ph. D dissertation, Faculty of Business, Edith Cowan University, Perth, Western Australia, Australia, for a detailed discussion of these studies.

characteristics as two decades ago. The last 20 years have seen an increasingly more diverse population of people in western countries having tertiary education and entering the professions. Changes in the structure and management of corporations have affected the job mobility and career paths for many professionals in positions of financial trust, factors that affect the composition of white-collar offenders.

Findings providing good support for Gottfredson and Hirschi's theory have recently been reported by Virta (2000) in a follow-up study of 927 white-collar offenders who were convicted in the years 1991 and 1992 in Finland. By the end of 1998 over half of them were convicted for conventional offences. According to Virta (2000), for this group of criminals, the choice of criminal activities is very broad and she refers to them as the "anything-goes criminals".

The studies mentioned thus far have involved surveying official records on white-collar offenders. Langdale (1990) reported an Australian study that used a case study approach. Langdale was concerned with two cases only. She attended the court proceedings, read the briefs of the case and followed an unstructured interview approach with the offenders and the victims. No concrete reasons or benefits are outlined for the methodology used and it is very unclear what the research was testing. Qualitative case studies of two cases can provide some useful insight into corporate criminal activity. Langdale found that the offenders did not see themselves as criminals; in fact they denied having deceived any of the victims. Such case studies, however, need to be followed up with quantitative research. It is doubtful whether the approach followed by Langdale provides the claimed "deeper understanding of corporate criminal activity" (p.16).

Zietz (1981) also reported using a case-study approach with 100 women inmates at the California Institution for Women serving sentences for embezzlement or fraud. She first interviewed the women and surveyed their prison records in order to examine whether the same conditions (antecedents) advocated by Cressey (1953) in *A Study in the Social Psychology of Embezzlement: Other People's Money* as necessary for male offenders to commit offences violating financial trust also apply to female felons. Cressey's antecedents for financial trust violators who had accepted a position of trust in good faith are: (1) conceiving of themselves as having a non-shareable financial problem; (2) being "aware that this problem can be secretly resolved by violation of the position of financial trust"; and (3) being able to apply their "own situation verbalisations which enable them to adjust their conceptions of themselves as trusted persons with conceptions of themselves as users of the entrusted funds or property" (p.30).

Cressey found that the most important of the three antecedents was whether someone was able to formulate, in advance, a rationalisation that would permit them to justify to themselves violating their position of financial trust. Regarding the nature of the unshareable financial problem, Zietz (1981:52-61) reported that the following financial problems, also identified by Cressey, underpinned the trust violation of the women in her study: problems resulting from personal failure, from business reversals, and problems involving pressure or persuasion by a significant person. However, Zietz also found that, unlike Cressey's male trust violators, none of the women in her study had been affected by: (1) physical isolation (though many had been adversely affected by emotional isolation); (2) problems resulting from employer-employee relations; or (3) a desire to gain status. Zietz concluded that the behaviour of the women in her study, unlike that of the male offenders described by Cressey, "seemed to have a Joan of Arc quality. They showed a willingness to be burned at the stake, if necessary, to obtain for a loved one the medical care he needed, or to buy, if possible, the love of a husband attracted to a younger woman" (p.58).

Having found that the female inmates studied did not share the same characteristics as those reported by Cressey (1953) for his heterogeneous group of 133 male financial trust violators (embezzlement and fraud offenders), Zietz attempted to develop a typology of female property offenders in general and embezzlement and fraud offenders in particular. She focused on the "problems" the female incarcerated felons tried to solve with their embezzlement or fraud and identified two typologies of such offenders. The first group consisted of a number of subtypes. First, there were "honest" women who breached financial trust in the context of: (1) shouldering their responsibilities as mothers and wives; (2) because they were romantic dreamers, e.g., obsessed with keeping a husband or a lover they loved too much to risk losing; (3) being greedy opportunists who defrauded in order to meet a financial need, and as a result came to enjoy a new lifestyle they got used to and, consequently, persisted in defrauding in order to go on enjoying the same lifestyle; and (4) women who came to violate financial trust as a result of having been pressured into or been persuaded to do so by another person.

The second group of women identified by Zietz also consisted of subtypes. There was the vindictive type who committed offences in order to benefit herself on the basis that this was justified by what she perceived to be childhood deprivations or hardships she experienced as an adult; there was the social entrepreneur who perpetrated a variety of fraud offences with or without an accomplice, who planned her crimes and justified them by pointing to similar practices by legitimate entrepreneurs in the business world or by referring to the criminal avarice of her victims. Another identified subtype was the reluctant offender who perpetrated a variety of property offences, but did not feel particularly responsible for planning them and blamed a husband or a lover as having pressured or talked her into committing the crimes concerned. Zietz reported that the two groups of women differed significantly in how they viewed themselves, in their motives, in what they valued in life and whether they engaged in a criminal lifestyle. A basic limitation of this type of research is how to ascertain the reliability of what one is told in interviews in general, especially by incarcerated felons. Inmates may well have their ideas about what are desirable answers to the questions and numerous factors influence how people attribute responsibility for their behaviour. Zietz failed to ensure adequately the reliability of her data. One way of doing so would be to interview the spouses/lovers of the women, where applicable. A final limitation of Zietz's study is that it is not clear whether the justifications offered by the inmates were the cause or the effect of their fraudulent activity. Despite its limitations, that study does provide some insight into the thinking of women imprisoned for deception offences.

Recasting the typology of female fraud offenders developed by Zietz (1981) in terms of components of a model of why people commit fraud (see Figure 1, Chapter 4), we have: (1) **motives** (e.g., domestic responsibilities, greed, financial pressure, or other pressure such as emotional or even revenge on the company by a disgruntled employee seeking personal justice); and (2) **justifications/ rationalisations** (so as not to lose a husband/lover, the company deserved it). Of course, given a person with a motive for committing fraud and being able to justify it to him/herself, an opportunity is needed for fraud to occur. What is lacking in Zietz's typology is some explanation of the reasons why, under the same circumstances, other women do not commit fraud. In other words, what personality attributes of the women rendered them crime-prone in combination with particular opportunities/conditions.

It can be seen that findings from five of the seven studies discussed (the exception being Weisburd et al., 1990, and Virta, 2000) contradict Gottfredson and Hirschi's general theory of crime. Therefore, one could conclude that white-collar offenders differ from common convicted offenders in terms of a number of important demographic and criminal justice characteristics, namely being older, better educated, likely to be first offenders, to have steady employment histories and, finally, to be less likely to have an alcohol or illicit drug abuse problem. However, Virta's recent Finnish study provides good support for the Gottfredson and Hirschi's theory and shows the need for further research before we are able to arrive at definitive conclusions about the validity of a basic premise of the general theory, namely that white-collar criminals are versatile and not specialists.

In considering these studies, it is important to bear in mind that different findings may reflect differences in the research method used, such as the definition of white-collar crime, the types of offences examined and whether the criteria of prior criminality or recidivism was used. Furthermore, the term embezzlement, as used in the U.S., may cover a broader range of offences than in Australia and New Zealand. It is also important to remember that the studies involve convicted white-collar offenders. It is unknown whether such offenders are representative of white-collar offenders in general since only a proportion of such offenders comes to the attention of the authorities and, of those, a number beat the charges against them or, if convicted, are not sent to prison. Consequently, a study that focuses on incarcerated fraud offenders, as Benson and Moore (1992); Marshall et al. (1980); Thomas (1992); Weisburd et al. (1990); Wheeler et al. (1988) and Zietz (1981) have done, can not justifiably extrapolate its findings to the general population of such offenders. The comment made (and which would apply less to research involving white-collar offenders investigated and prosecuted by the police, but not necessarily incarcerated, see Chapter 5) should not be taken to mean that such research should be dismissed; rather, that it should be treated with caution. Finally, there is still a lot we do not know about what factors motivate fraud offenders. Before considering a number of general theories of crime, it should be pointed out that:

> fraud occurs in many forms. A great deal of the published literature on fraud uses the term very loosely, often as a synonym for, or in the context of discussion of, white-collar crime, i.e., crimes against business. However, not all frauds would be classified as white-collar crimes (especially if they occur outside an occupational context) and there are white-collar crimes other than fraud. Fraud can also occur in the context of corporate crimes or crimes by business (Edelhertz, 1983; Levi,1987; Geis, 1991). (Thomas, 1992:123)

On the basis of the preceding discussion it can be concluded that there are conflicting findings regarding the adequacy of Gottfredson and Hirschi's general theory of crime in explaining fraud. Therefore, auditors wishing to improve their knowledge about why fraud occurs should consider other theories of criminal behaviour which have been proposed from different perspectives. A discussion of such theories follows but it needs to be pointed out that the theories concerned have not been tested on white-collar criminals. In the context of this book, the justification of discussing these theories is that they provide useful pieces of the jigsaw puzzle of fraud aetiology.

PSYCHOLOGICAL THEORIES OF CRIMINAL BEHAVIOUR

Psychologists' interest in crime goes back to the end of the nineteenth century. As Thomas (1992) points out, psychologists "do not appear to have considered fraud in the context of white collar crime in much detail" (p.123). In fact, as Blackburn (1993:2) reminds us, "crime has always been a minority interest among psychologists". Psychological research into criminal behaviour has concentrated on who becomes a criminal and why. Generally, psychologists have put forward positivistic explanations of criminal behaviour. Thus, they are subject to the same criticisms mentioned earlier with reference to positivism. It should be noted that critics of psychological theories tend to lump them together. However, as shown below, this can not be justified because such theories differ significantly.

In considering the psychological theories discussed below, one should remember that there is disagreement among criminologists as to whether researchers should be focusing on offenders, offences or both. The usefulness of psychologists' concern with individual offenders is appreciated more when one remembers that "acts and tendencies ... call for different kinds of explanation" (p.22). It should be emphasised that psychologists are interested in explaining individual differences. In this way, they supplement the sociologists' focus on social and cultural factors as determinants of criminal behaviour. After all, individuals who are brought up in the same environment do not necessarily exhibit the same behaviour.

Self concept/esteem/image and criminal behaviour[7]

Behaviouristic psychologists, who like to explain behaviour in terms of conditioning, frown upon the notion of the self as a separate "I" or "me" which people experience subjectively. Social cognitive theorists (see Bandura, 1989) conceive of the self as a structure that processes information actively. In other words, it is viewed as a *cognitive schema.* According to Blackburn (1993), the concept "refers to knowledge and beliefs about oneself including attitudes of affective regard or *self-esteem.* Since the self is generally believed to derive from and mediate social interaction, a deviant self-concept may also mediate antisocial behaviour" (Wells, 1978:197). Psychologists have constructed instruments that measure self-esteem (see Eyo's, 1981, "Tennesse Self Concept Scale"). Self-esteem is part of a person's social identity and is said to be inversely correlated with a person's degree of neuroticism (Watson and Clark, 1984). As mentioned below, neuroticism is a personality trait considered by Eysenck (1977) to be associated with criminal behaviour.

There are conflicting views about the exact nature of the relationship between self concept and criminal behaviour. One such theory is that a positive self concept insulates against deviant influences (Reckless and Dinitz, 1967). Another view is that people will commit offences if they believe that in doing so their self-image will not suffer. When one's self-esteem is low, one is more likely to commit deviant acts such as cheating when an opportunity presents itself (Eisen, 1972). Other authors (see Howells, 1978) argue that people are motivated to maintain their self-esteem or to augment it, even if it means committing deviant acts such as crimes. Finally, researchers have reported a significant correlation between low self-esteem/negative image and non-conformity in young offenders (Richman, Brown and Clark, 1984) and between low self-esteem and cheating (Aronson and Mettee, 1968 - cited in Feldman, 1993:287-288). One explanation as to why there are such conflicting views (and no identifiable prevailing or current view) between self image/esteem and deviant behaviour/offending is that there is "a lack of an adequate theory of self concept" (Blackburn, 1993:199).

Social identity theory (Tajfel and Turner, 1986) provides an explanation for the relationship between one's self-categorisation and behaviour. This theory maintains that much of people's social behaviour is motivated by the desire to understand and evaluate one's self, and that this desire is satisfied through social categorisation and social comparison. Social categorisation refers to how people simplify a complex social world by placing themselves and others into categories such as gender or successful business-person. Thus, one's social identity is defined by the social categorisation process. According to Vivian and Brown (1995), together with the need for self-evaluation and understanding, there may be a need for "self-enhancement". In other words, people are motivated by the desire to know and

[7] This section draws on Blackburn (1993:197-200).

evaluate themselves favourably in relation to others, to have a positive social identity and behave accordingly (see below).

Drawing on the psychology of self-concept and social identity, one could hypothesise that someone in management who regards themselves as competent and a high-achiever and is accepted as such by their colleagues enjoys high self-esteem. If such a person comes to perceive him/herself as having failed as a professional because the company is facing imminent bankruptcy his/her self-esteem will be low, he will accordingly be under pressure, and may well commit fraud to re-establish his/her self image/esteem/social identity (Kaplan, 1980).

Personality and criminal behaviour

Eysenck's Theory

Maddi (1980) defines personality as a set of characteristics, tendencies and temperament that have been formed by inheritance and by social, cultural, and environmental factors. On the basis of his assessment of available empirical findings from a number of criminological studies of offenders under the age of 21[8], Feldman (1993:160) states that "there seems, then, some basis for expecting personality measures to correlate with criminal behavior and to discriminate between offenders and controls". One view is that certain personality characteristics (e.g., being a neurotic extrovert, high on psychopathy, having a weak ego or inadequate superego, or being characterised by criminal thinking patterns[9]) facilitate the commission of antisocial acts. In other words crime-prone individuals possess certain identifiable characteristics/traits.

Caspi et al. (1994) examined the relationship between personality traits and crime in two studies. In New Zealand, they studied 18-year old males and females from an entire birth cohort. In the U.S., they studied an ethnically diverse group of 12 and 13 year old boys. In both studies they used personality tests (Multidimensional Personality Questionnaire (MPQ)) and a number of independent measures of delinquent behaviour: police records of contact, court records of convictions, self-reports, and reports from independent informants, parents and teachers (pp.166-7). Caspi et al. found that, irrespective of country, age cohort, gender and race, those high on Negative Emotionality (the tendency to experience negative emotional states[10]) and weak on constraint (i.e., having a strong tendency to behave impulsively) were more delinquent. Crime prognoses in terms of distinct personality traits, however, has not been examined with adult white-collar offenders.

A well-known theory of personality and crime was put forward by Eysenck (1977) and it is known as the Eysenck theory of crime and delinquency. This theory

[8] See, for example, McCord (1979).

[9] See Blackburn (1993) for a discussion of the relevant literature.

[10] Persons high on "negative emotionality" are said by Caspi et al. (1994:169) to have a "low general threshold for the experience of negative emotions such as fear, anxiety, and anger and tend to break down under stress".

(unlike psychodynamic theories such as that of Sigmund Freud - see below) is stated in a way that makes it possible to falsify it. Eysenck's starting position is that human beings are by nature antisocial, i.e., hedonistic, egocentric and destructive. Therefore, he asks: why doesn't everybody commit certain criminal acts? In other words, what is it that stops people from committing criminal offences? His answer is that it is people's conscience, which he takes to be a conditioned reflex. According to Eysenck, an individual's personality can be measured on three dimensions:
extroversion (E), *neuroticism* (N) and *psychoticism* (P). Each of these personality traits is said to have a biological basis and the three personality traits can be measured using the *Eysenck Personality Inventory* (EPI)[11].

This section draws on Feldman's (1993) and Blackburn's (1993) discussion of Eysenck's theory. The three determinant variables are:

i. *Extroverts* (E) are said to be low on cortical arousal (i.e., brain stimulation) and a high score on E points to a person who (in contrast to an introvert) is sociable, active, optimistic, outgoing and impulsive. Individuals who are high on E are said to be difficult to condition, will not have a strong conscience and, consequently, will show higher levels of criminal behaviour.

ii. The individual who is high on *neuroticism* (N) has a labile autonomic nervous system (i.e., jumpy), which overreacts to painful stimuli (e.g., when being punished for behaving in a particular way) and thus interferes with conditioning. They are prone to mood fluctuations, are sensitive to criticism, are anxious, restless, and rigid. A high N score is said to be associated with higher levels of criminal activity.

iii. As far as *psychoticism* (P) is concerned, people high on this characteristic tend to be loners who search for pleasure, are social misfits and do not feel remorse for the trouble they cause others and, finally, are incapable of empathy. A high P score is also said to correlate with higher levels of offending.

Eysenck's theory predicts that offenders will have higher E, N and P scores. Studies which have tested this hypothesis, comparing, for example, prisoners and, non-offenders as well as studies of self-report offending, have reported conflicting findings[12]. Farrington, Biron and Le Blanc (1982) reviewed 16 studies (including Allsopp and Feldman, 1974; Bartol and Holanchock, 1979; Buikhuisen and Hemmel, 1972; Eysenck and Eysenck, 1970; Farrington, 1979) which compared offenders with police records and control groups. They concluded that while in most of the studies the officially-known offenders scored higher on P and N, seven studies which used a self-report measure of offending reported a significant positive correlation with E, a smaller number of studies reported a significant positive correlation with P and, finally, there was no unequivocal relationship reported for N and offending. On

[11] See Blackburn (1993), Feldman (1993) and Williams (1991) for detailed descriptions and appraisals of the theory.
[12] See Blackburn, 1993, for discussion of such studies.

the basis of their own test of Eysenck's theory in London and Montreal, Farrington et al. concluded that it lacked empirical support.

Eysenck's theory has been criticised by Blackburn (1993) on a number of grounds. The following are some of the major criticisms made by Blackburn: (1) it only considers punishment and ignores the importance of praise, positive reinforcement, in shaping one's behaviour; (2) the EPI can be faked; (3) the P dimension as described by Eysenck contains a lot of ambiguities; and (4) it ignores the importance of social factors in explaining criminal behaviour.

Blackburn (1993:127) concludes his comprehensive evaluation of Eysenck's theory by stating that:

> It must be concluded that Eysenck's theory of criminality is not well supported ... the crucial prediction that the ranks of criminals are swelled by extroverts has not been upheld with sufficient consistency to justify confidence in the theory.

Eysenck's theory has not been tested with white-collar criminals. On the basis of this theory one would argue that:

i. not forgetting individual differences regarding one's E, N and P score and crime proneness, people would not feel guilty about perpetrating white-collar crimes such as fraud because they have not been conditioned through punishment to feel enough anxiety about it so as not to commit such acts; and
ii. white-collar crime is very widespread because most people do not disapprove of it.

While fraud victimisation studies[13] support (ii), whether white-collar offenders in general and fraud perpetrators in particular feel remorse about their offending remains an empirical question. Chapter 5 reports findings relevant to this issue. Eysenck's theory suggests some ways that link personality traits and criminal behaviour. Limited support for Eysenck's theory is found in the research finding that psychopaths are very similar to the extremely extroverted individuals described by Eysenck (Bartol and Bartol, 1994:323). Psychopathy is a controversial personality trait much discussed by psychologists and criminologists alike.

The psychopath and crime

Psychopath is a clinical term which has some validity as a behavioural pattern that is both identifiable and distinct. Psychopathy is often measured with the Psychopathy Checklist (Hare, 1991). According to Bartol and Bartol, psychopaths are generally of average or above-average intelligence, sociable, appear friendly, likeable, well educated with broad knowledge and interests (p.323). Additional features of the psychopath include an ability to remain calm and collected under extremely stressful conditions, they do not feel anxious, do not have a genuine sense of humour, and they appear emotionally flat (p.323). Behavioural patterns typical of

[13] See Cressey (1986), Dirkis and Nichol (1996).

psychopaths include: an inability to love and be affectionate towards others and to be extremely selfish; they are unable to learn from their mistakes and, when drunk, they "become vulgar, domineering, loud and boisterous" (p.323). Psychopaths are constantly under-aroused neuro-physiologically so they have an insatiable need for stimulation, excitement and, in this sense, they are very similar to the extremely extroverted individuals described by Eysenck. In psychoanalytic terms, a psychopath has a *weak superego* [see below] (Glover, 1960).

Psychopaths should not, be confused with *sociopaths* or people with an *anti-social personality disorder* (APD). As Bartol and Bartol (1994:323) point out, the terms sociopath and APD are commonly used to refer to recidivist offenders who exhibit a distinct inability to learn from experience. The psychopath, despite also sharing an apparent inability to learn from experience, may or may not commit criminal offences.

Most people would find psychopaths difficult to live or work with because they are irresponsible, unpredictable and thus unreliable. Their behaviour follows a cyclical pattern in that for a period of time a psychopath will appear responsible and be successful at whatever he/she is doing. However, quite unexpectedly, he/she will do something which endangers his/her status irrespective of the importance of the occasion and however serious the consequences of his/her impulsive behaviour. "Because of this cyclical pattern, psychopaths rarely pursue consistent, successful criminal careers. Rather, they are more likely to participate in capers or hastily planned crimes that offer immediate satisfaction" (Bartol and Bartol, 1994:323). In the light of the attributes of the psychopath (e.g., intelligence, charm, selfishness, lack of anxiety or remorse, sensitivity to monetary gains and a weak superego), one could hypothesise a significant positive relationship between psychopathy and a tendency to commit fraud.

Psychodynamic theory and criminal behaviour

Freud's ideas have influenced thinking in various disciplines. Blackburn (1993:11) points out that while Freud himself "had little to say about crime", other psychoanalysts have shown strong interest in criminal behaviour because of their general focus on individual pathologies which are expressed in crime. Consequently, a number of psychoanalytically-oriented authors have expressed views on causes of crime, however, there is no single psychoanalytic theory of crime (p.11).

Like Eysenck, Freud regarded people as antisocial by nature. This is because humans, whose behaviour is largely determined by how unconscious conflicts are resolved, are born with instincts (e.g., aggressive, sexual, death) that demand satisfaction. Freud advocated three personality structures and maintained that a child goes through a number of stages of psychosexual development (oral, anal, phallic), each of which is characterised by an erotogenic zone (i.e., a part of the body which can be the source of sexual pleasure). The first component of the personality structure is the *id*. This stands for our instincts. Inevitably, the *id* conflicts with demands imposed by our social natures. The need to control the demands of the *id* gives rise to the *ego* which mediates between the *id* and external reality. The *ego* can thus delay satisfying the demands of the *id* using fantasy and planning. In addition, the *ego* has at its disposal a number of defence mechanisms to help deal with conflicts experienced by an individual. The defence mechanisms include: denial, repression, regression, projection, displacement, sublimation and reaction formation.

An individual's superego represents the norms of his/her parents and social groups. The superego consists of two parts: a set of moral principles, a conscience, violation of which gives rise to guilt, and an ego-ideal, i.e., standards to which the self aspires, which provide the *ego* with values and goals (Blackburn, 1993:112). If the *id*'s demands are incompatible with a person's conscience, then the *ego* must either neutralise them or prevent them from reaching consciousness through the ego's defence mechanisms. For example, if the *id*'s demand is for someone to be aggressive towards a person they consider morally wrong to attack, then if this wish breaks through into consciousness or is acted upon, the person will experience guilt. The *ego*, therefore, needs to neutralise the energy generated by the *id*'s wish or redirect it by, for example, denying the unconscious wish or repressing it or displacing it. In channelling *id* drives, the *ego* is guided by the superego. "Superego formation depends on psychosexual and *ego* development through the child's relations with its parents, and is associated with the resolution of the Oedipal conflict around the age of five" (p.112).

Psychoanalysts explain criminal behaviour in terms of inadequate superego formation and functioning. More specifically, criminal behaviour may result from a harsh, weak or deviant superego. According to Blackburn, a person with a harsh superego may commit a crime in order to be punished (p.114), while a weak superego (i.e., a weak conscience) correlates with a person having a psychopathic personality, i.e., one which is egocentric, hedonistic, feels no guilt and cannot empathise. Finally, a deviant superego is one where a boy has a good relationship with his father, but the father is a criminal and the boy comes to adopt the father's norms and behaviour. People with a weak superego, i.e., those who have an underdeveloped conscience, are less able to channel their energies into socially approved pursuits and thus feel no guilt when committing antisocial acts (Albrecht, Romney, Cherrington, Payne and Roe, 1982:32).

Blackburn (1993) points out one major weakness of Freudian theory, namely that it does not provide a comprehensive theory of crime because it not only fails to account for several features of offenders such as their age but, also, not all examples of criminal behaviour can be attributed to unconscious conflicts - the fact is that many crimes involve rational decision making (pp.115,116). In other words, Freudian theory overemphasises unconscious processes. Other major weaknesses of orthodox Freudian theory are: (1) it ignores the importance of influences on a person's behaviour during adolescence and later on; (2) it is not clear whether criminal behaviour is a consequence or a cause of neurotic conflicts experienced by individuals; (3) it overemphasises the importance of unconscious processes; and (4) it is not possible to ascertain the effectiveness of psychoanalysis as a method of helping a person resolve their unconscious conflicts.

Despite such weaknesses, Blackburn (1993) concludes that:

> the psychodynamic hypotheses cannot be rejected out of hand. Psychoanalysis is the only theory which attempts to deal systematically with the phenomenon of affective experience, and contrary to the somewhat overdone positivist critiques, the theory has proved to be falsifiable, and has withstood the test in several respects ... The resistance of psychologists to the notion of unconscious processes has also begun to dissipate ... and with the 'cognitive' revolution, psychology has moved closer to psychoanalysis ... (p.116)

To the best of the author's knowledge, none of the psychological theories considered above have been tested in the context of white-collar crime. Each provides a useful insight into personality attributes of crime-prone individuals and thus goes some way towards explaining why people commit crimes. Such knowledge enables us to expand on existing models of the aetiology of fraud which, for example, talk about "attitudes" and "motivations" (Loebbecke et al., 1989) as a necessary prerequisite for fraud to take place, but fail to locate their explanation within a conceptual framework, treating the individual fraud offender in a vacuum.

In summary, it can be argued that the personality of the individual offender may be a significant component of a psychological explanation as to why people commit fraud. The psychological perspectives discussed provide some useful pieces to construct the personality mosaic of fraud-prone individuals. These include:

- weak superego/low self-control; low self-esteem; need for excitement;
- not being attached to other people; egocentricity; impulsivity;
- lying; lack of anxiety and empathy; over-sensitivity to monetary gain;
- being indifferent to the consequences of one's behaviour.

This list does not suggest that an individual must possess all the attributes for fraud to occur. Possessing some of them can be enough under the right circumstances of environmental opportunity and conditions.

SOCIOLOGICAL THEORIES OF CRIMINAL BEHAVIOUR

Sociologists have been concerned with which social groups become delinquent. Most sociological theories of crime have been concerned with explaining juvenile delinquency by lower-class male offenders. Such theories can be grouped into "learning", "strain", "control", "labelling", "conflict" and "radical" theories. Sociologists researching crime have traditionally been interested in identifying causes of delinquency in social structure and cultural factors (Blackburn, 1993:87). In other words, "they have emphasised the causal processes in the social environment" (p.88). This section considers three well-known sociological theories of crime: (1) differential association; (2) control theory; and, finally, (3) theory of drift (see Blackburn, 1993; Feldman, 1993, and Williams, 1991).

Differential association

In an attempt to explain white-collar crime (i.e., criminal offences by persons of high socioeconomic status), Edwin Sutherland (1939), put forward the theory of differential association (Sutherland and Cressey, 1970). This is a learning theory which explains criminality by asserting that crime is learned primarily by association with others. Such learning is said to take place in small groups and involves both the techniques for committing a particular crime as well as the values, attitudes, rationalisations and motives necessary for its commission. Williams, (1991:195) indicates that, "whether a person takes part in criminal activities depends on the amount of contact they have with criminal activities or with those who support or are sympathetic towards criminal activities".

The notion of differential association is useful in understanding the professional career conman who intentionally sets out to victimise a company. Such an offender would often get him/herself into a position of trust within the company (sometimes by forging qualifications and work references or would set up a company to prey on other company by exploiting the trust he/she manages to establish) or *vis-à-vis* the company. In their association with other criminals, such offenders can acquire skills and techniques useful in committing fraud, such as how to produce forgeries of various documents and how to otherwise deceive financial institutions. Another example of how the notion of differential association can be applied to the aetiology of management fraud is by focusing attention on the importance of the corporate culture that often condones unethical and illegal means of acquiring wealth, whether for oneself or the company. Adopting such a perspective, for example, might lead a researcher to ask about the processes by which a manager becomes aware of and adopts the norm that "it is okay to use insider information to trade in shares". A final example of how the type of people one associates with can facilitate the commission of fraud is the case where someone in a position of trust in a company that is vulnerable to fraud victimisation (e.g., due to weak internal controls) is befriended by a non-employee of the company (e.g., a real estate agent) and together they embark on a scam to defraud the company.

Williams (1991) discusses a number of criticisms of differential association theory (pp.197-198):

i. It cannot account for the first time a crime is committed because if the behaviour does not exist, it cannot be learned.

ii. It does not cater for individual differences when it comes to being influenced by one's associates. As Blackburn (1993:90) points out, differential association is "an incomplete theory, since it rests on vague psychological assumptions about human learning".

iii. It cannot account for crimes committed by individuals who have not associated with criminals or people who hold similar attitudes. Of course, as Williams points out, behaviour may be learned through observing others, watching television, from books, etc.

iv. "A further criticism is that this approach cannot explain irrational, impulsive, opportunist or passionate criminals, who would then be acting due to one of those factors rather than as a result of anything they have learnt" (p.197).

v. It is impossible to measure the effect of differential association as an explanation of why an individual has committed a particular crime.

vi. One cannot, on the basis of this theory, decide whether differential association is the cause or the effect of a person's criminal activities.

vii. Finally, differential association, as formulated by Sutherland (1939) and Sutherland and Cressey (1970), is not "concerned with the process of acquiring criminal attitudes and behaviors" or "with their performance and long-term maintenance" (Feldman, 1993:234).

Despite the above criticisms, according to Williams (1991:198) and Blackburn (1993:90), there is evidence for a link between differential association and criminal behaviour. The theory appears to be more useful in explaining white-collar or corporate crime. One could hypothesise, for example, that new business executives are "inducted" into the "executive subculture" and this includes attitudes and norms which are conducive for the commission of certain white-collar offences. Furthermore, placing one's self into the category of successful company director, bank manager, solicitor, or accountant, defines one's social identity favourably relative to what others in a similar occupational position enjoy in life.

Control theory

Control theorists in sociological criminology (e.g., Hirschi, 1969), like their counterparts within criminological psychology, start with the assumption that people are born free to break the law and that criminal activity is natural since the uncontrolled human tendency is to look for pleasure and avoid pain. The search for an account of why people commit offences is a search for constraints and/or controls on behaviour. Hirschi (1969) argued that four elements are necessary for someone to be a law-abiding citizen:

i. Attachment to other people. Evidence for this is to be found in one's conscience and the norms one has come to adopt, as well as whether one cares about what others think.

ii. To develop a commitment to conventional goals and the responsibilities that go with them.

iii. To be involved in conventional activities which are incompatible with law-breaking.

iv. To have a belief "in the moral validity of conventional values" (Blackburn, 1993:92).

According to Hirschi (1969), these four elements are important because they are associated with the bond between a person and society. If this bond is weak an individual will exhibit criminal behaviour.

Hirschi (1969) does not provide details about how bonds develop or break down or how weak bonds produce criminal behaviour or why an individual selects one kind of criminal activity rather than another (Williams, 1991:250). Blackburn (1993:92) states that empirical studies have reported conflicting findings regarding the negative relation between bonding elements and delinquency that control theory would predict. Finally, criminologists disagree on whether control theory can account for crimes such as Watergate and oil sanction busting in Rhodesia that are committed by the powerful (Box, 1981-cited by Williams, 1991:262).

Theory of drift

The American sociologist Matza (1969) reintroduced the notion of free will into criminological theorising with the idea of "drift". Matza's theory maintains that individuals choose to drift in and out of criminal behaviour or, to put it differently, to drift between law-abiding and criminal behaviour. In other words, offenders are not committed to criminal behaviour. Matza, too, has been concerned with explaining juvenile delinquency. His theory, however, has applications to adult offenders (Williams, 1991:239). According to Matza, there are constraints on offending and the state of drift is reached by means of a number of *techniques of neutralisation*. These are justifications which explain or neutralise the offenders' criminal behaviour. More specifically, they enable individuals to:

i. *Deny responsibility* for their offending by blaming factors beyond their control (such as poverty, their family background, influence of friends and so forth) for their behaviour.
ii. Claim that *no one has been harmed* by the crime(s) concerned because, for example, the victim can afford the financial loss and/or the insurance company will pay.
iii. Claim the *victim deserved the harm caused* because, for example, the victim also commits offences and/or because he/or she or the company provoked the offence.
iv. *Condemn the condemners* by claiming that they too commit crimes so they are in no moral position to condemn the offender and, finally,
v. Claim greater *loyalty to a particular group*. This justification may be used by delinquents to refer to their loyalty to a street gang, but a white-collar criminal could use loyalty to his/her company or family in order to justify a particular crime. This does not mean, however, that either the street gang or a company actually demands that a member or an employee commit a crime. Rather, the choice is up to the individual.

Matza's techniques of neutralisation are no different from the notion of rationalisations, justifications put forward by Albrecht, et al. (1995) or Cressey (1953, 1986) to explain why people commit fraud. The theory explains how it is possible for someone to lead a double life, commit fraud and see themselves as respectable members of the community. There is empirical support for his view that individuals are not necessarily committed to either criminal or law-abiding behaviour (Williams, 1991) and the theory is not deterministic in its predictions. As Williams puts it, most delinquents "have some area of choice as to whether they will perform criminal acts when both the opportunity and the temptation arise" (p.243).

It is possible for someone to initially get into trouble financially and, as a result, drift into criminal behaviour. For example, a bank manager may decide to lend someone more money than is justified by the type of security provided, in the hope that the excess funds will soon be paid back and/or because, due to a very heavy workload and/or incompetence as a manager, he/she had no time to do the necessary paperwork that would render the loan objectionable. Subsequently, however, the loan is not repaid and the manager ends up stealing from the bank to cover up the bank loan decision. In this sense, a person may be said to "drift in" to fraud rather than to commit the crime(s) on the basis of a rational, free-willed decision.

In concluding this brief discussion of these three well-known sociological theories of crime, it can be said that theories which attempt to explain juvenile delinquency can not readily be used to account for white-collar offenders and why they offend. However, particular concepts from these theories (e.g., differential association, weak self-control, a person's rationalisations that render criminal behaviour possible) can be used to explain causes of white-collar crime.

A SITUATIONAL THEORY OF FRAUD

Unlike the psychological and sociological theories of crime, which treat compliance with the law as a consequence of internalised norms or moral prohibitions, the situational approach to criminal behaviour is concerned with crime prevention (see Clarke, 1980; Clarke and Mayhew, 1980). More specifically, it "sees crime as the outcome of immediate choices and decisions, and [...] focuses on the proximal rather than the distal influences on crimes as specific events" (Blackburn, 1993:104). Without ignoring the importance of individual differences, advocates of the situational approach do not assume environmental determinism. The situational approach to understanding why people commit crime developed out of a disillusionment with theories that assume crime is the result of some disposition of the individual (p.104).

Seen from this perspective, the career, professional fraud offender is motivated to exploit and, if need be, to create opportunities. Most frauds, like most crimes generally, are best understood as "rational action performed by fairly ordinary people acting under particular pressures and exposed to specific opportunities and situational improvements" (Hough, Clarke and Mayhew, 1980 - cited by Blackburn, 1993:104). Conceptualising fraud offenders as rational decision makers focuses on the aetiology of fraud as the result of benefits outweighing the costs and could well lead one to advocate the use of deterrents to reduce fraud victimisation. Fraud reduction could be achieved by increasing one's subjective perception of risk of apprehension and severity of likely penalty upon conviction, so that the calculated costs of punishment are significantly greater than the individual's subjective benefits or profits of the fraud (See Braithwaite, 1989).

THE AETIOLOGY OF FRAUD: WHAT EXPLANATION?

Historically, it appears that fraud is more prominent when there is a recession, or an avalanche of corporate collapses (Clolery 1993). KPMG's (1995b) report of

Canada's 1,000 largest companies indicates the following reasons for alleged increases in fraud (multiple responses):economic pressures (88%); weakening of society's values (70%); more sophisticated criminals (56%); lack of emphasis on prevention (51%); staff downsizing (50%); and lack of government intervention (11%).

There may be cultural factors affecting the determinants of fraud. An international survey conducted by KPMG (1996:8) attributed the major reason for the increase in fraud to be

> society's weakening values. This was the number one reason given by the regions of Hong Kong, Middle East/Asia, Europe and Australasia. Consistent with the Canadian survey, North America and Africa listed economic pressures as the major reason for the expected increase.

The preceding discussion has shown that fraud offenders are different from common offenders in terms of a number of demographic and criminal activity characteristics. Despite a number of criticisms that can be levelled against the psychological and sociological theories of crime, each theory has something to contribute to our understanding of the reasons people commit crimes. This knowledge can be supplemented through the situational approach, which highlights situational factors and conditions providing opportunities for crime.

Prior research in criminology indicates that a single theory can not account for a broad range of criminal behaviours. Given that the term "fraud" covers a list of diverse situations and individuals, and because serious fraud offenders do not appear to be versatile, the best we can do is to provide a multi-disciplinary explanation for specific types of fraud offences. Elliott and Willingham (1980) also recommend that an interdisciplinary approach be taken when studying management fraud so as to better understand how such acts are committed, by whom, and in what type of organisations.

Reference was made earlier in this chapter to Blackburn's (1993) argument that "whether behaviour is a function of a person or a situation depends on what is meant by *behaviour*" (p.21, emphasis in the original). This point is very important to the work reported in this book and, therefore, Blackburn's argument is quoted at length:

> The claim that behaviour is a function of the situation usually refers to specific acts. However, a specific act or occurrence must be (at least) a function of the situation, because it depends on environmental opportunities and conditions: A could not have hit B without B's presence in that particular context. It is therefore tautologous to say that behaviour is "situation specific", because what identifies a specific act is the situational context in which it occurs. On the other hand, if "behaviour" means a tendency, it is clearly a property of the purpose: it is something he or she carries around with them, which is the product of their prior history. Terms such as "sociable" and "aggressive"... describe tendencies or capacities residing in the person, which are manifest only under relevant conditions ... Acts and tendencies therefore call for different kinds of explanations. A specific act is a function of the situation and the person. The situation is necessary to provide the conditions and

> opportunities for action, but only the person has the power to produce that action ... traits are weak predictors of specific acts ... traits summarise average and likely behaviour, and cannot reasonably be expected to predict single acts, unless other conditions are known ... Theories of criminal behaviour vary in whether they focus on crime, as the aggregate of criminal activities, crimes, as specific criminal acts or events, or criminality as a disposition to engage in such acts (Hirschi and Gottfredson, 1988) ... to contrast "situations" and "dispositions", or proximal and distal factors, as causes of "crime" is a false dichotomy. Clearly, early family experience cannot itself explain why an adult commits a specific criminal act. Equally clearly, some people have strong criminal dispositions, which can only be explained by prior history, not the immediate situation. (pp.21-23)

The studies cited above report correlates of white-collar crime, and characteristics of both the person and situational factors. On the basis of such data, one cannot predict with accuracy who will turn out to be a major fraud offender. What is needed for such a predictive statement is detailed and reliable data on both characteristics of offenders and specific situations. If enough such information were available to generate a predictive model, then one could attempt to provide a *probability explanation*, i.e., how was it inevitable that such an act should have taken place? In the absence of such detailed information on recurring behaviours or because the behaviour in question is a one-off event, the best one can hope for is a *possibility explanation* (Walker, 1977), i.e., how was it possible for someone to commit fraud? By virtue of being narrative, such an explanation is of an historical kind. The existing empirical literature on fraud offenders only allows for possibility explanations. In other words, in attempting to provide an answer to the question "Why is fraud committed?", the available empirical literature enables us to point to correlates of fraud that make it possible for the crime to take place. Such factors, whether operating alone or in combination, can be said to facilitate the commission of the crime. We cannot talk about direct single causes of fraud on the basis of relevant theories in criminology, psychology or sociology because no single feature of a person or a situation makes it inevitable that fraud will be committed. Rather, fraud is more likely to be the result of multiple factors operating contemporaneously.

CONCLUSIONS

This chapter has shown that a number of criminal behaviour correlates relevant to the offender's personality and situational factors have been identified by psychologists, criminologists and sociologists. The characteristics of offenders that are likely to be related to their criminal behaviour include the following: (a) psychological (weak superego/low self-control, low self-esteem, not being attached to other people, egocentricity, lying, lack of anxiety and empathy, over-sensitivity to monetary gain, need for excitement, being indifferent to the consequences of one's behaviour; and impulsivity); and (b) sociological (one's associates, being part of a criminogenic corporate culture, possessing techniques of neutralising one's guilt, and finally being prepared to exploit opportunities). Without ignoring the fact that the theories of criminal behaviour discussed have not been tested on white-collar offenders the present author argues that such correlates of criminal behaviour are also to be found among fraud offenders. The personality correlates of fraud identified together with the various motives discussed in the next chapter enable us to talk about fraud-prone individuals. The notion of fraud-proneness is used to refer mainly to a person with low self-control who is motivated to commit fraud. One's level of self-control (which renders a person crime-prone) in combination with crime opportunity appears to be worth investigating further as one mechanism that affects crime. The existence of an opportunity and pressure on someone to commit fraud are not enough to account for individual differences in who does or does not commit fraud.

Given the importance of an individual's personality and motives in any attempt to explain individual differences in why people commit fraud, as well as situational factors (e.g., opportunity), aetiological factors of fraud identified in this chapter are incorporated in the model proposed in Chapter 4 and tested in the research reported in Chapter 5.

CHAPTER 3

AUDITORS AND FRAUD DETECTION

- Auditor's ability to detect fraud.
- A critique of approaches to fraud detection

WHY FRAUD IS DIFFICULT TO DETECT

Due to the nature of auditing and its inherent limitations, fraud is very difficult to detect. Interestingly, a survey of British accountants by the Audit Faculty of the ICAEW found that the two areas considered as the most difficult to detect were transactions with related parties and manipulation of computer programs ("Fraud Fears", 1997:13). Possible reasons why fraud is difficult to detect are:

- it may be committed by people who are familiar with accounting procedures and can cover it up,
- auditors do not have the requisite education and background to recognise its characteristics (Wells, 1993: 93-94; APB, 1992),
- there is a built-in conflict since auditors are asked to investigate upper management who indirectly are the same group that hired them (Wells, 1993:93-94),
- the scope of audit testing and inquiries were inadequate; the scope of the auditors' work has been restricted by management; the auditors have failed to understand the company's business; failure to identify related party transactions; reliance on uncorroborated representations from management; and deceptions practised on auditors. (Knox, 1994:128[1]),
- time pressure which leads to increased reliance on management's representations (AICPA, 1978:114-121) " and may well prevent the auditor from following up large, unusual and infrequent transactions,
- due to tight reporting deadlines, senior personnel are spread too thin, hence having an impact on the effectiveness of the audit. Interestingly, according to Elliott and Willingham (1980:31)"large transactions near the end of a reporting period have been a feature of a number of fraud cases".

Despite the above-mentioned difficulties, there are some auditors who are able to detect fraud even though it might be well hidden (Bell, Szykowney, and Willingham, 1991; Jamal, 1991; and Johnson, Grazioli, Jamal and Zualkerman, 1992).

APPROACHES TO ENHANCING FRAUD DETECTION BY AUDITORS

A number of models have been developed to assist auditors to obtain expertise in fraud detection, even though it is a rather infrequent experience for them (Loebbecke et al., 1989). Different authors on the subject of fraud detection have

[1] Knox (1994) is an ex- deputy Director of the Serious Fraud Office in England.

taken different approaches and put forward a range of different suggestions aimed at enabling auditors to be more effective in detecting fraud. These can be differentiated into general approaches and specific models.

General approaches

There is a growing supply of published texts on how to detect and/or investigate fraud (see Albrecht et al., 1995; Bologna, Lindquist, and Wells, 1993; Fridson, 1996; Huntington and Davies, 1995; Schilit, 1993 and Thornhill, 1995). Similarly, some of the Big Five firms have recognised the need to survey fraud victimisation (see Ernst and Young, 2000, 1996 and KPMG, 1999, 1996, 1995a and b; 1993a and b), and offer fraud awareness training to their clients.

Fraud can be concealed in financial reports by means of one or more deceptive accounting methods and an auditor needs to possess the skills necessary to read and evaluate financial reports critically (see Fridson, 1996). Schilit (1993) refers to such deceptive accounting tricks as "financial shenanigans"; more specifically, he uses that term to describe "..actions or omissions intended to hide or distort the real financial performance or financial condition of an entity" (p.1). In his book he discusses the following seven shenanigans which enable management to manipulate income:

- Recording revenue before it is earned.
- Creating fictitious revenue.
- Boosting profits with non-recurring transactions.
- Shifting current expenses to a later period.
- Failing to record or disclose liabilities.
- Shifting current income to a later period.
- Shifting future expenses to an earlier period.

For his part, Arthur (1995) maintains that for external auditors to be proficient at detecting fraud, they should be able to use some of the techniques already developed by *pre-emptive fraud investigators*[2] According to Arthur, *Pre-emptive Fraud Investigation* "is a review intended to assess the vulnerability of an organization to fraud" (p.23). On the basis of his survey of suppliers (security firms) and users (accounting firms) of pre-emptive fraud investigation services, Arthur lists the following requirements for auditors wishing to be proficient at fraud-detection, they:

i. need to develop more effective inter-personal skills;
ii. should acquire investigative work experience;
iii. should use non-financial information and information external to the organisation under review;
iv. should use subterfuge (e.g., undercover methods, and surveillance); and
v. should adopt a more suspicious and proactive attitude towards fraud.

---

[2] See Sadgrove (1996:117-131) for an introduction to the topic of pre-emptive fraud.

Finally, he recommends that more experienced and senior auditors should be used "at the coal face" to review crucial documents and to carry out basic tests to detect fraud.

One weakness of Arthur's survey is that the security firms whose opinion was sought about external auditors' fraud detection ability had a vested interest in criticising auditors to justify the pre-emptive fraud investigations services their companies provided. Also, it is highly unlikely subterfuge will ever become an acceptable external audit tool because it raises important ethical and professional issues. Finally, the use of pre-emptive fraud investigation methods will add significantly to the cost of an audit, a major obstacle to introducing such methods into the audit process. According to the *Association of Certified Fraud Examiners Manual* (1994:1.601), to examine company books and records for fraud, one must know and understand the environment where the entity operates (i.e., the business, the industry, major customers, the methods of receipts, the procurement methods) and the accounting system (i.e., the system of internal controls, past, present and future, internal fraud, the audit trail).

The triangle approach in detecting fraud

According to Sorensen and Sorensen (1980:196-225), the triangle approach that can be used to detect management fraud centres on the `Triangle Model', which comprises three parts: (1) a strong, involved, investigative board of directors; (2) a sound, comprehensive system of internal controls; and (3) alert, capable independent auditors. If any of the points in the triangle do not function properly, the entire triangle will collapse, and the opportunity for management fraud is increased.

In order to avoid the triangle collapsing and the opportunity for fraud increasing auditors need to audit the Board where the Board members do not take an active role in the company's operations. Auditors need to ascertain the knowledge and understanding of its individual board members, and assess the board's composition and operation (e.g., how many non-executive directors are on the board, and whether board members attend meetings). In addition, companies should form audit committees to assure the adequacy and effectiveness of accounting and other controls as well as the objectivity of the financial statements.

Sorensen and Sorensen also recommended that auditors investigate management involvement in material transactions which are included in financial statements utilising red flags are tied to conducive economic factors (e.g., pressure to finance expansion via current earnings rather than through equity or debt) and business structures (management tendency to exert extreme pressure on executives to meet budgets). Finally, they also recommend using the risk-based audit approach, which requires the auditor to have an understanding of the overall economy, industry, and environment in which the client operates and a general knowledge of the operations of the client's business AUS 304 (AARF, 1995c).

Elliott and Willingham (1980:38) recommend that the audit team's detection effectiveness can be enhanced by:

i. Improving the "preparation of individuals entering the profession" (p.24).

ii. Audit firms ensuring that they have "measures of individual's sensitivity to evidence of potential fraud, the measures to be used to recruit and promote auditors with greater regard for their acuity in detecting fraud" (p.25).

iii. Varying the "audit procedures from year to year" (p.25) so that perpetrators of management fraud do not become familiar with the audit procedures.

iv. Learning auditing procedures that should have been performed in an audit where fraud is known to have been committed. To illustrate, following the McCusker (1990) report on Rothwells, once again the significance of debtors' confirmations became apparent.

v. The creation of a database of fraud cases to assist auditors in maintaining sensitivity to management fraud indicators.

vi. Appointing members to the audit team with a sociology or a psychology background to question employees on their role in the internal controls, or interviewing outgoing employees who would least fear reprisals.

Pincus (1994) recommends an individual approach. She claims that auditing firms need to recruit and select auditors who are sensitive to red flags. It is doubtful, however, that auditing firms can assess this sensitivity of auditors. She recommends combining this approach with Sullivan's (1993 - as cited by Pincus, 1994) frontal[3] and side[4] approach in order for auditors to be effective in fraud detection.

A practical suggestion about how to enhance auditors' fraud-detection capacity has been made by Davidson (1994) who argues that auditors ought to spend time in forensic accounting departments to gain knowledge about fraud detection.

There is undoubtedly a need for the effectiveness of these fraud-detection enhancement techniques/approaches to be ascertained empirically.

Manipulating trade-offs for the auditor

In an attempt to obtain more information on the relationship between the occurrence and detection of fraud and substantive testing versus compliance testing and audit fees, an experimental simulation was used by Matsumara and Tucker (1992) to gain some understanding about factors that impact on fraud detection by auditors. They developed a theoretical framework drawing on game-theoretic

---

[3] This approach uses increased "manpower and heavy artillery - such as larger samples and more detail tests" (Pincus, 1994:91). With this approach, while auditors will detect fraud, the cost of auditing will increase and, as Pincus claims, will have economic ramifications for the companies and the survival of auditing firms.

[4] This approach involves getting the auditors "smarter" about fraud (Pincus, 1994:92). Auditors need to know more about the nature of the client's business and the industry and auditing firms would need to invest in their auditors' training and improved decision making.

analysis and economic experimentation. The manager moves first by committing fraud. Unaware of the manager's move, the auditor plans his/her compliance and substantive procedures. Substantive testing allows the auditor to detect fraud with a probability that increases with the level of testing (p.753). They examined the importance of four independent variables on the auditor's tests of transactions and balances, fraud detection and incidence of fraud, namely: (1) the auditor's penalty (financial penalty or loss of reputation); (2) auditing standard requirements; (3) the quality of the internal control structure; and (4) the audit fee. They reported the following findings using 39 students (undergraduate business and MBA) as subjects who were asked to play the role of checker (auditor) and marker (manager):

i. Increasing the auditor's penalty decreased fraud occurrence, decreased tests of transactions, increased detailed tests of balances, and increased fraud detection.

ii. Increasing audit procedures increased audit costs, decreased discretionary testing, increased fraud detection and decreased fraud commission.

iii. With strong internal controls, auditors increased tests of transactions and detected fraud more frequently and managers committed fraud less frequently.

iv. Increasing the audit fee resulted in less fraud due to increased testing being done.

v. A direct relationship exists between the extent of tests and likelihood of fraud detection and, consequently, fraud prevention.

It should be noted that Matsumara and Tucker (1992) focused on irregularities in general, i.e., fraud (misrepresentation of fact) and defalcations (misappropriation of assets). Therefore, as they themselves admit, their findings cannot be generalised to management fraud (p.754). A methodological weakness of the Matsumara and Tucker (1992) experimental simulation study is its apparent low external validity because they used university students as subjects. In fact, they concealed the purpose of the study by referring to managers as "markers" and auditors as "checkers".

The Red-Flags[5] Approach

Under this approach, fraud indicators are cues ("red flags") meant to alert an auditor (i.e. make him/her more watchful and suspicious than usual) to the possibility of fraudulent activity, which could have a material impact on the financial statement in a given circumstance. The use of red flags is evident in textbooks on fraud detection (Albrecht et al., 1995, 1982; and Bologna and Lindquist, 1987) and in auditing standards AUS 210 (AARF, 1995a). Recognising the auditor's difficulty in detecting irregularities including fraud, AUS210 (AARF, 1995a) provides a checklist of fraud indicators that might alert the auditor to detect an irregularity.

---

5 Red flags are cues that may be picked up by external auditors or internal auditors which may put them on notice that someone in the company may be engaged in some form of fraudulent or improper conduct.

The notion of "red flags" has been conceptualised by the accounting profession in a very narrow way. Price Waterhouse (1985:31) defined "red flags" as "potential symptoms existing *within* the company's business environment that would induce a higher risk of intentional misstatement of the financial statement" [own emphasis added]. Such a definition ignores attributes of an individual holding a position of trust that point to his/her being crime prone, as will be shown later in this book (see Chapters 5 and 6). It also ignores various external pressures which have an impact on an individual and increase the likelihood of fraud being committed.

According to Sorensen and Sorensen (1980), the red flags approach began in the mid-1970's with Touche Ross designing a set of warning signs for fraud. Following an increase in the expectation that auditors ought to be responsible for fraud detection, some of the U.S. Big Six [then] audit firms developed the red flags approach within their practices (Pincus, 1989).

Uretsky (1980:90-91) emphasised that auditors must be alert for signals that management lacks integrity[6], conditions that may provide a motive for management fraud, and to signs that fraud has occurred. According to Elliott and Willingham (1980:28) red flags do not indicate the presence of fraud. Instead, they represent conditions commonly present in events of fraud and they therefore suggest that auditors should be more concerned with fraud when such indicators are present. Views similar to Elliott and Willingham have been expressed by Johnson, Grazioli and Jamal (1993:485), who argued that neither the use of red flags nor the development of specialised individuals have "been particularly successful" in fraud detection. Johnson et al. arrived at this conclusion on the basis that the problem of fraud detection is better solved "through reasoning rather than through recognition and experience" (p.486).

KPMG's (1993b) fraud survey of the largest companies in the U.S. found that the most frequent reason why frauds remained undetected was insensitivity to red flags. More specifically, it was found that approximately half of the reported fraud "could have been detected more quickly had red flags not been ignored" (p.2).

The effectiveness of the red flags approach depends on the auditor's interpretation of the fraud cues, and its correlation with other evidence found during the audit. Therefore, communication among audit team members is imperative to enable them to compare, analyse and correlate various signals. For a small audit team this might be easy, however, for a large audit team involving up to 100 audit staff, tax consultants and information technology advisers, in various offices or even

[6] A questionnaire survey of 156 auditors from a [then] Big 6 firm by Shaub and Lawrence (1996) found that situational factors that increase professional scepticism include: the existence of a related party transaction, client financial stress, prior client inaccuracies, and prior client-auditor communcation. It was also found that the professional scepticism of the auditors was counteracted when the client was important to the practice of the audit firm as a source of referrals (p.155).

states, it will be very difficult to achieve. As Pincus (1989:155) states, studies (e.g., Sorensen, Grove and Selton, 1983; Wallace, 1983; also see Jones and Maher, 1987 - cited by Pincus, 1989) "have not yet established impressive predictive ability" of the red flags questionnaire.

Pincus (1989) investigated the usefulness of the red flags approach with an experimental study. One hundred and thirty seven auditors, with an average of 18 months' experience at a large CPA firm, were asked to evaluate the possibility of fraud during the planning stage of an audit. An actual case was used. Subjects were asked to review a set of detailed background information for an audit client and to assess the likelihood that material fraud existed. In order to assist their assessment, about half of the subjects were provided with a red flags questionnaire comprising 73 questions (while the other half were not) and were given either a case where the current year financial statements were materially misstated due to fraud or were given a no-fraud case. Pincus found that: (1) the "subjects who used a red flags questionnaire to aid them in fraud risk assessment considered a more comprehensive and uniform set of potential fraud indicators than those subjects who did not use a questionnaire" (p.161); and (2) "there was no significant difference in the assessed fraud risk by questionnaire users and non-users for a no-fraud case, and the non-questionnaire users outperformed the questionnaire users for a fraud case" (p.160). In other words, the use of a red flags questionnaire did not impact significantly on the auditors' fraud risk assessment for the fraud case (p.160). One can argue, however, that the Pincus study did not prove the case against the usefulness of red flags for the following reasons: (1) the auditors used were relatively inexperienced;[7] (2) as Pincus herself admits, several fraud indicators listed by non-questionnaire users were not included in the red flags questionnaire; and, finally, (3) there is the possibility that "the red flags questionnaire used in this study may have underemphasised negative indicators" (p.162).

There is general agreement among authors on the limitations of the use of red flags. According to Pincus (1989:155), the predictive ability for red flags is limited by the nature of the approach. While red flags are associated with fraud, the association is not perfect. In addition, Pincus (1989) and Purvis (1987) pointed out that one major disadvantage of red flags is that they focus attention on specific cues and could prohibit the auditor from identifying or observing other reasons.

Regarding the advantages of red flags, Pincus (1989:155) is of the view that they: (1) are functional to the extent that they appropriately raise the auditor's sensitivity to the possibility of fraud; (2) add structure to the consideration of fraud; (3) provide consistency among auditors; and (4) could increase the possibility of detecting fraud.

---

[7] According to Bonner and Pennington (1990), in order to make reasoned assessments of the likelihood of fraudulent financial reporting, auditors should have at least eight and one-half years' experience.

In testing the predictive ability of red flags, Albrecht and Romney (1986) state that "this validation is important because most of the red flags were identified from single fraud cases rather than a statistically valid study" (p.324). As a result, they prepared "two questionnaires, each containing 87 red flags, (categorised into situational pressures, opportunity to commit fraud and personality factors). One questionnaire was written in the present tense and served as the control group instrument" (1986:324). It was sent to partners on engagements where fraud had not been found and was not suspected. The partners had to indicate whether the red flags were present. The major limitation which detracts from the survey is that the questionnaire was sent to 20 firms and data on 27 past frauds and 36 non-fraud cases were identified. The respondents were asked to rank the red flags, and as the authors themselves state, there "was an insufficient number of responses to statistically test the red flags" (p.331). It was found, however, that only one-third of the 87 red flags were significant predictors of fraud.

Fama and Jensen (1983) argued that the board of directors plays a crucial role in monitoring the actions of top managers and, furthermore, it constitutes the highest internal control mechanism that performs that task. They also argued that the presence on the board of outside directors (who are more motivated to discharge their monitoring responsibility and not to conspire with top managers to victimise shareholders) reduces the risk of financial statement fraud. Beasley (1996) examined the relationship between financial statement fraud (i.e., management fraud) and the composition of the board of directors. He utilised data on 75 fraud and 75 non-fraud firms matched for "size, industry, national exchange where common stocks traded, and time period". He also controlled for "differences in motivations for management to commit financial statement fraud and for conditions that enable management to override board monitoring to carry out the fraud" (p.445). It was found that the inclusion of a larger proportion of outside members on the board of directors (but not the presence of an audit committee) significantly reduces the risk of financial statement fraud.

Fraud Assessment Model

Loebbecke and Willingham (1988) and Loebbecke et al. (1989) developed a descriptive model based on empirical work conducted in two studies. A pioneering research project, it tried to identify as much information as possible on both management fraud and employee fraud.

One basic premise of the Loebbecke et al. (1989) fraud assessment model is that material management fraud (**MI**) occurs when the following three components are present: (1) conditions that provide an incentive (**C**); (2) person(s) in position of authority and responsibility have a reason or a motivation (**M**) to commit a fraud; and (3) person(s) in position of authority and responsibility have an attitude or set of ethical values that allow them to commit that irregularity (**A**).

$$\mathbf{P(MI)=\mathit{f}(C,M,A)}$$

In developing their model, Loebbecke and Willingham (1988) considered the content of the then relevant U.S. Auditing Guideline SAS 53 (AICPA, 1988) which identified factors to consider when assessing the likelihood of management fraud being present. They proposed a reorganisation of those red flags and developed a model which tested management fraud cases reported by the Securities and Exchange Commission (SEC), as well as by Accounting and Auditing Enforcement Releases. They recognised that their model was biased towards those cases investigated by the SEC. As a result, they extended their model in an attempt to gain more information on: "how often can an auditor expect to encounter fraud? Where is it encountered and how is it likely to be detected? What are the common types of fraud? What industries seem to be more fraud-prone than others?" (p.3). They surveyed 125 partners in one of the then Big Six firms and, *inter alia*, found the following:

Management fraud[8] was found to be more prevalent in public than in private companies as well as in technology and communications, transportation and manufacturing companies, but was less frequently encountered in the educational sector. It was mainly committed by top management and occurred in revenue, inventory, related parties transactions, other assets, and accounts receivable. Regarding *defalcations*[9], they were more likely to be committed by a variety of personnel at all levels in an organisation and tended to occur in payroll and cash receipts. Finally, like defalcations, management fraud came to light as a result of substantive tests. They also found that about 25% of instances of defalcation or management fraud occurred with new clients and with clients who had been audited for up to ten years rather than for those who had been audited for more than ten years (p.12). The authors concluded that since detecting a material irregularity is such a rare event, auditors need to maintain their vigilance and not fail to detect them due to a sense of complacency.

On the basis of their findings, they recommend the use of their assessment model on every audit as opposed to a check-list approach. Their model internalises the reasoning process. The work of Loebbecke and his associates has been important in highlighting fraud-vulnerability differences between different types of industries as well as between different financial areas within the same company. They also reported useful correlates of fraud, which can be used by auditors to help detect fraud.

Their model, however, contains a number of important limitations which detract from its usefulness. First, auditors need to make a subjective assessment on each of the three components, and if any one requirement is absent, the overall assessed likelihood is zero. Since it is a subjective assessment, there is the risk that an auditor might not be able to identify a condition(s) that would allow a material

---

[8] Management fraud is irregularities including fraudulent financial reporting undertaken to render financial statements misleading SAS 53 (AICPA, 1988).

[9] Defalcations are misappropriation of assets by employees SAS 53 (AICPA, 1988).

management fraud to occur. Furthermore, in practice, fraud can occur with only two elements being present (see Chapter 6).

Second, it has been maintained by Hackenbrack (1993) that how auditors assess the risk of fraudulent financial reporting using red flags is related to whether they are assigned to the audit of small or large companies. Consequently, since their model is based on a biased sample, it may not be useful to auditors who are routinely assigned to audit small companies.

Third, Loebbecke et al. assumed that the decision concerning whether an irregularity does or does not exist is a dichotomous one. However, this view ignores the fact that irregularities can be located at different points along a continuum and there is discretion in deciding whether there is enough evidence to constitute a material irregularity.

Fourth, their model conceptualises the perpetrator as a pathological individual with deviant attitudes and ethics. Criminologists, however, question such a simplistic perspective of deviance, especially one in terms of pathology (see Taylor, Walton and Young, 1973). The view that there are two types of people, honest and dishonest, can not be sustained given the amount of evidence from studies of criminal behaviour showing that committing offences (with the exception of a few very serious violent crimes) and breaking all sorts of rules and regulations is a characteristic of most people.

Finally, it is not possible to generalise the findings from Loebbecke et al. (1989) to auditors at large because it was based on the responses of audit partners who frequently do not perform the bulk of the audit work and make assessments on fraud indicators but simply review and approve the work of other auditors.

Type of audit experience and differential approach to fraud detection

Recognising some of the weaknesses in Loebbecke et al. (1989), Hackenbrack (1993) conducted two studies to determine the effect of experience with different sized clients on auditor evaluations of fraudulent financial reporting indicators. In a simulation study, the author administered a one-page description of a hypothetical company to 21 auditors with three years' experience in audit work in order to establish a baseline from which to evaluate 16 fraud-related situations. Each situation was based on a fraud-risk factor listed in the AICPA (1987) *Treadway Commission's Good Practice Guidelines for Assessing the Risk of Fraudulent Financial Reporting*. Each auditor had to rate how much each independent situation would increase the company's exposure to fraudulent financial reporting. After completing the rating task, the auditors categorised each of the fraud-related situations as either an incentive or an opportunity. He found significant disagreement about the amount of fraud-risk associated with the fraud related situations presented. None of the fraud indicators examined was found to be significant.

In a second study Hackenbrack (1993:103), examined possible systematic differences in auditors' opinions about the relative importance of incentives versus opportunities when making fraud-risk assessments as a function of whether an auditor's experience had been with small or large clients. Hackenbrack found that "audit seniors presented with the same facts and instances had different opinions about the risk of fraudulent financial reporting. The auditors, assigned predominantly to the audit of large companies, placed more emphasis on the opportunities than the auditors assigned to the audit of small companies" (p.108). The policy implication of this finding is that: (1) "such differences of opinion may lead to differences in planning decisions about the extent of supervision, the extent and selection of audit procedures, and the degree of professional scepticism to be applied on the engagement"; and (2) the need to develop fraud risk engagement tools with high utility cannot be overemphasised (p.108).

The findings of Hackenbrack's two studies, however, need to be treated with caution because: (1) what auditors say they do or influences them may be different from what they actually do and what factors influence them in real audit work; (2) the auditors who participated had on average 37 months' experience in auditing and only 33% of them had experienced fraud detection, i.e., the respondents were relatively inexperienced in fraud detection[10]; and (3) Hackenbrack did not instruct his subjects to make any assumptions about materiality levels, despite the fact that they were reminded that the definition of fraudulent financial reporting is intentional material misstatement. Hackenbrack's studies point to the importance of auditors' experience with different size clients (it could be argued that partners in the then Big Six firms would have bigger size clients than smaller tier firms, which indicates a possible weakness in the Loebbecke et al. (1989) study).

The cognitive approach to fraud detection

Briefly stated, the cognitive approach aims to understand people's decision making by focusing on how they process and utilize information available to them and explaining differential use of the same information. In other words, this approach concerns itself with the thinking and reasoning that underlies one's decisions. As will be shown below, the cognitive approach has been used to detect fraud by utilising information about an auditor's expectations regarding the likelihood that fraud has occurred, and his/her degree of perceptual field-dependence (see below Bernardi, 1994a). From this perspective, fraud detection by auditors is largely a function of the extent to which auditors selectively perceive, interpret and utilise information about fraud so as to justify to themselves carrying out additional tests. Another way the cognitive approach can be used to detect fraud is by enabling the auditor to think like the person who has perpetrated the fraud. The auditor is thus able to avoid being fooled by the fraud offender's deception tactics (see Jamal, Johnson and Berryman, 1995; Johnson et al. 1993).

[10] See Bonner and Pennington (1990).

Fraud detection: Psychological attributes of auditors

There is evidence that an auditor's perception of a client's integrity and competence are important factors in fraud detection (Anderson and Marchant, 1989; Kaplan and Reckers, 1984). Using a modified version of the case study used by Pincus (1990), Bernardi (1994a) tested the following hypotheses:

i. fraud will be detected by auditors at a higher rate when they are provided with low-integrity and competence information about their client;
ii. fraud will be detected by auditors at a higher rate when their prior expectations regarding the existence of fraud increase;
iii. fraud will be detected by auditors at a higher rate when they are more field independent (i.e., are able to recognise embedded figures within larger and more complex figures, as measured by the "Group Embedded Figures Test"), of high moral development (as measured by the short form of the "Defining Issues Test") and are of internal locus of control (as measured by the "Internal-External Locus of Control Test")[11].

The subjects in Bernardi's experimental study were randomly assigned to the experimental conditions (i) and (ii) described above, and comprised 152 managers and 342 seniors from five Big Six [then] auditing firms in the U.S. It was found that the auditors' fraud detection ability was significantly affected by perceptions of client integrity and competence only for high-moral development managers. Managers outperformed seniors but this difference was moderated by the latter's moral development, and finally, a positive relationship was found between an auditor's prior beliefs concerning the existence of fraud and fraud detection. Bernardi (1994a) concluded that "auditors should be more suspicious about the probability of fraud existing" (p.78) and that "accounting firms should develop specialized training aimed at increasing auditors' awareness of the probability of fraud" (pp.78-79).

In her discussion of the Bernardi (1994a) study, Pincus (1994) argued that the reason why no differences were found between field-dependent and field-independent[12] auditors may well reflect a shift towards a more field-independent population distribution for auditors. Furthermore, that shift may reflect more field-independent people being attracted to auditing as a career and/or remaining in the field and not so much the increase in computer technology in auditing. Pincus also questioned Bernardi's hypothesised relationship between an auditor's locus of control and fraud detection, on the basis that an auditor can influence outcomes and events in

---

[11] See Bernardi (1994a and 1994b) for details regarding these different tests.

[12] A field-independent person (the opposite of a field-dependent person) is someone who is good at recognizing figures which are embedded within larger and more complex figures (Bernardi, 1994a:71). Field-independent individuals have been found to be more efficient at constructing inferences, to be better at solving problems and, finally, to detect fraud at a higher rate (p.71).

the external audit despite his/her locus-of-control rating as far as everyday life is concerned (p.92).

Another criticism levelled against Bernardi (1994a) by Pincus (1994) concerned the finding that auditors who failed to detect fraud were insensitive to ethical attitudes of their client's management. Pincus argued that this finding was attributable to weaknesses in the research design used by Bernardi, namely the extreme manipulation of the client integrity/competence or that some of the subjects misinterpreted the moral development scales used or, finally, that adding the competence/integrity scale experimental manipulation was unrealistic. Pincus concluded that "further research on auditors' sensitivity to management integrity is the only means to determine whether Bernardi's results are disturbingly real or spurious" (p.94).[13]

Using general strategies

Managers are in a position, if they wish, to word/"frame" their annual report in such a way as to conceal fraud or to otherwise mislead financial statement users (Kahneman and Tversky, 1986 - cited by Jamal, Johnson and Berryman, 1995). According to Jamal et al. (1995:86), "a framing effect occurs when alternative descriptions (frames) of a problem activate different representations in the mind of a problem-solving agent". Thus, a "*framing effect*" would refer, for example, to the impact of changes in management's descriptions in the annual report on the auditor's decision making. In the context of an audit, a representation is a mental image of such task-relevant constructs as materiality and audit risk and their interrelationship. Kahneman and Tversky (1986) proposed that there are two ways a framing effect can be detected:

i. Using *multiple representations*, i.e., considering alternative representations of the particular problem (e.g., gains vs. losses). By being in a position to know the different solutions for different representations of the same problem, the auditor can identify which particular representation is likely to be invalid; and
ii. using a procedure that will transform all problems into a *standard representation*. An example of such a procedure is the conversion of different streams of cash flows into net present value (Jamal et al., 1995:87).

Jamal et al. reported that financial statement fraud can be better detected by converting alternative versions of a problem into a standard representation, instead of a multiple representation. Twenty-four audit partners were asked in a simulation study to think aloud while carrying out a concurring partner review in four cases in which client management had constructed a misleading frame (description of the company) and a financial statement fraud. All the (seven) auditors who used a standard representation were successful in detecting both management's frame and the financial statement fraud in all the four cases used. Auditors using a single

[13] See Bernardi (1994b) for his reply to Pincus (1994).

representation detected neither the frame nor the fraud. Four auditors who used multiple representations were only successful in detecting the company's overall company frame and not the fraud in the four cases. Jamal et al. concluded that their results suggest that a strategy that uses multiple representations may not be effective in complex task domains such as auditing (p.102).

Finally, Jamal et al.'s findings lend support to the idea that management has the power to deceive auditors by using framing effects. Over half (13) of the audit partners who took part in their study were deceived by management despite their training, experience and motivation not to be deceived (p.102).

Using specific strategies to counter management's deception tactics

Johnson et al. (1993) developed a cognitive model using an interdisciplinary approach. Their model transforms the problem of fraud detection by auditors into an adversarial information processing problem in the context of one auditor examining the financial statements of a company, the management of which is assumed to attempt to deceive the auditor. Their model proposes that while management attempts to deceive the auditor by utilising their knowledge of the business and accounting practices as well as deep cognitive strategies and tactics for constructing a deception, auditors can use strategies and tactics for detecting such deceptions. Furthermore, they claim that fraud detection requires knowledge which is not based on direct experience of fraud detection and consider fraud to be an instance of a deception created in order to cheat on a social contract. For an auditor to detect such a deception, they must first understand the strategies for constructing a deception. A deceiver can use "dissimulative deceptions [hiding the real]" or "simulative deceptions [showing the false]". For an auditor to detect such deceptions, they need to identify the misrepresentation created by the deceiver. Johnson et al. consider this an easy task since there are constraints created by the deceiver, for example, information which is not readily available to the auditor. Johnson et al. identified a number of "strategies and tactics that have been developed as a means of constructing a deception, and use them to specify constraints that must be processed by any agent that attempts to detect this deception" (p.469).

A basic goal of management is to create a favourable impression among financial statement users such as creditors and investors. Additional goals of management that can lead to the creation of a deception were suggested by Turner (1980:101 -104 - cited by Johnson et al., 1993:472) and include the following:
Table 1[14] shows seven deception tactics that can be used to cover up an overstatement of earnings.

[14] Reproduced from Johnson et al., 1993:472

Table 1: Examples of Deception Based on the Goal of Overstating Earnings

Strategies for Deception	Examples of Tactics for Creating Deception
Masking	•Failing to record or disclose an expense or a liability. •Eliminating differences with the target representation by deleting non complying items.
Double play	•Improperly applying Generally Accepted Accounting Principles, where an item is not individually material.
Mimicking	•Adding a misleading narrative about the company. •Spreading the extent of the fraud into small manipulations, individually not material.
Dazzling	•De-emphasizing issues by reporting them in the notes to the financial statements rather than reporting them in the financial statement.
Inventing	•Creating fictitious transactions or transactions without substance. •Creating external factors justifying attributes that deviate from the misleading representation.
Repackaging	•Changing the labels that characterize attributes in the financial statements. •Reframing issues to maliciously justify attributes that deviate from the target representation.
Decoying	•Creating "blind alleys"; anomalies which after a close examination turn out to be inconsistent with the misleading representation.

i. overstatement of earnings (e.g., in order to maximize compensation);
ii. obtaining financing (credit, capital) despite condition of financial distress (e.g., by fulfilling contractual obligations such as bond covenants);
iii. evading legal tax liability;
iv. manipulating the company's stock price;
v. consolidating management's reputation despite unsatisfactory performance (e.g., by increasing R&D investments);
vi. concealing the sale or assignment of fictitious or misrepresented assets;
vii. fulfilling regulatory constraints (e.g., portfolio restrictions);
viii. concealing illegal activities (e.g., bribes); and
ix. embezzling.

It would be useful if auditors had some way of identifying intentional misleading assertions made by management that constitute fraud. As a starting point, it would be helpful to know the tactics management use to conceal fraud in the financial statements. Johnson, Jamal and Berryman (1991) reported three such tactics, namely:

i. by describing a company as expanding rather than on the verge of collapse, for example, management deceives an auditor into having false expectations about the company; as a consequence, the auditor fails to notice inconsistencies;
ii. by presenting information about the company in such a way (creating a "frame") as to induce the auditor to test non-irregularity hypotheses in order to evaluate inconsistencies that are created; and
iii. breaking up an impropriety and presenting and rationalising a series of small manipulations to particular accounts in the financial statements (each one on its own immaterial) in order to minimise the likelihood of the auditor detecting the material misstatement.

According to Johnson et al. (1993), the strategies the auditor can use to detect deception fall into two categories:

i. Strategies for finding evidence suggestive of the process used to perpetrate the deception. The auditor can first look for "situational" red flags as signs that management's personal financial situation is in distress or that a manager's compensation scheme relies on the company's income, which would motivate management to deceive the auditor. Second, the auditor can look for signs showing manipulation activity such as a manager who insists personally on approving all payments of a particular kind.
ii. Strategies that utilise information contained in the manipulation environment. The auditor: (1) recognises cues that reveal a manipulation; (2) is cautious about what inferences he/she draws in order to avoid committing him/herself to accepting management's representations early on in the audit; (3) reduces the scope for management to deceive by making the audit both exhaustive and accurate (thus preempting management's attempt to deceive); and finally (4) focuses on the goals and limited actions management can take in order to concentrate on what and how a manipulation can be effected. The last strategy is known as the "intentional-based" strategy and is "one of the most likely to be uncovered in the concurring partner review task" (Johnson et al., 1993:475).

Johnson et al. go on to outline four deception tactics[15] and the line of reasoning actually used by their model to solve the case used in their study. Johnson et al.'s (1993) model of fraud detection makes use of the "risk hierarchy" from Johnson et al. (1992). Their model is a means of solving the problem of fraud detection through reasoning rather than through experience and recognition. Its main weakness is that it is time-consuming and imposes a high demand on human

[15] See Johnson et al (1993:479) for details of these deception tactics.

resources, as it requires that every inconsistency, however small, be evaluated as a potential fraud. Consequently, its wide adoption by auditors generally (as opposed to fraud auditors) is questionable. The model satisfies four independent basic information processing requirements, namely: (1) activation; (2) detection; (3) editing; and (4) revaluation[16]. Johnson et al. (1993) validated the model on four known cases and two clean cases. The model was also compared with the judgement of 24 experienced concurring partners. Their model was successful in detecting fraud in all five cases to which it was applied and it was found that the tactics used in the model to detect fraud are very similar with such tactics used by auditors who have been successful at detecting fraud. Johnson et al. (1993:485) concluded that neither the use of red flags nor the use of auditors who have specialised knowledge about particular industries to examine financial statements has been particularly successful in detecting fraud.

CONCLUSIONS

The usefulness of the various fraud detection approaches (i.e., general, triangle, manipulating trade-offs, red flags, fraud assessment, differential approach, and cognitive) described in this chapter will be enhanced if the various approaches are used to supplement one another. To illustrate, the counter-deception strategies advocated by Johnson et al. (1993, 1992) can be supplemented with knowledge derived using Loebbecke et al.'s (1989) fraud assessment model. To assist auditors, a fraud detection model is developed which integrates and expands on the merits of models discussed in this chapter. The next chapter describes and argues the case for (1) a *descriptive model of the aetiology of fraud*; and (2) an *eclectic fraud detection model*. Empirical findings about both models are reported and discussed in Chapters 5 and 6 respectively.

[16] Described in more detail, according to Johnson et al. (1993:476-478) the four requirements/stages are as follows: (1) in activation the auditor looks for cues in the financial statement, calculates expectations, identifies inconsistencies between cues and expectations, thus generating potential symptoms of manipulations; (2) in detection the auditor uses one or more deception-detection tactics to generate hypotheses about the manipulations of the environment, some of which concern possible goals of management; (3) editing, in the light of the manipulations hypothesized in (2) in using deception-detection tactics, the auditor edits the initial representation in (1) and for each inconsistency identified in (2) the auditor identifies a dollar value which expresses its likely impact on the operating income of the hypothesized manipulation. Finally, (4) in revaluation, the auditor makes a decision concerning the appropriate action to be taken, i.e., determines the materiality of the hypothesized manipulations and the conclusion reached is expressed in the audit opinion. The success of the method described is based on two principles: (i) coverage - this states that "success in the task of fraud detection is based on the use of the goals of a fraudulent management for interpreting detected inconsistencies", and (ii) composition - this states that "success in the task of fraud detection is based on the ability of combining cues that are functional to the achievement of management goals as elements of a larger manipulation" (Johnson et al., 1993:478).

CHAPTER 4

MODELS OF FRAUD AETIOLOGY AND FRAUD DETECTION

- Three fraud-aetiology models.
- A critique of three fraud-aetiology models.
- A new model of why people perpetrate fraud.
- A model of fraud detection.
- Conclusions

INTRODUCTION

The model/theory of why people commit fraud put forward in this chapter incorporates and expands on ideas from existing models. It is argued that we can identify factors which make the commission of fraud possible, but not inevitable. The factors are presented as "correlates of fraud" since a correlation indicates an association between two factors but not a causal relationship. The model depicts the three components necessary for fraud to occur. Systematic knowledge concerning the aetiology of fraud is then incorporated in a fraud-detection model to enhance auditors' fraud-detection ability.

THREE MODELS OF FRAUD: Albrecht et al. (1995), Cressey (1986), and Loebbecke et al. (1989)

As far as the concepts used by the three models are concerned, even though they all focus on workplace fraud they do not use the same terms for it. Cressey is concerned with embezzlement while Loebbecke et al. talk about management fraud and defalcations, whereas Albrecht et al. use fraud in such a way as to encompass both.

For Albrecht et al. (1995) the essential components are presented in the "fraud triangle" and consist of: (1) perceived opportunity to commit fraud; (2) financial and/or non-financial pressure; and (3) rationalisation. These are explained below:

i. *Perceived opportunity to commit fraud*, convert the fraud and conceal the offence. Albrecht et al. provide the following examples of opportunities: lack or circumvention of controls that prevent and/or detect fraudulent behaviour; inability to judge quality of work; lack of disciplinary action; asymmetrical information; ignorance and apathy, and no audit trail (p.27).

ii. *Financial and/or non-financial pressure*. *Financial pressure* includes factors such as greed, living beyond one's means, high personal debt, high medical bills, poor credit, personal financial loss, unexpected financial needs, (p.20). *Vice pressure* includes factors such as gambling, drugs, alcohol and expensive sexual relationships. *Work-related pressure* such as to get even with one's employer or somebody else, getting little recognition for job performance, experiencing job dissatisfaction, fearing losing one's job, being bypassed for promotion and feeling underpaid, (p.24). *Other pressures* such as having a spouse who insists (either directly or indirectly) on an improved lifestyle or a challenge to beat the system.

iii. *Rationalisation.* Albrecht et al. list the following examples: the organisation owes it to me; I am only borrowing the money and will pay it back; nobody will get hurt; I deserve more; it's for a good purpose, and finally, something has to be sacrificed (p.46).

On the basis of his studies of embezzlers, Cressey (1986) identified the following three components necessary for fraud to take place:

i. *Someone with an unshareable financial problem.* According to Cressey, people have problems of this nature "if it seems to them that they cannot turn to ordinary, legitimate sources for sorely needed funds" (p.199).

ii. *Someone who knows how to solve the problem* in secret by violating his/her position of financial trust. Cressey points out that, "everyone in a position of financial trust has hundreds of opportunities to violate that trust. That's part and parcel of being trusted - if there is no opportunity for people to steal, it is meaningless to say that they are trusted" (p.200). Furthermore, it is often the case with professionals in positions of financial trust that knowledge and techniques concerning fraud are taught as part of professional training courses.

iii. *Someone who possesses neutralising verbalisations* that render committing fraud "right", cast, for example, in terms of "necessity", "just borrowing the money", "don't care" or "business is business".

Finally, Loebbecke et al. (1989:5-7) suggested that the following three components of their model must all be present if management fraud in particular is to take place:

i. *Conditions* (i.e., the "degree to which conditions are such that a material management fraud could be committed"[1]). Examples of conditions listed by Loebbecke et al. (1989:6-7) include: management operating and financial decisions are dominated by a single person; management (particularly senior accounting personnel) turnover is high; organisation is decentralised without adequate monitoring; the existence of frequent and significant difficult-to-audit transactions or balances; a weak control environment; conditions that indicate lack of control of activities (e.g., constant crisis conditions, disorganised work areas, frequent or excessive back orders); a lack of control over computer processing; inadequate policies and procedures for security of data or assets; and complex calculations affecting the balance or class of transactions.

ii. *Motives* (i.e., the degree to which the person(s) in "positions of authority and responsibility in the entity have a reason or motivation to commit management fraud"). Examples of motives that may result in management fraud include: management places undue emphasis on meeting earnings projections; profitability of entity relative to its industry is inadequate or inconsistent; sensitivity of operating results to economic factors (inflation, interest rates, unemployment, etc.) is high; rate of change in entity's

[1] These are weaknesses in internal controls.

industry is rapid; solvency problems or other internal or external matters that question the entity's going concern; excessive emphasis on meeting targets so as to receive a substantial portion of management compensation.

iii. *Attitudes* (i.e., "the degree to which the person or person(s) in positions of authority and responsibility in the entity have an attitude or such set of ethical values that they would allow themselves - or even seek - to commit management fraud"). Loebbecke et al. list the following: management's attitude towards financial reporting is unduly aggressive; management places undue emphasis on meeting earnings projections; management's reputation in the business community is poor; frequent disputes about aggressive application of accounting principles that increase earnings; and evasive response to audit inquiries (pp.6-7). It should be noted at this point, however, that there is an inconsistency between Loebbecke et al.'s definition of attitudes and the examples provided. As argued below, in effect Loebbecke et al.'s *attitudes* can not be taken to mean *rationalisations*.

All three models postulate three components as essential for an explanation of why people commit fraud, except for Loebbecke et al's the three components of which are in fact two since it ignores "rationalisations". While the terms used by the different authors for each component are different (see Table 1), two of the three refer to the need to have a person with a motive who rationalises/justifies committing fraud by exploiting a perceived opportunity.

Loebbecke et al.'s "conditions" is synonymous with Albrecht et al.'s "opportunity". Cressey's "the knowledge of how to solve the problem in secret, by violating a position of financial trust" (p.199) appears at first glance to be different from "conditions" and "opportunity". However, the notion of opportunity is contained in Cressey's emphasis on someone with the know-how to commit fraud. This is because, as Cressey points out, someone can only be said to hold a position of financial trust if he/she has opportunities to violate that trust.

Table 1 : Necessary Components for Fraud to Take Place

Albrecht	Perceived opportunity to commit fraud	Financial and/or non financial pressure	Rationalisations
Cressey	Knowhow	Unshareable financial problems	Possesses neutralising verbalisations
Loebbecke	Conditions/ Attitude	Motive	

The way Loebbecke et al. define "attitudes" is synonymous with Albrecht et al.'s "rationalisations" and Cressey's "neutralising verbalisations". However the examples of "attitudes" they list (see above) are a set of company characteristics which are conducive for fraud to occur. Thus, unlike Albrecht et al. and Cressey, they fail to take into account the importance of rationalisations that make fraud possible for an individual offender. This omission is perhaps explained by the fact that they only surveyed audit partners, had no data on individual offenders and did not draw on relevant psychological, sociological, and criminological literature on the aetiology of fraud. Recasting Loebbecke et al.'s model in terms of the ROP model components (see below) we have only a crime-prone person with a motive (P) and opportunity (O).

Loebbecke et al. (1989) and Cressey (1986) both indicate that all three elements (as they state them) must be present if fraud is to take place. Albrecht et al. (1995) are the only authors who draw attention to their three elements as *interactive*. By interactive they mean that "... the greater the perceived opportunity or the more intense the pressure, the less rationalisation it takes to motivate someone to commit fraud. Likewise, the more dishonest a perpetrator is, the less opportunity and/or pressure it takes to motivate fraud" (p.19).

In their use of "attitudes" Albrecht et al.'s and Cressey's models utilise knowledge from such other disciplines as psychology, sociology and criminology pertaining to the type of person who is likely to be a fraud offender. However, they all can be criticised for: (1) not doing so within a psychological, sociological or criminological theoretical framework; and (2) not dealing adequately with the notion of traits that render someone to be crime-prone. In other words, no attempt is made to account for individual differences as far as the aetiology of fraud is concerned by considering the individual offender's personality traits which predisposes him/her to commit fraud under particular circumstances. This is a serious deficiency in their models. Their explanations of why people commit fraud are incomplete and, consequently, their practical usefulness for auditors who want to enhance their fraud-detection ability is limited. In addition, all three authors have also failed to conceptualise "opportunity" so as to include the broader socio-economic context in which fraud takes place and to locate it within a theoretical framework such as Clarke's (1980) situational approach to criminal behaviour.

The model of fraud developed in this chapter incorporates and expands on ideas in the three models discussed, including the notion of rationalisations, as well as incorporating the notions of a crime-prone person and situational factors that facilitate the crime.

A MODEL OF WHY PEOPLE COMMIT FRAUD

The model of fraud put forward incorporates the ideas of the three models discussed earlier but expands on them by making good their common drawback of ignoring individual differences in crime-proneness. The model also: (1) incorporates the emphasis on the three fraud elements being interactive; (2) emphasises the importance of a motivated crime-prone individual; (3) stresses the importance of offenders' rationalisations/ justifications of their fraudulent activity; and (4) acknowledges that the process by which employee or management fraud comes to be committed is not necessarily a straightforward one.

The model also acknowledges that fraud offenders are not homogeneous; some have no second thoughts about embarking on a spree of fraud offences; for others, however, it can be an agonising decision and then end up being serial fraud offenders when they only intended to commit a single offence. Finally, others continue to commit other fraud offences not out of a need to cover up those already committed, but because they come to enjoy the proceeds of their first offence and believe they can go on perpetrating fraud without getting caught. For this type of individual, greed has replaced the original need for money to pay a debt. In other words, offenders become overconfident, greedy and compulsive, thus continuing offending until they get caught.

Assumptions of the model

The following assumptions underpin the model:

i. Generally, fraud is made possible by the presence of three preconditions, namely, an opportunity to commit the crime (**O**); one or more motivated crime-prone persons (**P**) who is/are likely to be in a position of financial trust and who has/have the knowledge of how to commit the fraud, convert the money, and conceal the offence; and, the use of rationalisations (**R**)/justifications (i.e., the thinking processes) that enable the individual(s) concerned to carry out fraudulent activity by overcoming any inhibitions imposed by one's conscience or by one's perception of the risks involved (Albrecht et al., 1995; Cressey, 1986).

ii. Each of the conditions are correlated with fraud occurrence. However, if an opportunity for fraud does not exist, this does not necessarily stop a crime-prone person with a motive and the necessary rationalisations from creating such an opportunity. To illustrate, a professional career fraudster sets out to infiltrate a company, or even establishes one in order to perpetrate his crime irrespective of the state of the national economy, the financial pressures on the company or the system of internal controls.

iii. Fraud offences and offenders are characterised by a significant degree of heterogeneity (Cressey, 1953) and no single explanation can account for all frauds.

iv. Employee and management frauds are committed for a variety of motives such as having an unshareable financial problem, acting out of love for the company and the employees, financial pressure, acting out of greed, wanting personal justice, wanting a challenge and, finally, being a professional/career conman (Albrecht et al., 1995; Zietz, 1981).

v. The majority of potential fraud offenders have a perceived urgent need for money while a minority seeks some other non-financial reward.

vi. Correlates of fraud exist at different levels of analysis: society, the individual company, the individual perpetrator(s) and, finally, situational factors.

vii. There are individual differences in how a person in a management position will resolve a particular company financial problem and/or a particular personal problem that calls for the raising of money urgently (Cressey, 1986). People predisposed to dishonest behaviour are more likely to commit fraud as a solution to a financial problem they face, if they perceive an opportunity to do so and believe they will not be found out.

viii. There are individual differences in how a person in a non-management position will choose to resolve a particular individual/family problem that calls for the raising of money. Such differences are largely explained by the crime-proneness of an individual (Albrecht et al., 1995).

The model of employee and management fraud must account for established facts about the offence and the offenders as well as the processes by which the offenders come to commit the offence. It is known, for example, that demographic, criminal justice, and personality attributes of such offenders include the following:

- getting first convicted when of a mature age (Benson and Moore, 1992);
- being a specialist offender, i.e., only committing fraud (Thomas, 1992);
- being predominantly male of high educational status (Wheeler et al., 1982);
- having weak self-control (Gottfredson and Hirschi, 1990);
- having a weak superego (Blackburn, 1993);
- because of their socialisation into some aspects of corporate culture (Sutherland, 1949) there is often an absence of constraints on their behaviour because they are not committed, are not involved and do not believe in conventional values and goals (Hirschi, 1969);
- egocentricity, feeling no anxiety or remorse (Eysenck, 1977);
- insensitivity to the consequences of their behaviour (Eysenck, 1977);
- over-sensitivity to monetary gain (Bartol and Bartol, 1994); and
- an ability to rationalise their misbehaviour, neutralise guilt and so justify it to themselves (Albrecht et al.,1995; Cressey,1986; Matza, 1969).

Some of the apparent inter-relationships between the demographic offender attributes listed above are explained by the following: the upper echelon of the executive world is male-dominated, as are the accounting and legal professions; tertiary qualifications are almost essential for someone to acquire a senior position of trust within a company; it takes a number of years before one can lay claim to such a management position and, finally, having a prior criminal record as an adult correlates with leaving school early and not with completing a tertiary degree (Farrington, 1993).

A representation of the model is as follows:

$$Pr(Fraud)=f(R,O,P)$$

The probability of fraud is a function of the three components. The model will now be referred to by the acronym **ROP** (see Figure 1). The three components of ROP are elaborated on below. Two basic features of ROP are that it attempts to account for: (a) the interactive relationship between the different components; and (b) individual differences, i.e., not everyone who is motivated to acquire extra money and is presented with an opportunity to do so actually goes ahead and commits fraud. Another important feature of ROP is that it concedes that there is an overlap between the different components. To illustrate, the fact that someone has the knowledge to commit the fraud and conceal the offence can be considered either as a characteristic of a motivated crime-prone person or as part of the notion of opportunity. Also, as already mentioned, "motive", "opportunity" and "rationalisations" cannot be considered independent of the individual offender's personality.

To use an analogy, a law-abiding member of the public walking along a residential street sees houses, whereas a recidivist burglar assesses opportunities for breaking into houses and identifies lucrative targets. Similarly, a weak internal control remains just that to a manager or an employee with strong moral scruples, but it is perceived as a great opportunity to steal money by deception by someone with a weak conscience and thus predisposed to break the law if he/she believes he/she can get away with it.

It should be noted that "crime-proneness" as an attribute of an individual is not used in the ROP model as a dichotomous variable but is conceptualised as being located along a continuum. The existence of any one of the ROP model's three components is not enough for fraud to occur. Many people may become aware that there is a weakness in the system of internal control of a company but only those who are crime-prone will perceive it as an opportunity to commit the offence. Furthermore, a crime-prone individual will go ahead, exploit an opportunity and commit a fraud with or without accomplices if he/she can justify the deed to him/herself. A person who does not possess the necessary rationalisations would not be in a position to justify committing the crime to him/herself. In this sense, the components of the ROP model are interactive.

Drawing on Blackburn's (1993:21-23) distinction between acts and tendencies, it can be stated that:

i. there exist one or more acts/occurrences of fraudulent activity which depend on environmental opportunities and conditions for their occurrence;
ii. there are individuals who, for a number of psychological, sociological, and other reasons (e.g., financial pressure) are fraud-prone, i.e., given an opportunity to commit fraud they are likely to exploit it and justify it to themselves;
iii. only an individual, or two or more individuals conspiring together, has/have the power to commit an act of fraud;
iv. committing fraud is a function of the situation (i.e., opportunity in terms of both company characteristics and situational factors that facilitate the

commission of fraud) and the existence of a person with both the necessary predisposition and motive as well as rationalisations;

v. personality attributes of individuals by themselves are weak predictors of specific acts of fraud, but are useful red flags for auditors insofar as they summarise average and likely behaviour; and

vi. one could expect to predict a single act of fraud if one knew enough about an individual's personality traits that point to his/her tendencies to break the law, and if one had enough information about a given situation in terms of opportunities for fraud and relevant conditions.

Finally, the model needs to be viewed in the broader socio-economic context. The fact is that fraud increases during economic recessions when high interest rates exert financial pressure on both companies and individuals. In addition, the existence of multiple moralities within society and a largely utilitarian approach to ethics by the corporate culture (i.e., a state of "anything goes", of "ethical neutralism") in the competition for profit which expects a lavish lifestyle from its members, are conducive for fraud (Cressey, 1986). Consequently, a crime-prone manager/ accountant/ lawyer who cannot maintain mortgage payments on the family home because of drastic increases in interest rates may well exploit opportunities to commit fraud against clients.

The three components of the proposed model (see Figure 1).

Opportunity

Fraud is facilitated by: the existence of opportunities for individuals who collude to commit the crime; a lack of emphasis on fraud-prevention controls by a company; the absence of a code of conduct (KPMG, 1995a); and the presence of inadequately trained internal and/or external auditors.

Two characteristics that affect the opportunity for fraud are organisational structure and management style. Changes in management style such as the shift from a hierarchical, authoritarian one to a more democratic one, coupled with the influence of economic rationalism and staff downsizing, have resulted in flatter organisations where middle management (which used to watch out for fraud signs) has disappeared.

Undoubtedly, a poor control system provides opportunities for someone to commit fraud. Such opportunities include, for example, sloppy paperwork, the issuing of cheques payable to cash and giving discounts to clients who pay cash. The fraud surveys by KPMG (1999, 1996, 1995a, 1995b, 1993a, 1993b) found that poor internal control was the one factor that underpinned most frauds both in Australia and in 17 other countries. Albrecht et al. (1995) provide a comprehensive discussion of fraud opportunities within companies. Drawing on Albrecht et al., it can be said that such opportunities can take the form of:

i. Inadequate internal controls (improper management modelling; bad communication or labelling; ineffective hiring procedures; unclear organisational structure and assigned responsibilities, and an ineffective internal audit department).

ii. Lack of adequate control procedures that prevent fraud (e.g., inappropriate segregation of duties or dual custody; lack of a system of authorisations, independent checks, physical safeguards, and documents and records).

iii. Noncontrol factors that provide opportunities for fraud to be committed (e.g., inability to judge the quality of performance; failure to discipline fraud perpetrators; lack of access to information; ignorance, apathy or incapacity, and lack of an audit trail).

Cohen and Felson (1979) put forward the idea that crime can be understood in terms of people's daily routine activities. They also drew attention to the fact that criminal offences often take place due to the absence of capable guardians (e.g., police presence or other forms of surveillance) who increase the risk of offenders being apprehended, thus preventing the commission of offences being committed. Both internal and external auditors can be thought of as capable guardians. Auditors do not fulfil the role of the capable guardian when, for example, they come to rely more on management's representations due to reporting deadlines; and/or senior audit partners are spread too thin (i.e., they are deployed ineffectively as far as overseeing the quality of audit work is concerned) due to excessive time pressure. Under such circumstances fraud becomes more likely.

A theory of why fraud is committed must also account for the fact that employee and management fraud often involves more than one offender. KPMG's (1995a) national fraud survey found that collusion was involved in one-third of the cases and comprised 8% internal collusion and 24% collusion with third parties (p.11). Similar findings were made in the 1999 survey. Similarly, KPMG's (1996) international (18 countries) fraud survey reported that collusion between employees and third parties was the second most common element that allowed fraud to occur (p.12). Collusion in fraud cases against a company is often necessary for offenders to circumvent separation of duties, an impediment made easier to overcome by weak internal controls. Therefore, collusion between someone within the company and a client of the company or some other outside party is essential for some types of fraud to take place.

Situational factors such as a perceived low risk of being detected and a perception that upon conviction the likely penal sanction will be a relatively lenient one, contribute to fraud as they negate any notion of deterrence (Braithwate, 1989). A good reason why an offender may remain undetected is that there is a tendency for such individuals to not only hold positions of trust, but also to be hard working, not to take holidays and to be able to cover up their offences effectively (Loisel, 1996). Prosecution difficulties in convicting major fraud offenders means that such defendants are in a strong plea-bargaining position. The fact remains, however, that even though many people hold positions of trust in a company and are aware of opportunities to commit fraud, not everybody does it. Let us, therefore, consider what might explain such individual differences.

Person with a motive and a crime prone personality

The challenge for a theory of fraud is to account for individual differences. The fact is that not all crime-prone individuals who perceive an opportunity to commit fraud are motivated to do it. Also, not all motivated crime-prone individuals who perceive an opportunity eventually commit fraud because they may not possess the necessary rationalisations. As Albrecht et al. (1995:49) point out, some people commit fraud due to a lot of financial pressure while others do it "even though no real pressure or opportunity for fraud exists.... Most people are somewhere in between these two extremes". Excluding professional career conmen, it can be said that "When the combination of pressure, opportunity and rationalisation becomes severe enough, they cross the line of honesty and commit fraud" (p.49). It should also be noted that while for many fraud offenders the decision to commit the offence is a rational one, for a minority it is the result of a slow process whereby they half-heartedly commit the first offence as a quick-fix solution to an unshareable financial problem (Albrecht et al., 1995; Cressey, 1986). They experience a lot of guilt; they hope they will be able to pay the money back very soon and that will be the end of their misbehaviour, but they find they have to go on committing frauds to cover up those already committed, i.e., they sink deeper and deeper into fraudulent activity as they "rob Peter to pay Paul". Such offenders may well stumble across an opportunity to commit fraud (e.g., as when someone entrusts them with a large amount of cash), or they first commit fraud to misappropriate small amounts of money but the small thefts snowball and the offending gets completely out of control.

Drawing on a large number of fraud cases described in the literature[2] and on the basis of lengthy discussions the author had with MFG officers[3] regarding fraud offences and offenders they had investigated for major fraud and the different circumstances under which fraud occurs, the following types of individuals who commit fraud(s) as well as the circumstances under which they do so can be identified:

i. The offender is predominantly a highly educated male, of mature age when first convicted and is not versatile in his/her offending.
ii. The offender has weak self-control.
iii. The offender rationalises his/her criminal behaviour, justifies it to him/herself and feels no guilt for the crime.
iv. The offender is a professional, career conman, who infiltrates a company (or even establishes one, even though a bankrupt) and gets him/herself into a

---

[2] See Albrecht et al., 1995; Bologna, 1993; Cressey, 1986; Zietz, 1981.
[3] Det/Sgt Wayne Monk, Det/Chief Inspector Robert Cockerel, and Commander Allen Bowles.

position of trust in order to commit the crime. In other words, fraud is the goal from the moment this type of person enters a company.

v. The offender commits a fraud because of a belief, sometimes unrealistic, that he/she can get away with it and, also that he/she will be able to return the money to its rightful owner(s).

vi. The company faces financial problems and is in urgent need of money and someone in a management position rationally decides to commit one or more frauds to rescue the company, believing that he/she will be able to pay back the money to its rightful owner(s) and/or because of a belief that he/she can meanwhile conceal the offence(s) and not get punished. Here fraud is committed more out of love for the company than any animosity towards it or some egocentric motive.

vii. A company's financial problems lead a particular member of management to experience socioeconomic status disequilibrium and self-concept incongruence as he/she and/or his/her family can no longer enjoy the same lifestyle:
   a. but, due to strong self-control adjusts his/her expenditure accordingly and does not need to commit fraud; or
   b. due to weak self-control does not adjust his/her expenditure accordingly, and commits fraud once or repeatedly. For some people, being seen to be successful is more important than being honest.

viii. An individual in a position of trust persuades, or (by virtue of having weak self-control) is persuaded by, an outsider to embark on a scam to deceive and to share the money stolen.

ix. Fraud is committed by a crime-prone individual in response to a felt personal need, e.g., to buy a house because one is engaged to be married or in order to help loved ones.

x. Due to some vice pressure (e.g., gambling, drugs, alcohol, expensive sexual relationship) or for sheer excitement, an individual lives beyond his/her means. The financial pressure could also come from a spouse who insists (directly or indirectly) on a more expensive lifestyle than the individual can afford. Fraud is committed in response to such an unshareable financial problem by individuals who possess the necessary neutralising verbalisations to justify committing the offence.

xi. According to Albrecht et al. (1995), someone in management or an employee of a company commits fraud because of some animosity towards the company in order to get even. An employee may be disgruntled because of feeling underpaid, overlooked for promotion, job dissatisfaction, fear of losing his/her job, or getting little recognition for his/her job performance.

xii. Utilising an orthodox (i.e., Freudian) psychoanalytic perspective, the unconscious wishes of a high socioeconomic status individual, whose company is facing insolvency, may be sublimated and find expression by perpetrating a fraud which provides the needed recognition or status in the context of the corporate culture (Blackburn, 1993:114).

xiii. A person with an antisocial personality disorder (see Blackburn, 1993; Eysenck, 1997) is excessively egocentric, feeling no anxiety or remorse, and being insensitive to the consequences of committing one or more frauds on the victims. Such a person is predisposed to commit fraud under some financial or other pressure that call for the urgent raising of money if there exists an opportunity for fraud.

xiv. Finally, someone may commit fraud to prove they can beat the system, i.e., as a challenge (Albrecht et al., 1995).

Rationalisations

It needs to be emphasised that, as Cressey (1986) has argued, ultimately a trusted person with an unshareable financial problem who perceives an opportunity to commit fraud does so as a result of neutralising verbalisations that make possible frauds against or for the company. In other words, in order to commit fraud it is not enough for someone to be in a position of trust, with an unshareable financial problem and an opportunity to commit fraud in secret. By violating that trust, acting alone or with one or more accomplices, they need to talk themselves into a belief that, somehow, they have a "right" to perpetrate the crime. Therefore, it is the ability to rationalise and justify committing the offence(s) that ultimately makes fraud possible. In this context, how a manager feels towards the company (an example of motivation which may reflect one or more company characteristics) is important in understanding his/her *neutralisation techniques* (i.e., rationalisations) which make fraud possible[4].

Cressey's (1986) theory of why managers commit fraud involves a psychological process which includes among its three components "the ability to find a formula which describes the act of embezzling in words which does not conflict with the image of oneself as a trusted person" (p.199). Cressey called this "neutralising verbalisations", and argued that "they make up the most important element in the process which gets a trusted person in trouble, or keeps the person out of trouble" (p.200). Cressey stated that "every trust violator [he himself] interviewed used a neutralizing verbalization" (p.201). More specifically, Cressey found that imprisoned embezzlers made use of the notion that their case was one of "necessity", or that their loved ones were in a dire situation or that their employers "were cheating

[4] A past president of the Institute of Chartered Accountants in Australia (ICAA) at the time of writing, Rob Wylie, has warned that economic rationalism and staff downsizing have indirectly created the ideal climate for fraud ("A Climate for Fraud", 1996:9). The possible impact of these changes and staff downsizing includes fixed-term appointments, increases in job insecurity, a decline in corporate loyalty, low morale and the adoption by staff of a mercenary attitude to one's employers. These are factors that contribute to fraudulent activity.

them". However, such justifications were cast in terms of "borrowing", "ownership" or "don' t care" (p.201). He pointed out that rationalisations[5] used by fraud offenders are not made up by offenders on the spur of the moment but "they are learned, and are reflections of cultural ideologies pertaining to the propriety of committing crime under certain circumstances" (p.201). In this sense, the rationalisations one uses to justify committing fraud are related to both one's socialisation and personality (which encapsulates one's values, attitudes and behavioural patterns) generally as well as to socialisation into the contemporary corporate culture.

Cressey argued that neutralising verbalisations used by both management and employees who commit fraud are accounted for by Sutherland's (1949) differential association theory. According to this theory, people rationalise their behaviour in ways they have learned from associates. Cressey also argues that the source of rationalisations used by management who commit fraud for the company (e.g., to increase its profits) is a number of ideologies which permeate the business world. He lists four such ideologies: (1) honesty is the best policy but business is business; (2) it's all right to steal a loaf of bread when you are starving; (3) government regulation of business is socialistic and counterproductive (p.201); and (4) it's necessary (p.204). Thus, rationalisations are made possible, on the one hand, by the existence of widely-accepted ideologies that are part of the corporate culture and the socialising effect and, on the other, the socialising effect of differential association.

Rationalisations is the third element in Albrecht et al.'s fraud triangle, the other two being perceived opportunity and pressure. On the basis that generally "there are very few, if any, people who do not rationalize" (p.46), these authors maintain that "nearly every fraud involves the element of rationalization. Most fraud perpetrators are first time offenders who would not commit other crimes. Someway, they must rationalise away the dishonesty of their acts" (p.46). Such rationalizations sometime mean lying to oneself and sometimes to others (p.47). Albrecht et al. (1995:46) provide the following list of common rationalisations used by fraud perpetrators:

i. The organisation owes it to me.
ii. I am only borrowing the money and will pay it back.
iii. Nobody will get hurt.
iv. I deserve more.
v. It's for a good purpose.
vii. Something has to be sacrificed - my integrity or my reputation. (If I don't embezzle to cover up my inability to pay, people will know I can't meet my obligations, which will be embarrassing because I am a professional).

It needs to be emphasised at this stage that, as already argued above, that all three components of the model (opportunity, a crime-prone person with a motive, and rationalisations) are necessary for fraud to occur. As already mentioned, knowledge

[5] What he termed "vocabularies of motive".

concerning the aetiology of fraud would need to be integrated in a fraud-detection model in order to enhance auditors' fraud-detection ability.

A MODEL OF FRAUD-DETECTION

There has been an increasing amount of published literature on how auditors can become better at detecting material misstatements, including employee and management fraud. Fraud detection, of course, does not exist in a vacuum but needs to be considered in the broad context of audit work and against the backdrop of the knowledge of why people commit fraud. Having a definition of fraud detection helps to focus attention on the areas concerned. Albrecht et al. (1995) state that it "includes the steps or actions taken to discover that a fraud has been committed"; that "one of the most difficult tasks is determining whether or not a fraud has actually occurred", and that the "detection of fraud begins by identifying symptoms, indicators, or red flags that can be associated with fraud" (p.53). Recognising indicators of fraud is but the first step in detecting fraud, because the auditor then needs to pursue the indicators concerned until an unequivocal decision can be made as to whether fraud has in fact been perpetrated. Consequently, the availability of a checklist of red flags, however exhaustive, is not going to lead to more fraud being discovered than would otherwise be the case if the red flags are considered in isolation from other relevant information about fraud risk, and if the auditor is not inquisitive enough to pursue fraud indicators he/she has recognised.

Chapter 3 discussed different approaches that have been put forward to enable auditors to better detect fraud. While some of the approaches are very simplistic and do not warrant serious consideration, others have merits that point to the need of combining different approaches. For example, the practical usefulness of a comprehensive list of red flags is significantly diminished if an auditor has no knowledge of various deception strategies management can use as well as counter strategies he/she can use, to detect such deceptions. Similarly, complaints by a company's employees, clients or competitors, can provide the auditor with useful information/tip-offs that can alert him/her to the possibility that fraud may have been perpetrated.

The model developed in the next section is intended to: (1) bring together the essential components of a fraud detection strategy and guidance on the relevant tactics; (2) enhance auditors' ability to detect fraud by incorporating a component based on the *ROP model;* and (3) demonstrate how feedback from auditing experience in detecting fraud utilising the model can be used to train auditors in the task, as well as to set up and update fraud-detection data bases in order to keep up with the inventiveness of many fraud perpetrators.

The model's content

People commit fraud, therefore, an auditor needs to be aware of existing knowledge about why people commit fraud if he/she is going to detect it. The pattern-recognition/risk-assessment decision making process that precedes fraud-detection by an auditor would be incomplete without knowledge about the reasons people commit fraud. Hence, the ROP model is an essential part of the proposed eclectic fraud detection model as shown in Figure 2.

The phrase "adequate knowledge of a company's environment where the entity operates" means the auditor has an understanding of the overall economy and industry in which the client operates, and a general knowledge of the operations of the client's business as provided in AUS 304 (AARF, 1995c). Information of this kind should be incorporated into the auditor's overall fraud-risk assessment regarding the business, industry, major customers, methods of receipts, and procurement methods. Such knowledge would, for example, draw the auditor's attention to whether it is a high fraud risk industry or a high risk financial area within the company. The fraud survey by KPMG (1999:8) found that insurance, Communications, Retail, Education, Transportation, Government, Automotive, Tourism and Hospitality were the high fraud risk industries. Their previous surveys however (1996; 1995a; 1993a) found that high risk industries are manufacturing and finance and high risk financial areas are cash, inventory, revenue and expense cycles (see also Deakin University, 1995, and Loebbecke et al., 1989). The accounting and internal control symptoms of employee fraud and operational ones listed by Albrecht et al. (1995:76-93) are categorised under:

i. Irregularities in source documents. Common fraud symptoms involving source documents, such as cheques, sales invoices, purchase orders, purchase requisitions, and receiving reports include items such as missing documents, alterations on documents, duplicate payments, photocopied documents, etc.
ii. Faulty journal entries. The following are common journal entry fraud symptoms: journal entries without documentary support; unexplained adjustments to receivables, payables, revenues, or expenses; journal entries that don't balance; journal entries made by individuals who would not normally make such entries; and journal entries made near the ends of accounting periods.
iii. Inaccuracies in ledgers. Two common fraud symptoms related to ledgers are: a ledger that doesn't balance and master (control) account balances that do not equal the sum of the individual customer or vendor balances. The first symptom is indicative of fraud in which cover-up in the accounting records is not complete. The second ledger symptom is indicative of manipulation of an individual customer or vendor's balance without altering the master receivable or payable account in the ledger.
iv. Unexplained changes in financial statements such as a disproportionate increase in debtors when compared to sales growth.
v. Internal control weaknesses such as: lack of segregation of duties; lack of physical safeguards; lack of independent checks; lack of proper authorizations; lack of proper documents and records; overriding existing controls; and an inadequate accounting system.

vi. Fraud symptoms involving relationships with other parties include items such as significant litigation, a frequent change in solicitors or auditors, a high turnover of key management positions or board members, etc.

The part of the model dealing with fraud symptoms/indicators/red flags draws heavily on the work of Albrecht et al. (1995). Considering the various fraud-risk information sources from left to right, we note the importance of the auditor paying particular attention to information that someone in management, for example: has been/is under financial pressure; has a criminal record or his professional credentials are otherwise dubious, or leads an extravagant lifestyle beyond his means. Finally, the auditor should need information that someone in management exhibits behavioural changes such as sudden mood swings; is a heavy drinker; a heavy smoker; is on drugs; is unable to relax; suffers from insomnia; is unable to look people in the eye; is defensive; and argumentative. Albrecht et al. (1995) describe the "psychological aftermath of crime" as comprising "guilt > fear > stress > behaviour changes" (p.126). It can be argued, however, that there are people who do not feel any remorse after committing a crime (Eysenck, 1977). Information about an individual's employment history and contact with the criminal justice system can be easily obtained by means of background checks. Similarly, the auditor's fraud-detection ability will be enhanced by the company's relationship with its lawyers, auditors, board members, regulators and the Taxation Department, management, banks and other lenders, related parties and other companies and, finally, with its vendors or customers (see Albrecht et al., 1995:104-105). Useful intelligence information about a company's relationship with other parties and the life of its management or employees can sometimes come from tips and complaints by the company's employees, clients or competitors.

Albrecht et al. (1995) discuss fraud symptoms indicative of the following specific types of potential fraud:

i. Management fraud (operation performance anomalies, management characteristics that indicate possible motives, organisational structure anomalies, irregularities in relationships with outside parties)[6].

ii. Employee fraud (accounting anomalies, internal control weaknesses, analytical anomalies, extravagant lifestyle, unusual behaviour, tips and complaints).

iii. Investment fraud (e.g., "unreasonable promised rates of return, investments that do not make sound business sense, pressure to get in early on the investment..." (Albrecht et al., 1995:66).

iv. Kiting (e.g., signature and maker on kited cheques are often the same, area abnormalities, i.e., many out-of-area cheques; frequent deposits, cheques, and balance inquiries, escalating account balance, bank abnormalities, average length of time money is in the account is short)[7].

[6] See pp.60-64 in Albrecht et al. for further details.

[7] See Albrecht et al. (1995:70).

Authors on fraud detection emphasise the importance of the auditor and other fraud examiners looking out for, recognising and pursuing further "anomalies" of one kind or another. One such basic "anomaly" is an overly complex organisational structure which, according to Albrecht et al. "seems to exist without real purpose", but is intended to "mask financial statement frauds by not allowing auditors and other outsiders to understand that transactions were not at arm's-length and that substantial amounts of revenue and income were not legitimate" (p.95). Finally, the possible existence of fraud may be indicated by what Albrecht et al. term "analytical fraud symptoms, i.e., out-of-the-ordinary procedures and relationships that are implausible" such as increased revenues with decreased cash flows, increased inventory with decreased payables, etc.

If we take a look at the fraud detection model (see Figure 2) we also see that the auditor's endeavours to detect fraud are more likely to prove fruitful if: he/she has the support of his firm; the auditor possesses certain attributes and adopts a suitable approach to the task; addresses inherent risk before control risk which, in turn, should precede detection-risk assessment (Monroe, Ng, and Woodliff, 1993); and he/she is able to synthesise fraud-risk information from a variety of sources that point to "anomalies". If one or more of these ingredients are not present, fraud detection is likely to prove an elusive goal for the auditor. While the proposed model addresses the broad range of information-inputs into effective fraud detection, it does not claim to guarantee that, using it, an auditor will detect carefully-concealed frauds. It needs to be pointed out in this context that while, on the one hand, recognising even one fraud indicator can lead an auditor to discover fraud, on the other, recognising a number of red flags and pursuing them extensively may prove a false alarm.

For the proposed fraud detection model to be applied successfully, the auditor is required to process, evaluate critically, and synthesise a significant amount of information (including information contained in the ROP model) about a client. It is the ability to synthesise the information concerned that is essential for the model to work.

CONCLUSIONS

The interactive model of the aetiology of fraud holds that fraud is generally committed as a result of a combination of factors, namely, rationalisations, opportunities and person(s). It is argued that a variety of people commit fraud for a variety of motives and who the offenders are cannot be attributed to a random process. The model sets out the different ways in which fraud becomes possible when a crime-prone individual under financial pressure or with other motives, perceives at least one opportunity to commit fraud and the individual has both the knowledge to commit (alone or in collusion) and conceal the fraud and possesses the neutralising verbalisations that enable him/her to perceive committing the offence once or repeatedly seem "right". The need to locate the three sufficient components of ROP in a broader socioeconomic context is emphasised. Rationalisations constitute the most vital of the three components that make up the psychological process of information processing and decision making that precedes an act of fraud. By incorporating ideas from the existing models and expanding on them, by introducing the concept of crime-proneness and drawing on knowledge in other disciplines, ROP can be said to be a new model with high usefulness potential for auditors.

The need to enhance auditors' fraud detection ability cannot be overemphasised. Audit experience alone, however, cannot make auditors fraud-detection experts. The ROP model of the aetiology of fraud is an important part of the eclectic fraud detection model developed in this chapter. The model of fraud detection highlights the importance of having a competent, ethically-minded auditor, who is well versed in the aetiology of fraud, in management deception strategies and counter deception strategies, and who enjoys the full support of his/her firm as far as fraud detection is concerned. Moreover, an auditor should have a good overall view of the company's environment and internal control system, be alert to information about both individuals within the company who are high risks of potential fraud as well as about the company's relationship with outside parties and, finally, be aware of and guard against his/her own unintended biases in carrying out the audit.

Two studies were conducted to test the models developed in this chapter (see Chapters 5 and 6). The first study was concerned with demographic, *modus operandi* and criminal justice characteristics of major fraud offenders prosecuted successfully by the MFG in Melbourne. The first study also aimed to construct a two-component profile of the major fraud offender and to test the ROP model as well as Loebbecke et al.'s (1989) fraud assessment model. The second study involved a survey of 108 Australian auditors' experience of detecting irregularities including management and employee fraud. The second study also tested a number of hypotheses based on the fraud detection model proposed and examined the applicability of Loebbecke et al.'s fraud assessment model. The ROP model could not be tested in the second study as the auditors surveyed (see Chapter 6) were in no position to provide adequate data on offenders' crime-proneness and rationalisations.

Model of Fraud Aetiology

Figure 1:

Level 1- Descriptive Model of Fraud Aetiology
(ROP Risk Assessment Model)

Level 2 – A Detailed Account of the Descriptive Model of Fraud Aetiology (ROP Risk Assessment Model)

Fraud Detection Model

Figure 2:

Level 1- *Eclectic Fraud Detection Model*

Level 2- A Detailed Account of the Eclectic Fraud Detection Model

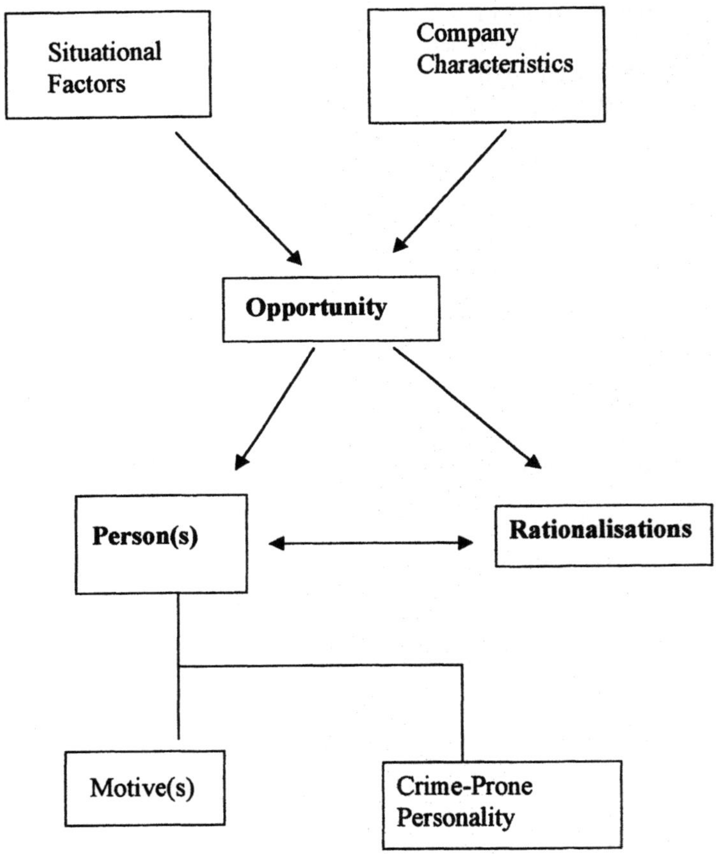

Figure 1- Level 1- *Descriptive Model of Fraud Aetiology (ROP Risk Assessment Model)*

Figure 1 Level 2: A Detailed Account of the Descriptive Model of Fraud Aetiology (ROP Risk Assessment Model)

Situational Factors:

- Collusion opportunities; absence of capable guardians; auditors rely excessively on management's representations; senior audit partners are spread too thin; perception of low risk of being apprehended for fraud; perception of lenient sentence if convicted.

Company Characteristics

- Collusion opportunities; lack of adequate control procedures that prevent fraud; non- control factors providing opportunities for fraud to be committed; lack of code of conduct; criminogenic corporate culture.

Motive(s)

- Non-financial pressure, e.g., need to be seen as successful.
- A disgruntled manager or employee.
- Acting out of love for the company and the employees (e.g., an individual in a management position commits fraud to rescue the company in the unrealistic hope that he/she can soon pay back the money borrowed or that the company will improve.
- Commits fraud in order to beat the system for a challenge, thrill.
- Financial problem (e.g., under financial pressure due to some vice or due to living beyond one's means or in order to help a loved one, or does not adjust his/her lifestyle and/or lives beyond his/her means)
- A professional conman
- Acting out of greed, alone or in collusion

Crime-Prone Personality

- Weak super ego/self-control; low self–esteem; not being attached to other people; egocentricity; propensity for lying; lack of anxiety, remorse and empathy; over-sensitivity to monetary gain; need for excitement; being indifferent to the consequence of one's behaviour; and impulsivity

Rationalisation

- Ability to rationalise their misbehaviour, neutralise guilt and justify it to themselves (e.g., the organisation owes it to me; I am only borrowing money and will pay it back; nobody will get hurt; I deserve more; it's for a good purpose; something has to be sacrificed)

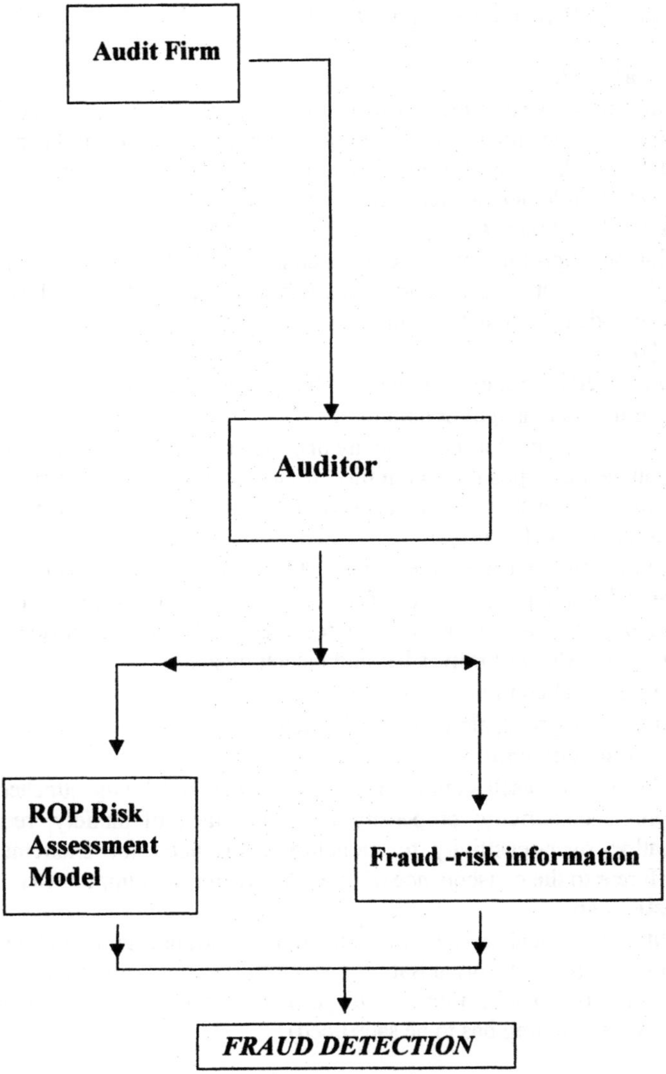

Figure 2 - Level 1 *Eclectic Fraud Detection Model*

Figure 2 Level 2 – A Detailed Account of the Eclectic Fraud Detection Model

Audit Firm

- Needs to provide incentives for auditors to probe fraud deep enough to counter the deterrent effect of such undesirable consequences of fraud detection as litigation; ensure that auditors are not under pressure to complete audits within unrealistic time limits; ensure that management has not restricted the scope of the auditor's work.

Auditor

- Does not rely on uncorroborated representations from management (London Oil Storage).
- Specifically assess the risk of material misstatment (AARF, AUS210, 1995a).
- Is both analytical and inquisitive (McCullogh, 1994).
- Is aware that his/her type of client audit experience can impact on how far the audit focuses on opportunities for fraud and knowledge on prior existence of fraud should be used (Bernardi, 1994a).
- Has adequate knowledge of the company's environment and its accounting system as well as being aware of high risk audit areas for fraud within a company (Loebbecke et al., 1989).
- Assesses inherent risk, control risk and detection risk in this order (Monroe et al., 1993).
- In assessing control risk evaluate management's integrity and competence, (COSO, 1990; Bernardi, 1994a).
- Assesses the composition of the Board of Directors and the characteristics of the Non-executive directors (Beasley, 1996).
- Individual approach (Pincus, 1994) in combination with frontal and side approach (Sullivan, 1993).
- Uses counter deception tactics to identify deception constructed by management (Johnson et al., 1993).
- If a control weakness is found the auditor should determine whether it has been abused and not just to correct it (Albrecht et al., 1995:58).

Fraud-risk information about (a) individulas and (b) the company (Albrecht et al., 1995): (a) a fraud-proneness profile of person(s) in position of trust that includes lifestyle, accomplices, criminal record, behavioural changes; and (b) accounting control of company; specific types of fraud e.g., management fraud, employee, investment kiting; company's organisational structure; relationship with other parties, (e.g., auditors, lawyers); tips and complaints.

CHAPTER 5

PROFILING MAJOR FRAUD OFFENDERS PROSECUTED BY THE POLICE

- Criminal profiling.
- A study of major fraud offenders.
- Representative vignettes.
- Offence, offender, victim and criminal justice characteristics.
- A taxonomy of major fraud offenders.
- Empirical support for the three components of the ROP model.
- Testing the applicability of Loebbecke et al.'s model.
- Discussion of results.
- Conclusions.

INTRODUCTION

An apparently untapped source of knowledge for auditors is to be found in official files on serious fraud offenders prosecuted by specialist police squads like the MFG in Melbourne or the Serious Fraud Office in London and in New Zealand and other such entities in the U.S and elsewhere. Who are these offenders who commit fraud for or against companies? What motivates their criminal behaviour? How do they justify doing what they do? Do they stand out in any way? If so, how can auditors use such information to assist them in detecting fraud? The criminological research reported in this chapter attempts to provide answers to these questions.

The film "Silence of the Lambs" popularised one approach to investigating serious crime known as "criminal profiling". The well-known British expert on criminal profiling, Professor David Canter, argues, in his 1994 book *Criminal Shadows: Inside the Mind of a Serial Killer*, that a profile is like a silhouette, a shadow, that an offender leaves behind at the scene of the crime. The profiling process developed by the FBI's Behavioural Science Unit (see Douglas, Ressler, Burgess, and Hartman 1986), also known as "psychological profiling" as well as by its technical term "criminal investigative analysis", is "an investigative technique by which to identify the major personality and behavioral characteristics of the offender based upon an analysis of the crime(s) he or she has committed" (Douglas and Burgess, 1990:1). Thus, while profiling does not yield the specific identity of the offender, it points to the kind of person most likely to have committed the offence(s) (Douglas et al., 1986).

The concept of offender profiling is based on the argument that "neither a crime nor an offender is completely unique" (Jackson and Bekerian, 1997:2). In other words, there are limits to the number of motives and the methods of carrying out a crime - there are always patterns to be identified and to be compared with those in other cases (p.2). In view of the fact that, as shown later in this chapter, fraud often involves serial offenders, offender profiling can provide auditors with useful knowledge to improve their fraud-detection ability. Profiling "can be based on clinical experience, research and statistical analysis of offender databases" (Jackson and Bekerian, 1997:3).

The profiling process

According to two FBI special agents Douglas and Burgess (1990) who have contributed to the development of criminal profiling, the technique is a viable investigative tool against violent crime. Criminal profiles draw on demographic and police data on particular categories of offenders and interviews with known offenders. In order to develop a psychological profile of a serious criminal it is essential that the crime scene be carefully studied. In the case of major fraud, the crime scene may be someone's office, one or more computers used by the offender and the system of internal controls. The weapon used by a fraud offender is his/her deception strategy and tactics. Turco (1990) emphasises the importance of being able to utilise demographic material based on population studies of known perpetrators of particular crimes when it comes to constructing a profile. In the case of major fraud, such data could include the type and style of deception used, the relationship between the offender, the victim(s) and the method(s) used to conceal the offence(s). The offender's motive(s) is an integral piece in this criminal jigsaw puzzle.

Criminal profiling (personality assessment) has been used to narrow the field and thus assist police in: managing hostage negotiations, identifying anonymous letter writers and individuals who have made oral or written threats of violence, investigating single and serial cases of arson, rape, and sexual homicide (Douglas and Burgess, 1990). Profiling has also been used with serious obsessive-compulsive offenders, including exhibitionists and kleptomaniacs (Reese, 1979 - cited in Blau, 1994). Finally, in an unusual proactive application of profiling, Hagaman, Wells, Blau and Wells (1987) developed a family homicide profile that could be used to predict such an event and possibly prevent the homicide. Proactive profiling has not been used with fraud. The research results reported later in this book show that the profiling technique could also be applied to such white-collar offenders as fraud perpetrators.

According to Copestake (1994:17), criminal profilers like Canter maintain that in order to understand and predict crime one needs to look for clues in the lives of individual offenders, in the "shadows" they leave behind. In order to understand the individual offender and their crime, one needs to assess the "distorted story about life each offender tells him/herself". "Distorted stories about life" refer to offenders' rationalisations that help them to: (1) justify their criminal behaviour to themselves and reduce, if not remove completely, any sense of guilt; and (2) resolve any discrepancy between, on the one hand, viewing themselves as successful and "respectable" citizens/professionals and, on the other, the knowledge that they are committing crimes.

Turco (1990:148) points out two limitations of profiles based on such data. First, an accurate prediction before the arrest of the subject is not possible since a large number of people fit the demographic characteristics of the profile but do not commit the crime in question. Second, there is no real theoretical basis for the profiles. Turco does admit, however, that such profiles allow organisation of material collected by police investigators. A theoretical basis is provided for the profile of fraud offenders put forward below.

According to investigative profilers at the FBI Behavioural Science Unit, profiling has been used by law enforcement in the U.S. "with success in many areas..." (Douglas and Burgess, 1990:1). Tetem (1989 - cited in Blau 1994) reviewed 193 cases where profiling was done and found that 45% of the cases, had been resolved. Of more interest, perhaps, is Tetem's finding that in 17% the accuracy of the profile was such as to identify the suspect. Tetem also reported that in 77% of the cases the profile had been of significant help to the investigation. Blau (1994) concluded his discussion of the usefulness of criminal profiling stating that it is a potentially useful tool. Of course, some of the demographic attributes of fraud offenders (e.g., age and educational status) are obvious. This is due to the time and qualifications normally required to acquire a position of financial trust in a corporation where one can effect major fraud.

Utilising data from police prosecution files on major fraud offenders, the study reported in this chapter attempts to: collect and analyse demographic, modus operandi and criminal justice data; identify clues to the frauds in the lives of the offenders and their rationalisations for their behaviour; construct a two-component profile of offenders consisting of: (1) at a general level, demographic characteristics; and (2) a classification in terms of offender typologies; compare fraud indicators in the ROP model and Loebbecke et al.'s (1989) fraud assessment model with those identified in the Major Fraud Group of the Victoria Police (MFG) cases; test Gottfredson and Hirschi's (1990) premises in their general theory of crime that: (a) white-collar offenders (like the major fraud offenders studied) do not specialise in one type of crime, but are versatile; (b) that a person's self-control in interaction with criminal opportunity, is the major cause of crime; and examine the validity of the eight assumptions underlying the ROP model of fraud correlates.

Drawing on the existing empirical literature, the study reported in this chapter investigates whether the following six propositions are applicable to the serious fraud offenders examined as well as the validity of one prediction of the ROP model.

i. generally, the probability of fraud occurring is a function of opportunity, a motivated crime prone individual and rationalisations (i.e., $PR(Fraud)=f(ROP)$);
ii. a serious fraud offender will tend to have weak self-control, be egocentric and indifferent to the consequences of his/her behaviour;
iii. some of their motives for committing the offence are such as to distinguish them from common offenders (i.e., persons perpetrating major index crimes other than fraud). More specifically, unlike common offenders like burglars or armed robbers, their motives will include greed, revenge and committing fraud as a challenge, i.e., in order to beat the system;

iv. they generally utilise techniques of neutralisation to reduce their status incongruence that arises out of their offending (Matza, 1969);
v. the majority are first offenders (Cressey, 1986);
vi. there are identifiable clues to the crimes perpetrated in the lives of such offenders; and
vii. a criminal profile of such offenders is possible.

The six propositions and the one prediction listed above were tested in a study of 50 major fraud cases prosecuted by the Major Fraud Group of the Victoria Police.

A STUDY OF 50 SENTENCED MAJOR FRAUD CASES

Methodological considerations

With the cooperation of the Major Fraud Group (MFG) of the Victoria Police in Melbourne, Australia, the usefulness of the fraud aetiology model that was constructed on the basis of existing knowledge was examined using prosecution data pertaining to fifty serious fraud offenders sentenced by the courts in the State of Victoria. Those major fraud cases (the average amount of money involved was $AUS 4.4M) were selected from a total number of 196 cases, covering the period January 1990-October 1994, where the occupation of the offender was known. Of those, the MFG had completed its investigation and a complete prosecution brief existed in 96 cases. The criteria for selecting a case for inclusion in the study were: (1) the offender held a position of financial trust; (2) the offender/s involved in a case had been sentenced by the courts and thus the information was public knowledge; (3) there was a complete prosecution brief available, and (4) the file could be accessed in the Metropolitan Melbourne region. If one of those criteria did not apply, a case was not included in the study. Thirty-seven cases not included in the study involved occupations that were either beyond the scope of the research or where the cases should have been included but were not because it proved impossible to locate the files.

A coding guide was used to code data for analysis on a total of 28 offence, (offender, victim and criminal justice characteristics see below) which had been identified in the literature review (ibid chapter 2). Quantitative data were collected to test the 'opportunity' and 'person' component of the ROP model. In addition, qualitative data on the culprits' rationalisations were also collected.

It was not considered necessary, as in Langdale (1990), to attend court hearings since the prosecution briefs had all the details required about the case and the offender. Unlike Langdale, the present study was not designed to look at "legal difficulties in alleged business fraud, the loss and hardship it may or may not cause, the offender's perspective and consequential media report" (p.17). In addition, as Langdale discovered, "the length of each brief was considerable and the fixed court date not less than eight weeks" (p.17), factors that made it impossible for the research to focus on additional aspects of fraud trials in view of the constraints on time and resources available to the researcher. The amount of money involved in a fraud case varied from $17,173 to $108,580,000 with the mean average dollar loss to the victim(s) per case being approximately $4.4 million. While the cases studied cannot be said to be representative of serious fraud cases investigated by the MFG in general, they can be said to be representative of major management fraud investigated by the MFG (e.g., misappropriation of trust accounts money, false valuations, false loans, stealing customers' money) and prosecuted by the Director of Public Prosecutions in Victoria.

Unstructured interviews were also conducted with thirteen MFG detectives to supplement the data on offenders available in the MFG briefs. The data were collected for the purpose of generating a taxonomy (i.e., a list of typologies) of such offenders. A total of 13 interviews were carried out with detectives who headed particular investigations and were responsible for preparing the prosecution brief.

Types of fraud involved

The types of fraud involved in the 50 MFG cases used in this study are: financial statement manipulation and theft of assets (46%), trust account fraud (28%), theft of assets (22%), financial statement manipulation (2%) and, finally, financial statement manipulation and trust account fraud (2%).

Data collection and coding

Following a pilot study of six cases, data were collected. The following variables were chosen[1] because they had been identified as relevant to the aetiology of fraud in the discussion of the empirical literature and/or because they form part of the ROP model:

i. **Gender**

Gottfredson and Hirschi (1990); Ross (1977); Wheeler et al. (1988, 1982); and Weisburd et al. (1990) discuss males as offenders of white-collar crime. Wheeler et al. (1988) argued that women offenders are under-represented among the highest tier of white-collar offenders, such as antitrust and securities fraud, because they occupy relevant organisational positions in lesser numbers than males. The Wheeler et al. (1988) sample was drawn from 1976-1978 records. Nowadays, however, women have higher educational achievements and are more likely to choose a professional career. As mentioned earlier, it has been claimed that women commit fraud for different reasons than men. Zietz (1981) reported that women who committed white-collar crime were more likely to do so due to family needs than to fund high living, unlike their male counterparts. However, limitations of the Zietz study (discussed in Chapter 2) mean that we cannot accept

[1] Some variables were dropped e.g., main sentence imposed, court of first instance, type of legal representation, how many months did it take to prosecute, under what law were the fraud charges, ethnicity as they were outside the scope of the present book.

unquestioningly her conclusion that women's criminality is motivated by family needs more than men's. Zietz (1981) was also testing Pollak (1950) and Reckless' (1961) findings that female crime has traditionally been underestimated in criminology (Pollak, 1950:161) as well as the claim that female crime is due to women being "more deceitful than men" (Reckless, 1961:8). Reckless argued that women belong to a "special order of criminal behaviour" (p.78) and findings should not be generalised. Gender differences in criminal behaviour have also been proposed by Barnes and Teeters, (1959:62) who stated that there is a group of women who are "calculating, fascinating and intelligent, who capitalise on their charm and femininity". However, the question of whether women white-collar offenders are more deceitful than their male counterparts cannot be answered on the basis of existing empirical evidence[2]. Gender was not used as a determining factor when the present author selected the sample of cases. Finally, on the basis of the existing literature, there is no reason why the ROP model should distinguish between male and female fraud offenders.

ii. **Marital status**

While neither Wheeler et al. (1988) nor Weisburd et al. (1990) investigated the marital status of the white-collar crime offenders, Ross (1977:32) wrote that the white-collar crime perpetrator is not anti-social and "is likely to keep his marriage vows, pay his debts, mixes well, stands by his friends, he is ready to protect maidens, or help poor widows". However, the study of female prison inmates by Zietz (1981:104) found that "all of the women in this group had one or more unsuccessful marriages and were currently living alone, with or without children, or with their parents". Marital status, as an indication of a defendant's social ties, is a legally relevant factor at the sentencing stage (Thomas, 1979), and may be useful in understanding offenders' motives and rationalisations. Both financial and non- financial pressures for someone to commit fraud can be related to their marital status.

iii. **Age**

In contrast to the majority of conventional/street offenders who tend to be aged under 18 (Feldman, 1993), the average white-collar offender in Wheeler et al. (1988) and Weisburd et al. (1990) was 40 years old. The average age for street criminals in Weisburd et al. was 20 to 30 years. Weisburd et al. (1990) also reported that white-collar offenders are likely to begin their careers later than street criminals. Undoubtedly, there is a link between age and white collar offending, since by the time one completes one's tertiary education and obtains sufficient professional qualifications and experience to command a highly paid position of financial trust such as accountant, solicitor, or bank-manager, one

[2] Gender is a factor that is taken into account by the judiciary in imposing sentences on convicted criminal defendants (Thomas, 1979). Discussion of the issue of sexism in sentencing is beyond the scope of this book.

would be at least 30 years old. There is, however, scope for age differences between different major fraud offenders. Interestingly, as far as female inmates serving sentences for fraud are concerned, Zietz (1981:114) found that "age did not appear to be a significant factor, although the majority were less than 30 years of age".

iv. **Occupation**

Wheeler et al. (1988) compared convicted white-collar and common crime offenders on a variety of social and demographic indicators. As would be expected, they found that white-collar offenders had a higher educational attainment than street offenders, and had histories of steady employment. Coleman (1987) believes that white-collar offenders use their occupation as an opportunity, but Spark (1994) goes a step further and argues that in addition to using one's job, if there is a complicated group structure or financial dictatorship then that is an added opportunity.

v. **Fraud charges and other non-fraud offences**

Korn and McCorkle (1959) pointed out that "the earliest and still the most common way of classifying criminals is in terms of the legal title identifying the criminal act" (p.142). The categories of fraud charges used most frequently by the MFG were obtaining: (a) property by deception; (b) financial advantage by deception; (c) theft; and (d) forgery.

One of the issues in the literature concerns the question of whether white-collar offenders are specialists or generalists (like street offenders) in the types of crimes they commit. Using official New Zealand data, Thomas (1992) reported that many fraud offenders reoffend; more specifically, 34.1% were later reconvicted for the same offence, and 68.2% reconvicted for fraud or any other crime (p.125). Benson and Moore (1992) concluded that white-collar offenders were a lot less involved in crime than street offenders. White-collar offenders were reported by Wheeler et al. (1988) as having a surprisingly high number of prior arrests and convictions, but were still lower in that regard than common criminals. Weisburd et al. (1990) found that more than one in seven securities fraud offenders had a prior felony conviction, as did more than a quarter of those convicted of credit fraud, false claims, and mail fraud. Even with the more elite population of white-collar offenders such as doctors, lawyers, accountants, office managers and owners of substantial capital, there was evidence "of criminal careers ... within a highly restricted population of elite white-collar offenders" (p.347). They reported that a nontrivial "proportion of white-collar offenders were found to be repeat offenders and some had serious and lengthy criminal records" (p.343). The same authors suggest that white-collar offenders do not specialise in white-collar crime.

vi. **Relationship to the victim**

The offender-victim relationship is of importance as far as both patterns in criminal behaviour and implications for its detection and prevention are concerned. It is also significant in sentencing because the violation of trust (a basic feature of many deception white-collar crimes) is an aggravating factor (Thomas, 1979). Regarding the type of victim, Wheeler et al. (1988:338) claimed that "common crimes victimise individuals. In contrast, the majority of federal white collar offences involves victimisation of organisations ... they are also likely to use an organisational form for their commission".

vii. **Number of accomplices**

For some deception offences to take place, more than one offender is needed because of a need for collusion. An example might be a bank manager and a real-estate agent operating a deception ploy, whereby the bank manager approves housing loans for properties he/she knows have been overvalued and is paid secret commissions by the real estate agent. Furthermore, an important question of interest to both police, detectives and the judiciary is whether an offender has been operating alone to commit a fraud or with accomplices. At the sentencing stage, having accomplices is an aggravating factor as it often points to more planning being involved (Thomas, 1979). Wheeler et al. (1988), the only researcher in this area to have looked at this variable, found that "only about nineteen percent of the common crimes involve five or more persons in addition to the defendant, while more than one-third of the white collar offences have as many participants" (p.339). It should be noted here, that any of the categories listed under "motives" in the ROP model could involve an offender with or without accomplices.

viii. **How the fraud was discovered**

Fraud is often carefully concealed and it would be of interest to know how it comes to light (e.g., who becomes suspicious and reports the matter to the police or someone else). Information about this variable was also considered in order to gauge the apparent involvement of auditors in fraud detection.

ix. **Motivation**

One of the essential components of the proposed ROP model is a crime-prone person with a motive for committing fraud. Offenders commit their crimes for many and various reasons. Business failures, drug addiction, gambling and particular lifestyles needing large amounts of money are important factors in understanding why someone might commit fraud. Other possible motivations might be revenge, greed and megalomania. Cressey (1986,1980) discounted gambling, alcohol or spending beyond one's means as causes of embezzlement, and reported that one of the offenders studied was willing to do anything to give his wife and children what they needed. For Cressey, "ascribing bad motives to behaviour does not explain that behaviour" (1980:121). According to Thomas (1992:125), family needs is more of an acceptable justification coming from women rather than men. As criminologists are not tired of telling us, drug addiction is a major cause of various criminal offences in society. Benson and Moore (1992:263-264) indirectly tested for this variable and found that "neither white-collar nor common offenders are likely to have drinking problems...only 6% of white-collar criminals are reported to have used illegal drugs, compared to almost half of the common criminals". Knowledge about vice(s)/motivation(s) of an offender helps to construct the offender profile and to develop a model to explain the reasons why major fraud is committed. Some of the vices identified for testing were: gambling, drugs, greed, to pay personal bills, to pay business bills, and lifestyle (e.g., leading a double life or otherwise living beyond one's means in order to maintain a particular self-image).

x. **Pre-trial status of the offender**

The decision to grant a defendant bail or remand them in custody indicates how the courts view a defendant (i.e., whether they pose a serious risk they may abscond, or whether they will commit another serious crime), a factor that can be expected to impact on sentence choice and severity.

xi. **Legally represented by a private lawyer or by a court-appointed lawyer**

This is to identify if the offender had the resources available to finance his/her legal defence.

xii. **Severity of sentence**

A lot has been written about white collar-crime offenders not receiving a fair punishment for their crime. Bologna (1993) claims that U.S. fraud offenders believe that "if you are going to be a financial crook be a big one...[since] the greater the offence against the capital, the less the punishment imposed by the sentencing judge" (p.7). Information about the type and severity of sentence imposed was collected because it is relevant to a discussion of deterrence theory. The severity of the sentence is looked at where applicable.

xiii. **Amount of money involved in the fraud**

Information on this factor was collected in order to throw some light on sentencing decisions, as it largely determines perceptions of harm done, i.e., perceptions of offence seriousness. Furthermore, it could be argued that the greater the money involved, the better the position the offender is in to bargain his plea with the police, who might be also interested in recovering some of the money involved in a spate of deception offences, so that the victims can recover some of their losses. Finally, that victims have recovered part or the total of their financial losses is a mitigating factor that the judiciary would normally take into account (Thomas, 1979). Information about this variable would also be useful in gauging the scale of the frauds investigated by the MFG.

xiv. **Type of irregularity**

As already mentioned above, one of the aims of the research is to test Loebbecke et al.'s fraud risk assessment model which differentiates between "defalcation" and "management fraud". Information on this factor was also collected because different types of irregularities have different implications for auditors, as far as their duty to detect and report such illegal acts is concerned.

xv. **Fraud-facilitating conditions** (i.e., fraud indicators)

Information was collected on this factor because of its potential importance for auditors. In addition, "conditions" is one of the components of the ROP model (O) and of Loebbecke et al.'s (1989) model being tested by this research.

xvi. **Rationalisations**

Possessing rationalisations (i.e., neutralising verbalisations) is a necessary component for fraud to take place. As Cressey (1986) pointed out, it is an individual's ability to rationalise and justify perpetrating the offence(s) that makes fraud possible. Qualitative data about the offenders' rationalisations was extracted from sworn written statements made to the MFG detectives investigating.

REPRESENTATIVE NIGNETTESS OF THE MFG CASES SURVEYED

Representative case summaries are provided below, with the ROP model components present being indicated, in order to provide the reader with an idea of the type of cases studied. The eleven cases described demonstrate a broad variety of circumstances under which fraud occurs. Cases where the facts are similar are not repeated. Due to a confidentiality agreement signed by the author, the cases are presented without any identifying details about the offender or the victim(s). The decision whether an offender had certain characteristics e.g., low self-control and his/her type of motivation (e.g., greed) was arrived at after careful examination of all the information in the MFG file, supplemented with interview data from the detectives who had investigated and prosecuted the cases.

Case one involved a fraud of $1,785,000 committed by a member of middle management in a finance company. He was engaged to get married and needed money (*Motive*: *financial problem*). The male offender had sole responsibility over computer assets, recording, and investments. When the company's bank lost the original authorised signature card with a specimen of the two signatories (*Person and Opportunity*), the perpetrator submitted one card with one signatory only thereby exploiting his company's weak internal controls, he submitted one card with one signatory only. He redeemed clients' Commercial Bills without their consent, paid them the interest due and paid the remainder into his personal account. He used the money to buy a house and a car for himself and his fiancée. After his first "success" he became both over-confident and more greedy and proceeded to commit more frauds. He justified the frauds on the basis that he would one day pay it back (*Rationalisation*). Realising he would not be able to pay back the money after all, one day he left his fiancée a note admitting having defrauded his company. She, in turn, informed the police.

The second case was for $1,600,000. The offender, was a director who was an undischarged bankrupt and a career conman (*Person*) who took advantage of the weak internal controls (e.g., inadequate screening of applicants for management positions) and deceived his two co-directors into signing blank cheques (*Opportunity*). He opened eight bank accounts in the names of each of the other directors with overdraft facilities of $200,000. He then debited each account with $200,000 and credited his own account with that sum of money. As far as he was concerned, he was entitled to whatever money he could get (*Rationalisation*).

Case three involved a fraud of $345,000. Perceiving a low risk of being apprehended (*Opportunity*), a crime-prone 40-year old married male solicitor (*Person*) deceived 17 clients (from conveyancing and divorce cases) into investing money in a company supposedly for better returns. He did not inform his clients that he owned the company concerned. He then misappropriated the investments. He covered up the frauds by making it appear that the clients had loaned him the money. His justification was that he had the clients' authority since there were only "technical deficiencies" in their trust accounts' (*Rationalisation*). He was found out when a client died and the beneficiaries asked for their money held in the trust account.

Case four was for $886,769. In this case the offender, a 50-year old consultant accountant, a professional conman who in the past had used three different aliases and was a compulsive gambler and a liar, purported to be a qualified accountant (*Person with a motive*). He was employed by a company (with weak internal controls to prevent fraud) as a consultant and was entrusted to requisition cheques as required (*Opportunity*). The offender would write up requisition forms, attach supporting documentation and write up the cheque details in erasable ink. Once the cheques were signed he would alter the payee and amount. The changes made were not obvious on the cheque. He forged a total of 341 cheques thinking of himself as a professional fraudster who was entitled to whatever he could get away with (*Rationalisation*). An auditor found him out.

Case five was for $100,327. This fraud was committed by a 42-year old male bank manager who perceived a low risk of being found out and being greedy for money (*Person with a motive*) took advantage of weak internal controls (*Opportunity*). He approved unsecured loans to two business partners above and beyond what he was authorised by the bank to approve. They had promised him a senior position in their company in the near future as well as a financial reward in return for his "services" to them. To cover up the unsecured loans, he also approved loans to fictitious customers. The money was paid into a number of accounts opened under assumed names. There was a need to avoid the excessive unsecured loans from being included by the bank's computerised internal control system on a list of loans that management would review regularly. That he did by using money from the fictitious accounts to reduce the balance of the unsecured loans. As far as he was concerned, what he was doing was justified as a means to an end (*Rationalisation*). He was found out by the bank's auditors.

Case six, involved a $1,250,000 fraud committed by a 47-year old grandmother accountant who had been dismissed by her previous employer for committing fraud. Acting out of greed (*Motivated crime-prone person*) she exploited weak internal controls. A lack of segregation of duties allowed her to be both in charge of personnel records as well as responsible for paying salaries (*Opportunity*). She defrauded her employer of the stated amount via fraudulent transactions. Using a variety of methods to cover up her frauds, she misappropriated cheques issued by her employer who was a foreign government and had them paid into her own account. She did this by getting subordinates to sign "pay cash" cheques or by forging cheques to alter the amount stated to a larger amount and have the difference paid into her account. She also misappropriated bills (meant to pay employees' salaries) upon their maturity by adding "or pay cash". She believed she had a very good chance of getting away with her frauds (*Rationalisation*). With a salary of only $27,000 and employment of 10 odd years the offender managed to own four houses in her name, buy another two for family members, pay school fees for grandchildren and to hold cash deposits of $1 million. It is unknown why a number of her assistants or even upper management co-operated with her and banked the cheques or even authorised the alterations. No charges were laid against those people. She was found out by the bank when she tried to have a bill paid into her own account which had already been paid. When interviewed by the police, she appeared naive and used the language barrier as an excuse not to communicate.

Case seven was a fraud of $1,063,900. This case involved a 55-year old married male bank manager with low self-control (*Crime-prone person*) who was at liberty to redeem clients' bills upon maturity (*Opportunity*). Acting out of greed (*Motive*) and believing he could avoid being found out (*Rationalisation*), he used three commercial bills owned by a friend and his associate for personal use. He paid off the bills and bought property. To cover up the frauds he transferred money (equal to the amount of the interest due) from one of his accounts to replace the stolen money. The friend who had invested the money was receiving the interest earned from the bills for nearly a year, but became suspicious when he decided he wanted to redeem one of the investments and another bank manager could not determine its existence.

Case eight involved a fraud of $1,141,104. A 37-year old professional conman, practising as finance consultant (*Crime-prone motivated person*). He believed he was justified in defrauding people because that was his job (*Rationalisation*). He used 11 aliases to open 16 separate bank accounts in three banks and utilised the serviced offices and business name of some reputable accounting practices around Melbourne (he created the *Opportunity*) in order to commit frauds as follows:

i. He scrutinised share registers to find personal details of large shareholders, assumed their identity and, using a series of false documents, he changed address and amended the share register accordingly.

ii. Following the alteration to the share register, he informed the share registry that due to the change in address the original share certificate was lost and a new one was issued to him.

iii. Upon receipt of the duplicate share script, the shares were sold to innocent shareholders and he managed to obtain $432,000 which he banked in his personal account.

He was found out as a result of one company's practice of confirming a "change of address" with the shareholders. In addition to this fraud, he was charged with involvement in a fraud he committed in 1990 in another state.

Case nine involved $340,000. This fraud was committed by middle management. The company's fleet cars were to be sold at public auction or traded-in against the purchase of a new vehicle (*Opportunity*). The transport office would obtain three quotations from various dealers and submit a requisition for a new vehicle. In collusion and acting out of greed, three single male employees in their 30's and of low self-control (*Crime-prone persons*) authorised documentation, drew and signed cheques, advertised and sold the trade-ins to family members or innocent purchasers. New vehicles were purchased for family members but paid for by the company. Their justification was that "nobody would get hurt" by the frauds (*Rationalisation*). They were found out by the internal auditor.

Case ten was for $4.5 million. A 57-year old married male chief executive officer[3] of a multinational company had weak self-control (*Crime-prone person)*. He had been with the company for over 30 years and nobody dared question him. Acting out of greed, and believing he was entitled to the money (*Rationalisation*), he renovated his house using company funds. Exploiting the company's weak internal controls (*Opportunity*), he instructed one of the managers to charge $4.5 million of renovations to various company stores. However, he was not aware that the Chief Accountant also renovated his house and some of the expenses were hidden into his expenses. A disgruntled builder whose invoice was questioned and who realised what was going on informed the police. He believed that the company owed him the luxury he sought to have (*Rationalisation*).

Case 11 involved a fraud of $3,700,000. A 46-year old male general manager with low self-control (*Crime-prone person*) colluded with the marketing manager (*Opportunity*) and approved invoices twice to a particular supplier who maintained two sets of books for tax purposes. The general manager was acting out of greed and justified the fraud as "a means to an end" (*Rationalisation*). One set was paid into the computerised accounting system of the supplier and the

[3] The chief executive officer received a 4 year jail sentence, including a minimum term of two and one-half years, despite the fact that he has repaid $3.453 million of the funds misappropriated. While delivering the sentence, Justice Eames emphasized the fact that the person in question was "motivated by greed" and while he "engaged in fraud upon the company" he expressed concerns to the rest of the members of staff of the problem of theft (Phesant, 1997:1 and 8).

other into his personal manual system. The marketing manager was only doing it to keep her job and the general manager was receiving secret commissions.

MFG SURVEY FINDINGS

Characteristics of major fraud offenders and a two level profile

The majority of offenders studied shared some characteristics one would normally have expected them to have by virtue of the fact that they needed to be in occupational positions where they could, alone or with accomplices, effect major fraud. To hold such positions, they almost invariably had to be professionals with tertiary qualifications and over 30 years of age. As expected, the great majority were male (92%), married/defacto (63%) and aged 31-45 inclusive (65%). As far as their occupation is concerned, 24% were company directors, 20% were solicitors, accountants made up 18%, office/bank managers 18%, finance managers 8%, bookkeepers 4%, sharetraders 4%, brokers 2% and other[4] 2%. These findings support similar results reported by Wheeler et al. (1988). Rather interestingly, it was also found that most of them had acted alone in perpetrating their fraudulent acts against two or more people they knew well and only committed deception offences, in other words, they were specialists and not versatile. These general characteristics comprise the first of two components of the profile constructed. The second is the taxonomy of offenders and circumstances (i.e., a set of typologies, categories and sub-categories) reported below. The two components are meant to be used in tandem by auditors.

The majority (91%) of the offenders examined were convicted under state legislation[5], with 44% convicted of 10 fraud charges or less while a significant proportion (39%) were convicted of 20 or more charges. Approximately half (51%) of the cases involved one or two victims, but in 26% of the cases the offender defrauded 10 or more separate victims. The presence of one or two victims in a prosecution does not, of course, mean the offender only committed one or two frauds, because a single victim may have been repeatedly defrauded.

As far as the treatment of the perpetrators by the courts is concerned, most offenders (73%) pleaded guilty, were granted bail (85%), all were legally represented at the trial and most (89%) were represented by a private lawyer. Slightly over half (52%) of the cases were tried by a higher court, namely the county or supreme court. Overall, the MFG had a high conviction rate (84%). As far as sentencing by the courts is concerned, the majority of the offenders studied were imprisoned (68%), 14% were given a good behaviour bond, 11% a suspended term of imprisonment, 4% a fine and, finally, 3% were given a community-based order. Of those who were sent to prison, the majority were sentenced to five years or less[6].

---

[4] This involved a person with an assumed identity and who practised as a solicitor.

[5] Crimes Act, 1958 (Victoria).

[6] The Chi-square test of association when dealing with frequencies was used to test the

Cross-tabulations of the main variables for which data were collected in the MFG study yielded the following findings: accountants were more likely to be sentenced to a longer (more than five years) term of imprisonment than other occupational categories[7]. The most likely explanation for that is to be found in the fact that accountants were convicted of more fraud charges and not because they defrauded a larger amount of money. Because an offender was convicted of more than one charge against the same victim, it is better to talk about victimisation per fraud. It was found to be one in over one-third (36%) of the cases, two victimisations (15%), 3-10 victimisations (23%) and over 10 victimisations in 26% of the frauds. One rather prolific offender was convicted of 98 charges. There was some limited evidence that those with a relatively "small" number of victimisations per fraud (i.e., < 10 victims) were more likely to plead not guilty.

In support of U.S. research, most (70%) of the offenders did not have prior criminal convictions while about one-third (30%) were also charged with a non-fraud (mainly theft) offence. Company directors and accountants were more likely (though not statistically significant) to have a prior criminal record. There was some indication that those who had a criminal record were more likely to perpetrate frauds netting a "larger" amount of money (more than $500,000) than were first offenders and that first offenders generally acted more out of greed and were more likely to plead guilty.

Of the professional groups involved, accountants and solicitors (unlike bank managers or company directors) were the most prolific in terms of the number of deception offences they were charged with[8]. Most of the offenders (70%) perpetrated the fraud(s) acting alone and of those that had accomplices, the tendency was to have one only accomplice. In contrast to bank managers and company directors, the rest of the occupational categories (e.g., accountants, solicitors, finance managers) were significantly more likely to perpetrate their fraud offences without accomplices[9]. As a rule, accountants and company directors were significantly more likely[10] than other occupational categories to have "specialised" in such deception offences as obtaining property or financial advantage by deception.

---

statistical significance of the relationship between pairs of characteristics pertaining to the offence, the offender, the victim, and the imposition of sentences by the courts. In all the reported results the significance level (p) is with one degree of freedom (1df) and for a two-tailed test. In some instances, small numbers in the cells of the frequency tables has meant that, even though a relationship between two variables was significant at least at p = 0.05, the result was dismissed in order to comply with the requirements of the chi-square test (e.g., having less than 20% of the cells in a table with frequencies of less than 5). Such cases are indicated with an *.

[7] Chi-square = 6.82105, p = 0.009*
[8] Chi-square = 3.65350, p = 0.05
[9] Chi-square = 11.72959, p = 0.0006*
[10] Chi-square = 12.82184, p = 0.0003

Regarding the relationship with the victim, in 25% of the cases the victim was the employer, a client/customer (61%), a fellow company director (6%) or a stranger (6%), but only 2% were employees of the offender.

Unlike conventional offenders, most (87%) of the offenders studied were not versatile, as Gottfredson and Hirschi (1990) would have predicted, but specialists, i.e., they perpetrated only particular deception offences, hardly changing their modus operandi. The specialist fraudsters (i.e., those committing only deception offences) were significantly more likely than their versatile counterparts to have a criminal record [11], and were significantly more likely to be imprisoned[12].

The fraud came to be investigated because a victim suspected the offender (40%), or because of the work of an auditor (13%) or as a result of a bank (14%) or a colleague/fellow co-director 11%, a client (11%) or the Law Institute of Victoria (9%) or, finally, the police (2%) becoming suspicious/acting on information received. While half of the solicitors involved were suspected by the Law Institute of Victoria, accountants and company directors were significantly more likely than all the other occupational categories to be suspected of having perpetrated fraud by one of their victims [13].

These inter-relationships indicates a need to desegregate major fraud offenders. The findings suggest that, at a general level, such offenders differ from common offenders in a number of significant ways, such as in being employed, specialists and first offenders. However, the way they go about committing their crimes, how many offences of the same kind they commit, whether they act alone, whether they plead guilty and what sentence they receive, appear to be related. In combination with the taxonomy of fraud offenders described below, these findings go some way towards painting the picture of the major fraud offender. In this sense the research can be said to have succeeded in profiling such offenders. This knowledge could be used to alert auditors to potential management fraud risks and their likely modus operandi against the backdrop of fraud-prone companies and areas within companies detailed in the next chapter.

Criminal typologies

The criminological literature contains a number of criminal typologies. The main concern has been with typologies of male juvenile delinquents (see Gibbons, 1975) and prison inmates (see Schrag, 1961). Typologies of white-collar offenders has been a neglected topic in criminology. In considering the typologies yielded by the MFG study it should be remembered that they are aetiological ones, i.e., they identify the types of persons in positions of financial trust who perpetrated fraud and the circumstances under which fraud is done.

---

[11] Chi-square = 5.45185, p = 0.0195*
[12] Chi-square = 3.47222, p = 0.0624
[13] Chi-square = 7.07087, p = 0.007

A taxonomy/Typologies of major fraud cases

Close examination of the 50 cases and the interviews with the detectives yielded the following taxonomy of major fraud cases described next. The taxonomy shows that if a profile of fraud offenders is to be useful in fraud detection, it needs to accommodate a broad range of categories and, in some cases, sub-categories of cases, which result from the combination of particular types of offenders committing different types of fraud under different circumstances[14]. The fact is that many professionals of the age group and with the types of pressures mentioned below do not resort to fraud. Consequently, if a profile of fraud offenders does not include information on particular combinations of different types of professionals, committing different types of irregularities under different circumstances, then it will not be of much use to an auditor. In other words, the taxonomy of types of fraud offenders and circumstances reported below can be thought of as enriching the sketch broad outline of a person who is likely to be a fraud risk, and is therefore likely to be of use to an auditor.

The predator/professional fraud offender. For example, an accountant with a record for committing fraud against a previous employer also defrauds his/her latest employer of a much larger amount of money. Another type of predator gets a position in a company in order to commit the fraud. In other words, the offender has the opportunity, is crime-prone due to the absence of a strong self-control as evidenced by his/her previous criminal activity of a similar nature, and justifies the fraudulent activity in terms of "I can make better use of the money than the company". Another example is where a career fraud offender (with a record for identifying, selecting major shareholders, assuming their identity, and selling their shares) sets up a company to defraud a bank. Here we have a crime-prone individual who creates the opportunity for fraud, commits deception offences and justifies the crime as "this is what I do for a living". Another example is where one individual who, after defrauding a company in his own country, flew to Australia to repeat his scheme. Again, we have a predator who sets up a company purporting to offer a service for a fee, collects a lot of money from clients and then simply disappears and, like serial killers, sees nothing morally wrong with what he does. Eight cases were perpetrated by predator, professional offenders who, like some of the other categories, stop offending when caught.

An opportunist professional with low self - control and without a previous record for deception who is in a position of trust. The second largest category identified is where a person with a predisposition to commit fraud as a result of having low self-control, perceives an opportunity to acquire additional money.

---

[14] According to Gibbons (1975), the main criteria a typology must satisfy in order to be useful are: clarity and objectivity; mutual exclusiveness; and comprehensiveness and parsimony (p.143).

Acting out of greed, he/she exploits it alone or with one or more accomplices, in the belief they will get away with it. For example, a bank manager steals a friend's commercial bills and converts them to money. The opportunity lies in the fact that people trust him with their money, the crime-proneness stems from a lack of a strong conscience and, finally, the fraudulent activity is rationalised in terms of "It's easy money to pay off bills and buy property" and avoid being found out. Another example is where, motivated by greed, an insurance company manager in collusion with two outsiders exploits weak internal controls to commit a long series of frauds against the company. A weak conscience predisposes him to exploit the opportunity provided by the weak internal controls and the frauds are justified in terms of "If I can make money and get away with it, why not?".

Fraud under an assumed professional identity. Irrespective of whether living a fantasy or not, an individual presents himself as qualified to practice law and enjoys the status and salary that comes with the job until unmasked (one single case).

Isolated fraud in response to unshareable financial pressure on the family. Cognisant of his family's financial circumstances and need for money, one of the parents in a position of financial trust and of low internal control avails himself of an opportunity, commits an isolated offence, and then ceases the criminal activity (two cases).

Serial fraud in response to unshareable financial pressure on the family. Also cognisant of his family's dire financial circumstances and need for money, a crime-prone professional commits fraud, gets over-confident that he can get away with it, and commits more frauds. Having satisfied the financial need of the family his real motive now for continuing to commit fraud offences is sheer greed (five cases).

Fraud as personal justice. A disgruntled, vindictive ex-employee exploits an opportunity and commits a fraud to get back what he believes the company owes him (one case).

Isolated fraud as response to unshareable financial pressure on one's self. Motivated by a need to resolve financial difficulty of a personal nature (i.e., not a family need and not a business need) an individual with weak self-control seizes an opportunity and commits fraud but does not become a serial offender (two cases).

Serial fraud. Motivated by a wish to solve a financial problem of a personal nature, a person (e.g., an overoptimistic lawyer driven by greed) commits fraud by exploiting an opportunity in the belief that there will be an upturn in the economy, his/her investments will improve and he/she will thus be able to pay the money back into his/her clients' trust accounts (four cases).

Serial fraud due to a vice. Motivated by a need to solve a serious financial problem due to big losses at the gambling table, a compulsive gambler commits fraud time and time again, as he sinks deeper into financial trouble, and stops when discovered (two cases). One case involved a 40-year old male (Mr. L), married with three children, was the manager of the accounts payable of a company. He worked there over 20 years but had a gambling habit. In 1993, the manager of business systems had difficulty reconciling an account. He found that seven cheques drawn on the company's name of $136,161 had unlawfully been paid into Mr L's account. Mr L then admitted that in his role as manager, he was able to access the computer system, create fictitious accounts/files, and make unauthorised alterations and/or deletions to this information. This unauthorised activity allowed Mr L to generate seven cheques of various amounts drawn on the company's account and payable to his personal account. He did this to feed his compulsive gambling habit.

Another case in this typology is the case of a married woman living with her unemployed husband who was socialising in an extravagant manner with her lover. She bought him expensive gifts including a house. The lover was not aware how Mrs X obtained the funds. He just thought she was wealthy. She worked for an insurance company and once a file for a car accident was completed she would re-open it, use someone's password to re-enter an invoice, use a third person's password to approve it and draw a cheque to herself or her husband. She would then retrieve the cheque from the printer which was on another floor in the same building. No one found out for some months until the internal auditor noticed some inconsistencies.

Fraud to restore social identity. A megalomaniac type of individual who cannot not endure the status incongruity brought about by some disastrous business investments, believes he can commit the crime and not get caught and exploits an opportunity to commit an isolated fraud to ensure his social identity does not suffer (one case).

Serial fraud by an unscrupulous deceiver. A first-offender psychopathic megalomaniac high flier of low integrity commits frauds against close friends, clients and business partners repeatedly, without having any qualms about it. A total of seven cases belonged to this category.

Serial fraud to assist loved ones with a financial problem. An example is where a finance manager falsifies payment vouchers and misappropriates money from his employer's bank account. He uses the money to pay university fees for his brother and to assist his sister who lives overseas. He justifies the frauds in terms of "nobody will get hurt" (four cases).

Interestingly, the cases examined did not include a case of someone committing fraud as a challenge to the system, as a thrill, even though such cases have been reported in the literature.

The typology findings obtained show that where fraud is committed, there is a significant likelihood that it is not an isolated event. The explanation for this finding is that (1) the offender(s) will only stop when found out, irrespective of whether the offender(s) is/are without a criminal record or of the predator/career kind, and (2) the former type of offender finds more frauds need to be committed to cover the money missing while the latter feel no remorse about stealing as much money as possible. It needs to be borne in mind, however, that the frauds studied were frauds which had been discovered. Therefore, caution is needed in extrapolating this finding to all fraud. The same typology findings also document the heterogeneity of both the type of persons committing major fraud as well as the circumstances under which they offended. The largest category (30%) is the predator career fraud offender and the second largest (24%) the opportunist unscrupulous first offender, with low self-control, in a professional occupation and holding a position of financial trust, commits fraud alone or with accomplices, motivated by greed. The third largest category (10%) involves cases where in response to unshareable pressure on the family, a person with low self-control exploits an opportunity and embarks on a spree of frauds against people he/she knows well. We see that the predator career fraud offender comprises a large proportion of such offenders whose frauds could be reduced significantly by means of better vetting of job applicants by employers. However, it needs to be emphasised that even if a person in a position of financial trust does not have a criminal record, it does not mean that he/she is not crime-prone. Therefore, in selecting candidates for such positions, one could administer them written tests of degrees of self control (see Grasmick et al., 1993) in order to identify those who are fraud risks. Finally, what the typologies identified make clear is that an effective preventative measure against fraud is undoubtedly strong internal controls.

In summary, the categories of people in positions of trust who commit fraud comprise a variety that includes: over-optimistic opportunists; the vindictive type; professional conmen who are likely to have a criminal record; people who commit an isolated offence (and others who become greedy and commit a number of offences) to solve a serious financial problem of a personal or family or business nature; unscrupulous high fliers, and investors or compulsive gamblers whose excessive optimism that "things will soon improve" leads them into committing a spate of deception offences. Fraud is made possible by the existence of the three components depicted in the ROP model, namely a motivated crime-prone individual, opportunity and rationalisations. The classification offered above should be treated with caution since: (1) there is some degree of overlap between some of the categories of offenders (e.g., a married compulsive gambler has a financial problem which impacts on his family); (2) the offenders were not interviewed; and (3) because of the sample of cases studied. The typologies offered do, nevertheless, support the view that major fraud offenders comprise a range of categories of offenders who perpetrate their crime(s) under a broad range of circumstances, for a diversity of motives and use different *modus operandi*.

Type of irregularity by deceptive action used

As in Loebbecke et al.'s study (personal communication with the main author), the terms "defalcation" is used to refer to employee fraud, embezzlement, and larceny while "management" fraud encompasses deliberate fraud committed by management that injures investors and creditors through materially misleading financial statements. The class of perpetrators in management fraud is management. It should also be noted that misappropriation of trust accounts by lawyers and accountants was classified as a defalcation not a management fraud.

Table 1 shows that in order to commit the irregularity a perpetrator carried out more than one deceptive action[15]. This explains why N = 88 and not 50. For all perpetrators, the average number of deceptive acts for the 50 cases reviewed is 1.8 More specifically, the average for defalcations and management fraud is 1.2 and 2.6 respectively. In agreement with Loebbecke et al's findings, largely the same deceptive actions underlined both defalcation and management fraud. The fact that the findings obtained in the present study are very similar to those reported by Loebbecke et al. is interesting given that their study was based on a survey of auditors whereas the findings of the present study have been obtained from prosecution briefs of major fraud cases. The implications of this observation for auditors are that: (1) the modus operandi of serious fraud offenders is very much the same whether they operate in Australia or United States and (2) upon discovering evidence of a deceptive action an auditor should assume that it is not an isolated event underpinning an irregularity.

[15] Unlike Loebbecke et al.'s study, "revenue or other credits recognised improperly", "specious accounting judgement made", or "transactions in the wrong period" and "disclosures omitted or misleading" were not contained in the irregularities included in the sample of MFG cases.

Table 1: Classification of the Fifty Cases into Irregularities by Deceptive Action

Type of Irregularity	All cases		Defalcations		Management Fraud	
	No	% of 50	No	% of 30	No	% of 20
Assets overvalued or incorrectly valued	2	4	2	7		
Transactions/events not recorded	1	2			1	5
Expenses recorded incorrectly	5	10	1	3	4	20
Liabilities understated	1	2			1	5
Misappropriation of funds	20	40	13	43	7	35
Theft of cash receipts	26	52	7	23	19	95
Falsified and altered records	33	66	13	43	20	100
Totals	**88**		**36**		**52**	
Average per occurrence	1.8		1.2		2.6	

Table 2 provides information about the incidence of different types of deceptive action by type of irregularity. With few exceptions the fraud offenders studied are prolific serial offenders. A review of Table 2 reveals that the offenders averaged 30.8 irregularities each. More specifically, the average number of charges for defalcations was 13.9 and 56.3 for management fraud. However, these averages are inflated by the presence of one management fraud offender who was charged with 340 counts of falsifying and altering records and with as many theft offences. Similarly, another offender was charged with 91 counts of misappropriating funds. Excluding those two offenders the average number of irregularities per occurrence of major fraud is 17.7. The implication of this finding is that upon discovering evidence for an irregularity an auditor should assume that many more have also been perpetrated.

Table 2: Classification of *Number of Charges* for the Fifty MFG Cases into Irregularities Committed by Deceptive Action

Type of Irregularity	All cases		Defalcations		Management Fraud	
	No	% of 50	No	% of 30	No	% of 20
Assets overvalued or incorrectly valued	12	24.0	12	40.0		
Transactions/events not recorded	1	2.0			1	5.0
Expenses recorded incorrectly	26	52.0	5	16.7	21	105.0
Liabilities understated	2	4.0			2	10.0
Misappropriation of funds	330	660.0	220	733.3	110	550.0
Theft of cash receipts	603	1206.0	112	373.3	491	2455.0
Falsified and altered records	568	1136.0	68	226.7	500	2500.0
Totals	1542	3084.0	417	1390.0	1125	5625.0
Average per occurrence		30.8		13.9		56.3

Empirical support for the three components of the ROP model

It needs to be acknowledged that using the MFG cases to test the applicability of the ROP model provides a useful but limited test of the model. The reason for this is that the MFG cases involved fraud convictions; in other words, they involved a person with a crime-prone personality who exploited opportunities to perpetrate fraud. This is a limitation of the methodology used.

Data analysis provided support for the three components of the ROP model. Regarding the *Opportunity component*, findings show the importance of a number of both "situational factors" (i.e., perception of low risk of being apprehended, absence of capable guardians, existence of gullible people willing to trust strangers with their money, perception of lenient sentence and collusion opportunities) and "company characteristics" (i.e. lack of adequate control procedures that prevent fraud, non-control factors providing opportunities for fraud, criminogenic corporate culture, collusion opportunities, and inadequate screening of applicants for management positions). These fraud indicators had been predicted by the model as facilitating the commission of fraud. Regarding the situational factors, the great majority (80%) of the offenders perceived a low risk of being apprehended. This finding provides empirical support for deterrence theory (Walker, 1980) according to which a potential offender is discouraged through fear of consequences from committing a particular crime if he/she perceives a high risk of being apprehended and expects a severe enough sentence upon conviction. It should be noted here that, on the basis of their statements during the police interviews as well as on the basis of lengthy discussions the present author had with MFG investigators, the majority of the offenders studied perceived a low risk of being apprehended and the issue of the likely penalty if convicted did not seem to have concerned them.

In support of Clarke (1980) and Cohen and Felson (1979), it was found that the absence of capable guardians (36%) is another significant situational factor. A closer look at the cases concerned, revealed that as long as the Law Institute of Victoria failed to audit solicitors' trust accounts regularly, it allowed enough solicitors (in ten cases) to perceive a low risk of being found out and to defraud their clients by stealing from their trust accounts. Similarly, so long as there were no regional managers to inspect the work of bank managers, it made it easier for five of them to defraud their own bank whether by colluding with outsiders or to steal money from their clients (see below). Of course, both solicitors and bank managers, like accountants in private practice, enjoy the trust of their clients and the existence of gullible people is another situational factor that made fraud possible in 34% of the cases.

In addition to situational factors, the *opportunity* component of the ROP model includes "company characteristics". The ROP model correctly predicted the importance of lack of adequate control procedures (90%) that prevent fraud. This supports the KPMG (1999, 1996, 1995ab, 1993ab) fraud surveys which found that poor internal control was the one factor that underpinned most frauds both in Australia and in 17 other countries. In addition to a lack of adequate control procedures, the ROP model also correctly predicted the importance of non-control factors (64%) that provide opportunities for fraud to be committed. Such factors include, for example, inability to judge the quality of performance; lack of access to information; ignorance, apathy or incapacity, and lack of audit trail.

Further support for the ROP model is the finding that 36% of the offenders belonged to a criminogenic occupational/corporate culture which appears to condone solicitors or accountants who "borrow" money from their clients' trust accounts or bank managers who authorise unsecured loans or loans far in excess of the amounts they are authorised to approve for clients they know well and trust. Weak internal controls may well mean that collusion between a number of company employees is possible. There was a total of six (12%) such cases. Three separate bank managers conspired with outsiders: two approved loans for "trusted" clients on the basis of information they knew to be untrue, and one approved excessive loans to a company in return for secret commissions. In another case, an employee of a disposal company paid secret commissions to the operator of a rubbish tip for lower rates per truck load. There were two cases of collusion within a company: three employees in a ministry conspired to steal cars that should have been traded in when new ones were purchased, and the manager of a credit corporation who sent all printing work to the same company and in return was being paid secret commissions.

Regarding the *person* component of the ROP model, findings obtained provide support for both its constituent parts, namely "motive" and "crime-prone personality". About the former, while 30% were professional, unscrupulous deceivers, the motive in 40% of the cases was a financial problem. There was only one case involving the restoration of social identity and one in order to obtain personal justice respectively. In further support of the ROP model, according to the police detectives interviewed, and the analysis of data in the study, the most frequent characteristics of a crime-prone person who has perpetrated fraud are a propensity for lying (92%) and weak self-control (62%), egocentricity (34%), someone having a strong sense they are entitled to whatever money they can get by deceiving others (28%) and low self-esteem (20%). As would be predicted using the ROP model, the cases studied involved a variety of *motives*. The two main motives were: being a professional fraudster (30%) and sheer greed in the case of opportunistic offenders (24%). A category of predator, professional conmen (N=15) had no moral scruples and therefore felt no guilt for committing the crime but justified committing the offence using a variety of *rationalisations* (in Cressey's, 1986, term *neutralising verbalisations)*.

Cressey (1986) considers rationalisations the most vital component of an explanation for why people commit fraud. Cressey interviewed imprisoned embezzlers in the U.S. about their rationalisations. No interviews were conducted with any of the imprisoned major fraud offenders included in the MFG study due to time constraints and lack of necessary resources. Therefore, information about such offenders' rationalisations was extracted from sworn written statements made to the MFG detectives investigating. This means that what is reported about rationalisations (see Figure 3 in Chapter 7) must be treated with caution. Offenders made their sworn statements, which were subsequently used in evidence during the trial, presumably acting on advice from their lawyer. It is possible that how they rationalised their fraudulent activity in the course of police interviews may be different from how they really justified the fraud(s) to themselves at the time. With this limitation in mind, it is interesting to note that the study identified more rationalisations (see Figure 3) than had been listed in Figure 1, in Chapter 4, on the basis of the literature discussion in Chapter 3.

Table 3: Offenders' rationalisations (N=50)

Indicators	% of cases with components in the MFG cases
Rationalisations	
Deceiving is what I do for a living; I am entitled to whatever money I can get / I can make better use of the money than the company	30
The end justifies the means/ It's for a good purpose/It's to: save the company/pay the staff/I'm doing it for the family	16
Nobody will get hurt/I am not really hurting anybody/the bank won't miss the money	12
I am only borrowing the money and will pay it back	12
I just need the money, there's no other way	8
It's OK to borrow from client's accounts because he/she does not really need the money	6
I can get away with it	6
The potential reward is worth it	2
The company owes me	2
I've deceived no one; these are only technical deficiencies	2
I, too, have a right to enjoy my life	2
Others do it too	2

Table 3 shows the different types and frequency of rationalisations used by the MFG offenders. The most frequently used rationalisations were: "I am entitled to whatever money I can get" and so forth (30%) that characterised predator, career offenders; "the end justifies the means/It's for a good purpose" and so forth (16%); "nobody will get hurt" an so forth (12%) and, finally, "I am only borrowing the money and will pay it back" (12%). The most common rationalisations in this study are almost identical to those reported by Cressey (1986) in the U.S.

In considering the rationalisations listed in Table 3, it needs to be remembered that in classifying the rationalisations as articulated by the offenders, an attempt was made to convey the essence of the justification used as they would often give a long answer to the question "why did you do it?". It should also be remembered that an apparent belief that the risk involved was low and the offender could avoid being found out was common to the majority of cases. However, in only three cases was that belief actually spelled out by the offenders.

The reader should also note that the rationalisations definitely existed after an offender was apprehended by the police. Future research should investigate the existence of rationalisations before an offender is apprehended and whether they predict fraud. To understand fraud victimisation further, future research should study more systematically the rationalisations used by different typologies of fraud offenders and explore the different styles of interpersonal interaction learned by fraud offenders in childhood and adolescence and/or as part of their socialisation into particular subcultures in the workplace or elsewhere.

In the light of the findings regarding *rationalisations* (R*),opportunity* (O) *and a motivated crime-prone person* (P), the MFG study has shown the importance of all three components of the ROP model in understanding the aetiology of fraud and demonstrates the model's applicability to the MFG cases, as had been predicted. Regarding crime opportunity, as Gottfredson and Hirschi (1990:12-13) would have predicted, it is particularly important where: the offence produces immediate rather than delayed gratification; committing the crime is easy in terms of the mental and physical effort required; and, finally, in situations where the perceived risk of being found out is minimal. In other words, in most cases, situational circumstances (e.g., strong internal controls) could mute or counteract the effects of a person's low self-control. However, the findings obtained emphasise that it is the interaction of both self-control and crime opportunity that largely explains the genesis of fraud. Of the two factors, however, and contrary to what Gottfredson and Hirschi (1990) and Grasmick et al. (1993) would have predicted, a crime-prone person with a motive and the necessary rationalisations is a better predictor of fraud than opportunity for fraud.

Finally, careful interrogation of the MFG data indicates that whether someone in a position of financial trust will commit fraud appears to vary to some extent independently of self-control or opportunity. The motivation for crime appears to influence the extent to which people perceive situations as constituting criminal opportunity as well as the extent to which low self-control produces crimes, given the opportunity.

Without ignoring the limitations of the MFG cases studied, the policy implication of the findings reported above is that the ROP model can be used by auditors to enhance their fraud-detection ability by alerting them to particular characteristics of individuals and companies that are associated with fraud. The successful test of the ROP model highlights the importance of the auditor utilising information contained in all three of the model's components when planning the audit.

Testing the applicability of the Loebbecke et al. model

One certain way of advancing knowledge is by falsifying existing theories, models and so forth. In order to test the applicability of the Loebbecke et al. fraud assessment model to the fifty MFG cases, fraud indicators were categorised as: (1) *conditions;* (2) *motives;* and (3) *attitudes* to determine if the Loebbecke et al.

model holds true in the 50 major fraud cases. Loebbecke et al. assert that for material management fraud to occur, all three components have to exist. If any one of the requirements is absent, then it would be deemed highly unlikely that a material irregularity has taken place or is likely to do so (1989:4).

Loebbecke et al.'s fraud-risk assessment model was tested as follows. First, the fraud indicators present in the major fraud cases were checked against Loebbecke's reported indicators (see Table 4 below for details). Second, an assessment was made of the degree to which all three components of Loebbecke et al.'s model (i.e., conditions, motivations and attitudes) were present in the cases examined.

It was found that:

- 6 out of the 24 indicators listed (weak internal controls, dishonest management, difficult to audit transactions, conflict of interest, dominated decisions, and major transactions) had a frequency of greater than 50%.
- The following red flags occurred with high frequency in both studies: dominated decisions; weak internal controls; conflict of interest, and difficult to audit transactions.
- In support of Loebbecke et al., high management turnover occurred with low frequency in both studies.
- The following three red flags occurred with high frequency in Loebbecke et al. but did so with very low frequency in the present study: the company is in a period of rapid growth; significant contractual agreements, and industry decline. It could be argued, of course, that, excluding "industry decline", the other two red flags would not be relevant in cases where accountants and solicitors steal from trust funds

A basic premise of the Loebbecke et al. model is that all three of its components must be present for fraud to occur. It was found, however, that one only component of the ROP model was present in 12% of the cases, only two in (52%) and all three components were present in 36% of the cases; in other words, contrary to what the Loebbecke et al.'s model predicts, in the majority of the cases (64%) fraud occurred despite the fact that all three components were not present. It can, therefore be concluded that in most cases the presence of any two components is sufficient for management fraud and defalcations to occur. Of the three components depicted, the average number of conditions-related indicators is higher than for motivations and attitude ones, irrespective of the number of components present. This finding emphasises the importance of the opportunity component of the ROP model in the aetiology of fraud and has implications for fraud prevention.

Table 4: Indicators and their Frequency of Occurrence by Loebbecke et al.'s three Components

Indicators	% of component in the 50 cases
Conditions:	
Weak internal controls	90
Difficult to audit transactions	72
Conflict of interest	70
Dominated decisions	64
Major transactions	62
Inexperienced management	48
Related party	36
Significant judgements	20
Decentralised organisation	10
Assets subject to misappropriation	8
High management turnover	6
New client	2
Rapid growth	2
Motivation:	
Industry decline	22
Inadequate profits	18
Significant contractual commitments	14
Emphasis on earnings projections	8
Attitude:	
Dishonest management	74
Lies or evasiveness	42
Aggressive attitude toward financial reporting	28
Personality anomalies	6
Prior year irregularities	4
Poor reputation	4
Emphasis on earnings projections	4

Since in 88% of the cases examined two or three components were present (i.e., conditions, motives and attitudes or a combination of two), in their efforts to assess whether there is fraud, auditors can utilise both information about profiles of fraud offenders as well as about the type and frequency of fraud indicators present. The justification for auditors' utilising such information lies in the finding that, as in Loebbecke et al., as the number of indicators increased, the chance of fraud increased. As far as Loebbecke et al.'s assessment model of irregularities is concerned, the findings of the Major Fraud Group study contradict one of its basic premises, that all three components need to be present for an irregularity to occur.

MFG CASE RESULTS AND THE ROP FRAUD RISK ASSESSMENT MODEL

The findings' provide support for the validity of the eight assumptions of the ROP model constructed in Chapter 4 and indicate that heterogeneity is a basic characteristic of fraud offenders and their crimes. In addition, crime-proneness (in the form of low self-control) is an essential component of fraud offenders and a broad variety of motives underpins the aetiology of fraud; while financial pressure is the most frequent motive, correlates of fraud exist at different levels of analysis and supplement one another. Finally, there are individual differences in how a crime opportunity and a rationalisation is constructed.

The results highlight the importance of the three components of the ROP model - a motivated crime-prone person (P), crime opportunity (O), and rationalisations (R) - in the aetiology of fraud. Considering first crime-proneness as an attribute of the offenders, the findings confirm the crucial importance of low self-control. More specifically, the results reported add some support to the following components of self-control proposed by Gottfredson and Hirschi (1990:89) and as re-defined and measured by Grasmick et al. (1993):

i. *impulsiveness*: this is evident in those cases where an offender exploits an opportunity that presents itself and commits fraud without any reservations;
ii. *risk-seeking*: many of the offenders appear to have perpetrated their frauds in a way that betrays a tendency to be adventuresome;
iii. *preference for simple tasks*: many of the offenders exhibited a preference for easy gratification of their desire for money; and
iv. *being self-centred*: a large number of the offenders can be described as self centred, insensitive to the suffering and needs of those they victimised.

DISCUSSION OF RESULTS

The results of this study show that the research into the MFG offenders achieved its seven designated aims. The results obtained show the validity of all seven propositions/assumptions of the ROP model tested in the survey. More specifically, the data analysis confirmed the importance of all three components of the ROP model in understanding why people in a position of financial trust commit fraud. When comparing the fraud indicators present in the ROP model with those in Loebbecke et al. (1989) it was interesting to find that the modus operandi of serious fraud offenders is very much the same whether they operate in Australia or in the U.S.

While results of the study support Gottfredson and Hirschi's (1990) emphasis on crime opportunity and low self-control, no support was found for their claim that fraud offenders are versatile or that crime opportunity is a better predictor of fraud than a crime – prone person with a motive.

All six assumptions and the one prediction of the ROP model appear to be valid. The two-component profile of the serious fraud offender that emerges from the study and which includes the taxonomy of cases is a lot more detailed than has hitherto been reported in the literature. To illustrate, Robertson (1996:294), for example, claimed, that white-collar offenders have these characteristics:

> Likely to be married, probably not tattooed, educated beyond high school, range in age from teens to over 60, employment tenure from 1 to 20 or more years, not likely to be divorced, member of a church, no arrest record, socially conforming, usually act alone.

Auditors need more details of such a profile in order to improve their fraud detection ability. The profile of fraud offenders reported in this book has been developed from data pertaining to actual major fraud offenders prosecuted by the police. Offenders and their crimes exist in a context. A profile that focused solely on features of the individual and ignored the interaction between a particular individual offender and particular circumstances and conditions (such as type of opportunity, type of victim) would not have much utility for auditors. The present research indicates that, at a general level, a fraud offender is one who: (1) is likely to be a male first offender; (2) aged 31-45; (3) occupies a position of trust; (4) acting alone and mainly out of greed, breaches that trust and commits a spate of deception offences defrauding a number of victims; (5) is in a position to bargain with those that prosecute him (see Katz, 1978); and (6) ends up going to prison for a relatively short period of time. The findings pertaining to demographic characteristics and lifestyle, criminal history, modus operandi and "distorted stories" of the major fraud offenders examined, indicate that a criminal profile incorporating all this information is possible. The profile constructed comprises information at a general level and an account of 12 specific offender typologies. The auditor, of course, needs to look for the most frequent factors associated with fraud. With this need in mind, the two-component profile constructed in the MFG study will assist auditors to enhance their fraud-detection ability, but not if it is used by itself. This is because what the general profile describes could be any professional in a position of financial trust. Rather, it ought to be used in combination with: (1) the knowledge concerning the inter-relationship found between offence, offender and victim characteristics; and (2) the fraud-detection model reported in the next chapter.

Contrary to what Gottfredson and Hirschi's (1990) *General Theory of Crime* predicts, most major fraud offenders are not immersed in crime in the sense of being recidivist career offenders. It is possible, of course, that an offender has been perpetrating fraud and/or other offences for much longer but managed not to come to police attention. Future research should aim to identify and interview major fraud offenders whose crimes remain part of the dark figure of white-collar crime.

The findings, however, support Gottfredson and Hirschi's theory to some extent in so far as the offenders in this study evidenced low self-control and exploited opportunities available to them. Future research should interview fraud offenders in order to explore the different styles of interpersonal interaction learned by such individuals in childhood and adolescence and/or as part of their socialisation into particular subcultures in the workplace or elsewhere. Such data would throw some light on the question of how it is possible for fraud offenders to be insensitive to the needs and suffering of those they victimise in order to explain the use of different rationalisations by them. Future research should also explore personality differences amongst fraud offenders (e.g., in terms of Eysenck's three personality traits-see Chapter 2) to add to our understanding of their offending. The offender-circumstances typologies identified by the MFG study need to be explored further in an attempt to produce "social profiles" of the offenders. Regarding the career/professional fraud offender, future research should examine the possibility that, as a profiler would predict, the way such offenders carry out their crimes on one occasion has some characteristic similarity to the way they carry out their crimes on other occasions. Finally, there is a need to investigate further the relationship between a person's characteristics and their fraud. Initially, one could focus on simple one-to-one relationships. It might then be possible to build on such simple relationships and generate canonical equations which provide an objective way of analysing the relationship between two sets of variables such as a person's characteristics and his/her actions (see Canter, 1995:345).

The offenders did not, as the general theory of crime would have predicted, engage in a variety of criminal acts but stuck to fraud. It becomes apparent that the offenders studied comprise a number of typologies of major fraud offenders, many of whom experienced situational pressures (e.g., high personal debts, financial losses) and who rationalised their offending to make it acceptable to them and thus to continue to perceive themselves as successful professionals in their fields. Also, it should not be forgotten that solicitors, accountants and bank managers, operate in an occupational culture that values wealth and corporate success, considers failure quite unacceptable, and, at the same time, provides opportunities for major fraud.

Whether the sentences imposed by the courts on such offenders (mostly five years' imprisonment or less) serve the purpose of individual and/or general deterrence is impossible to say on the basis of the research carried out. However, an examination of voluntary statements made to the police by the offenders indicates that a term of imprisonment of five years or less is unlikely to be a deterrent because: (1) they fancy their chances of not being apprehended; (2) if charged, believe they "can beat the charges" against them; and (3) even if they are incarcerated they know they would be unlikely to serve their full sentence. Without a perception by serious fraud offenders that there is a high risk of being detected and that the likely penalty upon conviction will be severe, a court would not be justified in imposing a very severe sentence on an individual offender in order to discourage him/her and/or other potential offenders from committing the same crime (Braithwaite, 1989). The two-component offender profile yielded by the data analysis is that the commission of fraud is not a random process and that a number of individuals who share a number of demographic characteristics (gender, age, marital status, occupation) and criminal justice features experience pressures to raise money for themselves, or their companies, or their loved ones. Since by virtue of their occupational position, they have the opportunity and the knowhow, they often do not require accomplices, and proceed to commit a number of deception offences following a characteristic modus operandi. Furthermore, they rationalise their behaviour in ways that neutralises any guilt they may feel as a result of their frauds. Finally, a sizeable minority of the offenders are best thought of as predators who feel no guilt for perpetrating fraud.

It is not claimed that armed with the criminal profiling results obtained, auditors can identify an offender and significantly increase their fraud-detection effectiveness. This is simply because, on the basis of existing knowledge in this area, it is just not possible to predict accurately who in a company will commit or has been committing fraud. Without ignoring its limitations, what the research reported in this chapter can do is to increase the fraud awareness of auditors and point to some indicators, i.e., red flags, which should alert auditors to an increased possibility of fraud. Together with empirically obtained knowledge about other sets of red flags pointing to vulnerable types of industries/companies as well as vulnerable areas within particular types of industries/companies, the red flags inherent in the offender profile provided above can be used to alert an auditor to a greater likelihood of fraud and thus negate an auditor's sense of complacency.

The findings obtained in the study reported in this chapter suggest that auditors played but a rather limited role in the detection of the frauds involved. The eclectic fraud detection model proposed in this book (see Chapter 6) shows how auditors can improve their fraud detection ability. Future research should expand the two-component profile of major fraud offenders constructed by the research, using in-depth psychological interviews with such offenders and develop a prediction model. Given that most frauds involve financial pressure on an individual and that factor plays such an important part in contributing to fraud taking place, a simple income-expenditure assessment of professional people in positions of trust should help to identify potential/actual major frauds. Future research should also consider fraud by a variety of officially-known and self-reported offenders in order to identify the factors that best explain their specific nature and prevalence.

CONCLUSIONS

Without forgetting its limitations, the MFG study has tested and demonstrated the applicability of the ROP model and its three components. It is the first time a comprehensive model of the aetiology of fraud (in terms of the components that are necessary for fraud to occur) has been proposed and tested successfully. As already stated, Loebbecke et al.'s model has nothing to say about rationalisations and one of its basic premises has been shown to be wrong. As far as it has been possible to ascertain, the ROP model is the only one which accounts for the broad range of persons who perpetrate fraud and the circumstances under which they do it. Future research should test the ROP model with a larger and more representative sample of fraud cases involving people in positions of financial trust. The fraud indicators identified for O and P can be used by auditors to enhance their fraud-detection ability.

A profile of major fraud offenders would be useful to auditors if used in conjunction with other relevant knowledge about fraud risk such as different industries and financial areas. The findings of this study show that the modus operandi (deceptive action) of serious fraud offenders is very much the same whether they operate in Australia or in the U.S. and that the offenders are very prolific.

Tabulation of data concerning fraud indicators shows that the presence of any two of Loebbecke et al.'s (1989) three components is usually sufficient for fraud to occur. This finding is contrary to a basic premise by Loebbecke et al. that for fraud to occur all three components (CMA) of their model must be present.

Reflecting the importance of opportunity, most of the offenders (94%) victimised someone they knew. Approximately one-third of the offenders had a criminal record, and that was especially the case with managing directors. This finding points to the importance of screening applicants for position of financial trust through background checks, to reduce the risk of fraud victimisation. The finding that about one-third of the offenders had accomplices means that for such offenders the decision to commit fraud follows group discussion, a factor catered for in the ROP model.

The findings show that it is not appropriate to talk about major fraud offenders as a homogeneous population. Future research should explore further patterns identified between offence, offender, victim and criminal justice characteristics with a larger sample of offenders in order to replicate the two-component criminal profile reported above and, also, to measure fraud offenders' level of self-control using the instrument developed by Grasmick et al. (1993). The next chapter reports a broad range of empirical findings from a survey of Australian auditors' experience in detecting material irregularities including fraud.

CHAPTER 6

A SURVEY OF AUDITORS' DETECTION OF MATERIAL IRREGULARITIES

- **Research method used in survey.**
- **Structure and content of the questionnaire used.**
- **Respondent characteristics and audit experience.**
- **Six types of irregularities encountered by auditors.**
- **Patterns in irregularity-detection.**
- **Usefulness of red flags.**
- **Correlates of fraud proneness.**
- **Reporting fraud.**
- **Use of fraud auditors and forensic accountants.**
- **The eclectic fraud detection model revisited**
- **Conclusions.**

INTRODUCTION

Despite the importance of auditors' detecting and reporting material irregularities, there is not a great deal of information in the professional or academic literature about these matters. No work has been undertaken of such a magnitude in Australia and the only other comparable work is that by Loebbecke et al (1989). In the first study of its kind worldwide, Australian auditors' experience in encountering irregularities and their knowledge about the perpetrators and the aetiology of irregularities generally was obtained by means of a self-administered structured questionnaire[1]. The questionnaire collected data on auditors' experience in detecting a broad range of irregularities, in the mid 1990's namely: management fraud, employee fraud, other illegal acts, other acts which contravene the constitution of an entity including non-compliance with trust deeds or memorandum and articles of association, intentional but not fraudulent or other illegal misstatements, and errors which are unintentional mistakes (see AUS 210 (AARF, 1995a, para. 05)).

RESEARCH METHOD

The questionnaire

The questionnaire was modelled on the one used by Loebbecke et al. (1989). As a result their findings can be compared, despite the fact that each study used a

---

[1] According to Moses and Kalton (1981:257-259), compared to other research methods, mail surveys have some advantages that include the following: they are cheaper, take less time to do, and avoid such sources of error as interviewer bias. Such surveys, however, face the difficulty of a low response rate, generalizability of the findings, not knowing that a respondent completed the questionnaire alone, and that the researcher is in no position to probe the respondent's answers further (see also Judd, Smith and Kidder, 1991:216).

different sample of auditors. Before the questionnaire was sent to auditors, it was piloted by administering it to a group of auditors known personally to the author.

The questionnaire comprised three parts. *Part I* collected summary information about each of the irregularities which the respondent had experienced during the last five years. This information was collected to increase our knowledge about auditors' experience with material and immaterial irregularities, their nature and frequency of occurrence, as well as whether they had a material impact on the financial statements of the clients involved.

Respondents were provided with a definition of: (1) *irregularities* and (2) *code of corporate conduct* to ensure consistency. Respondents were asked about the following: a management fraud[2] (to provide a description); the number of times that irregularity was encountered; the industry the client operated in; what alerted the auditor to the irregularity; whether there were effective internal controls in place; whether a code of conduct existed and, finally, whether there was a material financial impact on the accounts. They were asked to repeat the exercise for the remaining five types of irregularities[3].

The information collected on the different types of irregularities was expected to throw some light on both the types of industries that are prone to particular frauds as well as on the question whether having a code of conduct or effective internal controls assists in combating fraud.

Part II requested information about one material irregularity selected by the respondent which had been encountered in the previous 12 months.

The respondents were asked to:

- describe how the irregularity was committed; who was involved;
- the industry and the status of the client[4]; audit areas affected by the irregularity;
- how long the audit firm had been an auditor of that client when the irregularity was discovered;
- over what time period that particular irregularity had been committed;
- the audit procedures first indicating the irregularity;
- whether the presence of a fraud auditor or forensic accountant on an audit team would have assisted in discovering it earlier than it had been;

---

[2] In the survey of auditors' experience with detecting irregularities reported in this chapter management and employee fraud were treated as two categories of fraud to enable a comparison of the results obtained with Loebbecke et al.'s (1989) findings and the KPMG fraud surveys.

[3] It is interesting that the exposure intending to update ISA240(IFAC,2000) does not distinguish between the different type of irregularities. In fact the term "fraud" (par.4) "refers to an intentional act by one or more individuals among management, employees, or third parties, which results in a misstatement in the financial statements. Fraud may consist of fraudulent financial reporting or misappropriation of assets".

[4] The industry designation used is the one found in the Australian Bureau of Statistics (1993) *Australian and New Zealand Standard Industrial Classification.*

- a profile of the perpetrator; and
- to whom the material irregularity was reported.

The respondents were in no position to provide data on offenders' rationalisations (R) or crime – proneness and motives (P). Therefore it was not possible to test the ROP model, drawing on auditors' experience.

Part II also provided participants with a list of red flags that comprised those mentioned in AUP 16 (AARF, 1993)[5]. With reference to one particular material irregularity they were asked to tick the indicator(s) applicable to the engagement and relevant to the irregularity and whether it alerted the auditor during the planning phase. The categories "applicable ... ", "relevant ... " and "whether alerted ... " were independent but not mutually exclusive.

In *Part III*, the respondents were asked to provide demographic data about the respondent and his/her experience, which included: state of residence; gender; current position; number of years of experience as an auditor; position in the partnership; number of years in current position; approximate number of engagements worked on; industry specialisation; size of employer (e.g., Big Six-applicable at the time); whether the audit firm provides forensic and fraud auditors and their qualifications; and number of times a fraud auditor/forensic accountant had been required by the respondents themselves or their client in the last 12 months.

The respondents and data-collection procedure used

The respondents were external and internal auditors as well as public sector auditors. They were accessed as follows: first contact was made with the managing audit partner in several large, medium and small firms to seek their co-operation in the study. Initial contact was made with 117 partners in the Big Six, medium tier firms, and small practices in Australia in the middle of September 1995. The practices were selected from the yellow pages and telephone contact was made to identify the partner in charge of audit in a particular practice. Personalised letters were sent to the 117 partners stating the research being carried out and soliciting their firm's participation. A follow-up telephone call was made two weeks later. A total of 76 partners (65% of firms initially approached) agreed to participate. At the end of October 1995 they were provided with 433 questionnaires to distribute to their staff. The letter to the partners made mention of the fact that the Major Fraud Group of the Victoria Police was actively supporting the research into fraud and a letter to that effect by the then Commander of the MFG, Allen Bowles, was attached to the questionnaire.

[5] Since the study was concerned with Australian auditors' experience in fraud detection it was considered appropriate to use the fraud indicators (red flags) provided in the Australian Auditing Standard (AARF, 1993) which are the same as in AUS 210 (AARF, 1995a) rather than the ones provided by Loebbecke et al. (1989). In comparing the different red flags, however, it became apparent that the Australian list of fraud indicators is a lot more comprehensive (it covers the EDP area as well) than the one used by Loebbecke et al.

In order to avoid duplication of data, it was agreed with the participating partners that they would distribute only one questionnaire per fraud investigated. Partners were also asked to distribute questionnaires only to those who had some experience in fraud detection, or worked on a fraud investigation. Where firms employed fraud auditors or forensic accountants they were asked to distribute a questionnaire to them as well.

In addition to financial auditors, the Western Australian and Victorian Auditor General's offices were approached to participate in the research, the former participated in the survey the latter declined. Given that a lot of fraud is identified by the internal auditors, 25 questionnaires were distributed at a meeting held by the Internal Auditors' Association on fraud detection addressed by Commander Bowles.

A total of 125 questionnaires were returned, 108 (86%) completed ones and used for the data analysis. The low (23%) response rate is probably due to the fact that: (1) as Loebbecke et al. reported, it is rarely that auditors detect a material irregularity (including management and employee fraud); (2) only one questionnaire was distributed by the participating partners per fraud; and (3) mail surveys generally have a low response rate. It should also be noted in this context that the response rate "is not the only consideration in evaluating the quality of data from a survey" (Judd et al., 1991:217). Even though the response rate is low, since it rises above 20% the failing is not so critical as to make the survey results of little value (Moses and Kalton, 1981:268).

Of the 108 useable respondents, 87 (80.5%) completed all sections of the questionnaire while the remaining 21 completed only parts I and III. Part II asked respondents to discuss only material irregularities encountered by them in the last 12 months. It is assumed that those who did not complete Part II either had not come across a material irregularity in the last 12 months or might have felt that they were to give away too much information about their client if they did[6]. Part III of the questionnaire collected demographic data about the respondents and their audit experience.

Overall, it can be said that the survey had a relatively high response rate most likely due to the fact that partners solicited the respondents' participation in the study. The process by which the 108 respondents came to participate in the survey, and whose data form the basis of the findings reported below, means that as a sample they can not be considered a random sample of auditors with experience in detecting irregularities, including management and employee fraud. At the same time, however, it is clear from discussions with numerous partners that fraud-detection is such a specialist field that the proportion of fraud-experienced auditors in accounting firms is very small.

[6] Loebbecke et al. (1989) assumed that those auditors who did not participate in their survey did so because they had not encountered an irregularity (p.7).

The respondents

Most respondents resided in Victoria (40%), Queensland (17%), New South Wales (15%), South Australia (15%), Western Australia (8%), Australian Capital Territories (3%) and Tasmania (2%). The majority (85%) were males. While 39% held manager positions, 28% were partners, 13% seniors, 12% supervisors and 8% assistant managers.

Regarding their position at the time of the survey, most (82%) were financial auditors, 7% public sector auditors, 7% fraud auditors and 4% internal auditors. Forty-two per cent had been auditors for 11 years or more, 38% had been in their position for over three years and there was no one with under three years' experience. About three quarters (73%) were working for one of the [then] Big Six firms.

About half (52%) had worked on more than 50 engagements and about two-thirds (67%) had specialised in auditing more than three different industries. The following are some interesting characteristics of the auditors who participated in the survey and should be borne in mind when interpreting the findings reported below:

Table 1: Respondents' Fraud Experience

Average audit experience (in years)	10
Average years in current position	3
Average number of engagements worked on	106
Average number of engagements where an irregularity had been encountered	5
Average number of engagements where a material irregularity had been encountered	39
Engagements where an irregularity had been encountered as a % of all engagements worked on by the respondents	19%

The participants in the present study, are slightly younger in age, with fewer years' experience in audit and with less experience in encountering irregularities, compared to those in Loebbecke et al. (1989). The reason for these differences is that Loebbecke et al. surveyed only partners whereas in the present study partners made up 28% of the respondents.

As already mentioned, the sample of auditors who took part in the survey did so because they had experience in detecting irregularities, including management fraud and defalcations. Furthermore, the auditors concerned are a heterogeneous sample by virtue of the fact that they belonged to different firms, had different lengths of audit experience, and held different positions. The nature of the sample, therefore, limits the extent to which the findings obtained can be generalised to auditors in general. Unlike the auditors in Loebbecke et al. (1989) and Pincus (1989), however, the respondents in the present study did not come from one single firm. Hence, it is argued that the research findings can be cautiously generalised to auditors experienced in detecting irregularities (including management fraud and defalcations) more justifiably than in the case of Loebbecke et al. (1989) and Pincus (1990).

SURVEY RESULTS

Part I of Survey: Irregularities Encountered by Auditors and Discussion of Findings

Regarding the auditors' experience with encountering irregularities within the last five years, 19.6% had come across none, 20.6% one, 16.7% two, and 43.1% three or more; in other words, 80% had come across at least one immaterial irregularity. As far as the respondents' experience with material irregularities is concerned, 34% had come across none, 34.9% one, 13.2% two, and 17.9% three or more; in other words, 66% had encountered at least one material irregularity. By comparison, Loebbecke et al. (1989) found that 40% of the 277 audit partners who participated in their survey had not encountered a material irregularity of any kind and, of those, only 11% had done so on more than five occasions (p.8). In the present study of those who had encountered a material irregularity, 8.9% had done so on five or more occasions. The results obtained support Loebbecke et al. (1989) who also found that for many auditors encountering a material irregularity is a rare event. One could, therefore, argue that it is not reasonable to expect the average auditor to be proficient in detecting such irregularities as fraud when he (she) does not seem to have the necessary experience. Experience in fraud detection is one of the attributes needed since fraud detection is without doubt a "multi-attribute, high-level judgement task that requires knowledge, experience and reasoning" (Loebbecke et al., 1989:3).

When asked to provide detailed information in respect of specific irregularities, the 108 respondents indicated they had come across 768 incidents of irregularities during the past five years which comprised: 305 management fraud (39.7%), 185 (24.1%) employee fraud, 146 (19%) other illegal acts, 32 (4.2%) other acts, 52 (6.8%) intentional but not fraudulent or other illegal misstatements and, finally, 48 (6.2%) errors. These are the irregularities the respondents chose to discuss. It is possible, of course, that there might have been some irregularities they did not want to divulge or did not remember well enough to discuss in Part I of the survey.

Management fraud

Management fraud was defined in the questionnaire as an act which involves the use of deception to obtain an illegal advantage by management[7]. The respondents had encountered a total of 305 cases of management fraud during the last five years (i.e., 39.7% of the total irregularities encountered by those

[7] This term is not specifically defined in AUS 210 (AARF, 1995a, para.05) which only defines fraud as "an act which involves the use of deception to obtain an illegal advantage" and, since it is "management", it was added by the author that it ought to be committed by management. The same definition of "management fraud" was used by Loebbecke et al. (1989) [personal communication], namely "the material, intentional misstatement of financial statements to defraud users".

surveyed) and provided detailed information on 153 (50.1%) of them. The types of management fraud encountered were as follow (N of cases=153): window dressing (20.2%), misappropriation of funds (17.6%), cash spent without approval (9.2%), manipulation of reconciliations (9.2%), kickbacks (7.8%), conflict of interest (7.2%), other (6.7%), theft of equipment (5.2%), overstatement of sales/revenues/debtors (5.2%), overstatement of stock (5.2%), payroll fraud (3.9%), and theft of stock (2.6%).

We see that the most frequently encountered management frauds in the present study were window dressing and misappropriation of assets. Loebbecke et al. (1989) reported that assets overvalued or incorrectly valued (which is similar to window dressing) was the highest ranking management fraud.

Concerning the industry classification used in the present study, it should be noted that the respondents provided a long list of industries in which their clients operated in, responding to Part I of the questionnaire. A number of industries did not belong to any of the categories listed in Table 2 and subsequent tables which are based on the Australian Bureau of Statistics (1993) classification. Such categories included, for example: Fuel distribution, aviation, international service provider, "various", and subsidiary company. Such categories were assigned to the "Miscellaneous Industry" category because they were very few in number to show separately in the analysis and did not come under any of the ABS classification. To this category it was also added "fund management and trusts" which the respondents had listed on its own as a separate category worthy of attention, despite the fact that it would be listed under Financial Services.

Table 2 indicates that most management fraud occurs in the manufacturing and construction industries. This may be because there are more companies in these two industries than in most others. In manufacturing it often takes the form of window dressing, overstatement of stock, theft of cash and equipment, payroll fraud and cash spent without approval. In construction, management fraud involves window dressing, misappropriation of funds, cash spent without approval and kickbacks.

Table 2 also shows that there is no relationship between the type of industry, the type of fraud and which audit procedure(s) alerted[8] the auditors. It can be seen, however, that management review and tests of controls are two audit procedures most likely to detect such fraud.

[8] It should be noted that the auditors' responses regarding the different ways they were alerted to the existence of different irregularities are presented below as they were stated, i.e., where two such ways overlap (e.g., "substantive testing" and "audit test of balances") no attempt has been made to merge or reclassify the two terms.

Table 2: Type of Industry by Type of Management Fraud (MF) and Ways of Being Alerted and their Incidence

Industry	% of MF	Types of management frauds committed	Main ways of being alerted
Manufacturing (N=25)	16.3	Window dressing; overstatement of stock; theft of cash and equipment; payroll fraud; cash spent without approval	Analytical and management reviews, stocktake, whistleblower
Miscellaneous Industry (N=20)	13.1	Window dressing; misappropriation of funds; cash spent without approval; kickbacks; overstatement of stocks	Tests of controls and/or management review
Construction (N=19)	12.4	Window dressing; misappropriation of funds; cash spent without approval; kickbacks	Analytical; management review; substantive testing; and/or knowledge of client
Government Administration and Defence (N=13)	8.5	Misappropriation of funds; kickbacks	Substantive and tests of controls and/or management review
Finance and Insurance (N=10)	6.5	Misappropriation of funds	Management review and/or tests of controls
Accommodatio, Cafes and Restaurants (N=9)	5.9	Conflict of interest; manipulation of reconciliations	Management review; tests of controls/ substantive testing
Retail Trade (N=8)	5.2	Window dressing	Substantive testing; co-worker
Wholesale Trade (N=8)	5.2	Window dressing	Tests of controls and/or anonymous caller
Health and Community Services (N=7)	4.6	Misappropriation of funds	Anonymous caller; substantive testing
Property and Business Services(N=6)	3.9	Misappropriation of funds	Financial analysis; tests of controls and/or management review

Personal and Other Services (N=5)	3.4	Cash spent without approval	Tests of controls; management or analytical review
Transportation and Storage (N=4)	2.6	Window dressing	After balance date review; analytical and management review
Communication Services (N=4)	2.6	Manipulation of reconciliations; misappropriation of funds	Tests of controls; substantive testing; and/or management review
Education (N=4)	2.6	Misappropriation of funds; conflict of interest; manipulation of reconciliations	Substantive and tests of controls and/or management review
Mining (N=4)	2.6	Cash spent without approval; misappropriation of funds; conflict of interest	Tests of controls and/or analytical and management review
Electricity, Gas and Water Supply (N=3)	1.9	Misappropriation of funds; window dressing; manipulation of reconciliations	Financial analysis and/or tests of controls and/or management review
Cultural and Recreational Services (N=2)	1.4	Cash spent without approval	Tests of controls and/or management or analytical review
Agriculture, Forestry and Fishing (N=2)	1.3	Theft of equipment; window; window dressing	Review of asset register

Manufacturing also had the highest incidence of management fraud in the KPMG (1995a) fraud survey and in the Loebbecke et al. study. The other industries with a relatively high incidence of management fraud in the present study were construction, government administration and defence as well as finance and insurance. In KPMG (1995a), the financial services and the mining industries reported the second and third highest average fraud per occurrence respectively, whereas in Loebbecke et al.'s study they were merchandising and banking. The industries with the lowest incidence of management fraud in Australia are cultural and recreational services, electricity, gas and water supply, agriculture, personal and other services.

Close scrutiny of the data on which Table 2 is based found that the four most common types of management fraud across the different industries in order of prevalence were misappropriation of funds, window dressing, cash spent without approval, and manipulation of reconciliations. In contrast, the KPMG (1995a) survey reported that, out of 14 types of management fraud, the four most common were: expense account (16%), purchase for personal use (15%), theft of inventory/plant (13%), and conflict of interest (11%). The difference in prevalent fraud types between the present study and KPMG (1995a) is probably attributable to their different sample of companies and sample of respondents[9]. Interestingly, the Ernst and Young (2000) survey[10] found that 60% of the respondents feared computer fraud (i.e., "manipulation of data records held on a computer to disguise the true nature of a transaction, hacking into an organisation's computer system to steal or manipulate organisation information, manipulation of computer programs to disguise the true nature of a transaction, and unauthorised transfer of funds electronically" (p.4)).

Cross-tabulating the type of management fraud with whether the fraud had a material impact on the accounts, it was found that window dressing (24%), manipulation of reconciliations (21%), misappropriation of funds (16%) and overstatement of stock (12%) were the main types of management fraud that had a material impact on the accounts.

The present study found that auditors were more likely to be alerted to the possible existence of management fraud as a result of management review (14 out of 18), followed by tests of controls, which featured in 12 out of the 18 industry categories listed, and, finally, substantive testing in 7 out of 18 industry categories (see Table 2). This is different than Loebbecke et al., who highlighted the utility of substantive testing.

Further analysis of the data investigated whether a company belonging to a particular industry category lacked: (1) an effective system of internal control and (2) a code of conduct as well as (3) whether the management fraud impacted materially on the accounts (see Table 3). The Spearman's rank correlation coefficient test was carried out to test whether there is a statistically significant relationship between (1), (2) and (3). The same analysis was carried out for the other five types of irregularities reported below. As several of the categories reported in Table 3 have small sample sizes, caution must be exercised in interpreting the results. With this caveat in mind, a significant relationship was found between a company having an ineffective system of internal control and

[9] In the KPMG survey the respondents comprised the following categories: chief financial officer (36%), chief executive officer/ managing director (24%), company secretary (11%), internal auditors (11%), other (10%), general manager (4%), chief operating officer (2%), and head of security (2%). As already stated, most (82%) respondents in the present study were financial auditors.

[10] Questionnaires were sent to senior executives in 10,000 major organisations in 15 countries. They received 739 responses.

lacking a code of conduct (p = 0.000) and between each of those features and the management fraud having a material impact on the accounts (p = 0.000).

Table 3: Industries Involved in Management Fraud by Ineffective Internal Controls, Without a Code of Conduct and the Management Fraud Having a Material Financial Impact on the Accounts. (No % is given due to N being very small in each industry category)

Industry (N)	With ineffective internal control N	Without a code of conduct N	Material impact on Accounts N
Miscellaneous Industry (20)	16	12	8
Agriculture Forestry and Fishing (2)	2	2	1
Mining (4)	3	2	1
Manufacturing (N=25)	16	19	14
Electricity, Gas and Water Supply (3)	3	2	0
Construction (19)	13	12	11
Wholesale Trade (N=8)	5	6	4
Retail Trade (8)	5	4	4
Accommodations, Cafes and Restaurants (9)	3	4	2
Transport and Storage (4)	3	1	4
Communication Services (4)	2	3	1
Finance and Insurance (10)	8	6	5
Property and Business Services (6)	3	2	3
Government Administration and Defence (13)	9	6	4
Education (4)	2	0	2
Health and Community Services (7)	7	1	7
Cultural and Recreational Services (2)	1	0	1
Personal and Other Services (5)	4	4	1

These significant relationships lend support to the view that an ineffective system of internal control (as was also found in the MFG study, see Chapter 5) and the absence of a code of conduct do indeed facilitate the commission of management fraud. Consequently, any steps taken to reduce fraud must include both improving internal controls and implementation of a code of corporate conduct. These two fraud-prevention steps were the two most frequently reported as having been taken in the KPMG (1995a) survey.

Employee fraud

Employee fraud was the second type of irregularity respondents were asked to comment on[11]. Employee fraud was defined in the questionnaire as an act which involves the use of deception to obtain an illegal advantage by an employee. The terms "employee fraud", "defalcations", "employee theft" and "embezzlement" are, used as synonymous in the context of this thesis. A total of 185 incidents of employee fraud had been encountered by the 108 respondents in the previous five years. This was the second highest category after management fraud, making up 24% of the total number of irregularities discussed in this chapter. The respondents provided information on a total of 93 (50.2%) cases. Wrong expense claim was the most common example of employee fraud (as in Loebbecke et al.), followed by product theft and cheque forgery. This contrasts with the KPMG (1995a) survey, which found that theft of inventory or plant was the most common type of employee fraud, occurring almost twice as often as manipulation of petty cash, the next most common fraud. In the present study employee fraud did not include any assets overvalued or transactions not recorded, as in Loebbecke et al., but did have a relatively high incidence of cheque forgery. The types of employee fraud encountered (N=93) were: wrong expense claim (26.9%), stealing cash (25.8), product theft (15.1%), cheque forgery (11.8%), payroll fraud (7.5%), lapping (6.5%), kickbacks (3.2%), and 'other' (3.2%).

Table 4 indicates both the type of industries that are prone to employee fraud by the type of such fraud to affect each industry as well as the ways the auditors were alerted. It shows that manufacturing makes up the largest share of employee fraud out of the 16 industry categories, followed by government administration and defence and finance and insurance. In Loebbecke et al., banking and savings was the most employee fraud-prone industry.

---

[11] This term is not specifically defined in AUS 210 (AARF, 1995a) but it was considered appropriate to distinguish between fraud committed by management and employees to see if there is a difference in the types of fraud committed. In Australia, unlike in the U.S., this term is not commonly used in the professional literature but it is understood more clearly than the term "defalcation" which is used in the U.S.

Table 4 also shows that management review and/or tests of controls was the audit procedure most likely to detect employee fraud. However in Loebbecke et al. it was substantive testing.

Table 4: Type of Industry by Employee Fraud (EF) and Ways of Being Alerted

Industry	% of EF	Types of Employee fraud committed	Main ways Alerted
Manufacturing (N=20)	21.5	Cheque forgery, payroll fraud, cash and product theft, lapping	Reconciliations, management and/or analytical review and/or substantive testing and whistleblower
Government Administration and Defence (N=12)	12.9	Steal cash, lapping, wrong expense claim	Management review and/or substantive/ tests of controls and/or reconciliations
Finance and Insurance (N=10)	10.7	Wrong expense claim, steal cash	Reconciliations and/or discussions with management and/or tests of controls
Miscellaneous Industry (N=7)	7.5	Steal cash and products	Tests of controls and/or management review
Health and Community Services (N=6)	6.5	Steal cash	Internal audit
Retail Trade (N=5)	5.4	Wrong expense claim, stealing cash, lapping	Reconciliations and cash counts
Accommodation, Cafes and Restaurants (N=5)	5.4	Stealing cash	Management review and/or test of controls
Personal and Other Services (N=5)	5.3	Wrong expense claim	Management review, tests of controls
Transport and Storage (N=4)	4.3	Wrong expense claim	Management review
Communication Services(N=4)	4.3	Wrong expense claim	Tests of controls and/or whistleblower
Education (N=4)	4.3	Steal cash, cheque forgery, payroll fraud, kickbacks	Analytical review, and/or discussion with management

Electricity, Gas, and Water Supply (N=3)	3.2	Product theft	Whistleblower
Construction (N=3)	3.2	Steal cash	Internal audit, reconciliations
Wholesale Trade (N=2)	2.1	Cheque forgery, wrong expense claim	Analytical and/or management review
Mining (N=2)	2.1	Product theft	Internal audit and management review and whistleblower
Agriculture, Forestry and Fishing (N=1)	1.3	Wrong expense claim	Tests of controls, and/or discussions with management

The next question addressed by the data analysis was the relationship, if any, between a company lacking both an effective internal control system and a code of conduct and whether the employee fraud had a material impact on the accounts (see Table 5).

Table 5: Industries Involved in Employee Fraud by Ineffective Internal Controls, Without a Code of Conduct and the Employee Fraud Having a Material Financial Impact on the Accounts. (No % is given due to N being very small in each case)

Industry	With ineffective internal control N	Without a code of conduct N	Material impact on Accounts N
Miscellaneous Industry designation (N=7)	5	5	2
Agriculture Forestry and Fishing (N=1)	1	1	1
Mining (N=2)	1	1	0
Manufacturing (N=20)	13	10	5
Electricity, Gas and Water Supply (N=3)	2	1	0
Construction (N=3)	3	3	3
Wholesale Trade (N=2)	2	1	1
Retail Trade (N=5)	5	4	1
Accommodation, Cafes and Restaurants (N=5)	4	2	3
Transport and Storage (N=4)	1	2	0
Communication Services (N=4)	2	3	0
Finance and Insurance (N=10)	6	4	1
Government Administration and Defence (N=12)	11	10	2
Education (N=4)	2	2	0
Health and Community Services (N=6)	4	3	0
Personal and Other Services (N=5)	4	3	0

Spearman's rank correlation coefficient tests carried out yielded a statistically significant relationship between having an ineffective internal control system and lacking a code of conduct ($p = 0.000$) as well between having an ineffective internal control system and the employee fraud impacting materially on the accounts ($p = 0.001$). Having no code of conduct was also positively related to whether the employee fraud impacted materially on the accounts ($p = 0.008$). The following industries exemplify the relationships found: manufacturing, accommodation, government administration and defence. A number of government departments (government administration and defence; health and community services; education) appear to be prone to employee fraud and to be lacking an effective system of internal control and a code of conduct to a significant degree.

Other illegal acts

Other illegal acts refers to "acts which involve non-compliance with laws and regulations which may, or may not result in misstatements including omissions of amounts or other disclosures from an entity's accounting records or financial reports" (AUS 210, AARF, 1995a, para. 05). This was the third highest irregularity (N=143) encountered by the participating auditors comprising 19% of the total 768 irregularities reported in the survey. The respondents provided detailed information on 31 (21.6%) other illegal acts. The types of other illegal acts (N=31) encountered were: non-compliance with accounting standards (45.1%), breach of security and insurance industry regulations (29.3%), fictitious stock and invoices (6.4%), lending on false information (3.2%), trust accounts regulations altered (3.2%), non-lodgement of ASC documents (3.2%), money laundering (3.2%), non-maintenance of statutory registers (3.2%), and 'other' (3.2%).

As shown in Table 6, finance and insurance accounts for the largest proportion (32%) of other illegal acts encountered, followed by manufacturing (16%). Auditors were alerted to the existence of other illegal acts (most often non-compliance with accounting standards) mainly by substantive testing and/or a statutory records' review. As with the previous two types of irregularities, there does not appear to be a clear relationship between ways of being alerted and industry designation or type of other illegal acts. Data analysis also addressed the question of whether there were adequate internal controls in place and a code of conduct as well as whether the other illegal acts had a material impact on the accounts.

Table 6: Type of Industry by Other Illegal Acts and Ways of Being Alerted

Industry	% of other illegal acts	Types of other illegal acts committed	Main ways of being Alerted
Finance and Insurance (N=10)	32.3	Non compliance with accounting standards and breach of securities and insurance industries legislation	Audit tests of balances and/or statutory records review and/or tests of controls and substantive testing
Manufacturing (N=5)	16.2	Non compliance with accounting standards	Substantive and/or tests of controls
Property and Business Services(N=4)	12.9	Breach of securities and insurance industries legislation	Audit tests of balances
Health and Community Services (N=3)	9.6	Non compliance with accounting standards and breach of securities and industries legislation	Test of controls and substantive testing
Miscellaneous Industry (N=3)	9.6	Non compliance with accounting standards, fictitious stock, non maintenance of records	Substantive testing and statutory records review
Wholesale Trade (N=2)	6.5	Non compliance with accounting standards	Statutory records and review
Communication Services (N=2)	6.3	Non lodgement of ASC documents	Statutory records review
Retail Trade (N=1)	3.3	Non compliance with accounting standards	Statutory records review
Personal Services (N=1)	3.3	Trust account violations	After balance date review

Spearman's rank correlation coefficient tests carried out found a non-significant statistical relationship between an industry category (finance and insurance and property and business services) without a code of conduct and the other illegal acts having a material impact on the accounts ($p = 0.068$). However, in view of the small number of cases per industry concerned the findings obtained need to be treated with caution.

Other acts

Other acts are defined in AUS 210 (AARF, 1995a, para. 05) as acts "which contravene the constitution of an entity including non-compliance with trust deeds or memorandum and articles of association". The respondents reported having come across within the last five years a total of 32 other acts within the last five years (comprising 4.1% of the irregularities reported in the survey) provided information for about 15 (46.8%) of them. Of those, six involved non-compliance with trust deed, three non-compliance with memorandum and articles, two incorrect accounting treatment, two non-compliance with applicable legislation, one unintentional non-compliance with trust deed, and one 'other'.

Companies in the 'miscellaneous industry' category (which comprised mainly trusts and fund management and finance and insurance industry) accounted for 6 out of the 15 other acts encountered. In three of the six industries, auditors were alerted to other acts as a result of a review of records. Statistical analysis found no significant relationship between a company belonging to a particular industry category lacking a code of conduct and an effective internal control system and/or the other acts having a material impact on the accounts.

Intentional but not fraudulent or other illegal misstatements

Intentional but not fraudulent or other illegal misstatements are acts "which include omissions of amounts or other disclosures from an entity's accounting records or financial reports" AUS 210 (AARF, 1995a, para.05). The auditors participating in the survey had come across 52 such irregularities, comprising 6.7% of the total irregularities encountered. Respondents provided information on 26 (50%) cases. Caution is, therefore, warranted in interpreting the figures given below due to small numbers in each industry category. The types of intentional but not fraudulent or other illegal misstatements encountered were: accounts did not add up (19.2%), overstatement of debtors (15.4%), balance date window dressing (11.5%), falsifying items (11.5%), other errors (11.5%), non-disclosure (7.7%), understatement of provisions (7.7%), non-disclosure of contingent liabilities (7.7%), recognising sale in the wrong period (3.9%), and unintentional omissions from the financial statements (3.9%).

Table 7: Type of Industry by Type of Intentional but Not Fraudulent or Other Illegal Misstatements, and Ways of Being Alerted

Industry	% of other illegal acts	Types of other illegal acts committed	Main ways of being alerted
Miscellaneous industry category (N=10)	38.4	Accounts did not add up; non disclosure of contingent liabilities	Review of financial statements and/or knowledge of client
Manufacturing (N=8)	30.7	Overstatement of debtors; accounts did not add up; understatement of provisions; falsifying items	Review of financial statements and records and/or knowledge of client and/or cut off tests
Retail Trade (N=2)	7.7	Overstatement of debtors	Review of financial statements and records
Finance and Insurance (N=2)	7.7	Balance date window dressing; unintentional omissions	Review of financial statements and/or review of records
Construction (N=1)	3.9	Balance date window dressing	Review of accounting records
Government Administration and Defence (N=1)	3.9	Accounts did not add up	Review of financial statements and knowledge of client
Health and Community Services (N=1)	3.9	Falsifying items	Review of financial statements and/or cut off tests
Agriculture (N=1)	3.8	Accounts did not add up	Review of financial statements and/or knowledge of client

Table 7 also shows that companies in the "Miscellaneous Industry" designation made up the biggest share of intentional but not fraudulent or other illegal misstatements (38.4%), followed by manufacturing (30.7%). As shown in Table 7, a review of financial statements and/or accounting records is the audit procedure most likely to identify the various types of intentional but not fraudulent or other illegal misstatements in the industries concerned

Table 8: Industries Involved in Intentional but not Fraudulent or Other Illegal Misstatements by Ineffective Internal Controls, Without a Code of Conduct and the Intentional but not Fraudulent or Other Illegal Misstatements Having a Material Financial Impact on the Accounts

Industry	With ineffective internal control N	Without a code of conduct N	Material impact on accounts N
Miscellaneous industry designation (N=10)	2	5	6
Agriculture Forestry and Fishing (N=1)	1	1	0
Manufacturing (N=8)	4	3	3
Construction (N=1)	1	1	1
Retail Trade (N=2)	1	0	1
Finance and Insurance (N=2)	1	0	1
Government Administration and Defence (N=1)	1	1	1
Health and Community Services (N=1)	1	0	0

Spearman's rank correlation coefficient tests carried out revealed that the intentional but not fraudulent or other illegal misstatements have a material impact on the accounts of those industry-category companies which lacked a code of conduct ($p = 0.001$).

Errors

The Exposure Draft to update ISA 240 (IFAC, 2000: par.3) defines errors as "unintentional misstatements in financial statements, including the omission of an amount or a disclosure". This definition does not differ from that used in AUS210 (AARF, 1995a). The respondents provided information on 48 incidents of errors (6.25% of the total irregularities) they had encountered in the last five years. Where possible, the findings obtained about errors will be compared with similar findings reported by Entwistle and Lindsay (1994) and Sender and Moray (1991). The main types of errors encountered were: financial statement errors (27.1%), omitting creditors (16.6%), omitting disclosure (10.4%), related party transaction errors (10.4%), non-compliance with new AAS (8.3%), understatement of creditor's accounts (6.4%), understatement of doubtful debts (6.4%), overstatement of stock (6.4%), overstatement of sales (4%), and mistakes in estimates (4%). Cross-tabulating the type of error by industry (see Table 9) found that the companies that mainly fell into the "Miscellaneous Industry" category (i.e., unit trusts, fund management, marketing and electronics) accounted for most of the errors, followed by manufacturing.

Auditors were most frequently alerted to the existence of errors as a result of a review of financial statements, followed by detailed review and analysis of accounts. No clear relationship was found between the different audit procedures which alerted the auditor and type of error or type of industry. However, a statistically significant relationship was found between a company having an ineffective internal control system and lacking a code of conduct ($p = 0.005$). Entwistle and Lindsay (1994) concentrated on "large dollar-value misstatements and found them to be concentrated in relatively few accounts and to have arisen primarily from judgement error or biases". They also suggest that non-recurring transactions such as cut-offs are more risky than recurring ones as far as errors made in financial statements are concerned. Entwistle and Lindsay found manufacturing to be an error-prone industry with cut-off errors, and judgement errors or mechanical errors being the main types. The present study found that the most frequently reported errors were financial statement errors, or errors regarding related party transactions.

Table 9: Type of Industry by Type of Error and Ways of Being Alerted

Industry	% of Error	Type of errors committed	Main ways of being alerted
Miscellaneous industry category (N=26)	54.2	Financial statement errors; omitted creditors; omitted disclosure; related party; understatement of doubtful debts; non compliance with new Australian Accounting standards	Review of financial statements and records and/or review of debtors and/or detail review and analysis
Manufacturing (N=11)	22.9	Financial statement errors; related party; mistakes in estimates; omitting creditors; non compliance with new accounting standards	Review of financial statements, and/or detail review and analysis
Finance and Insurance (N=4)	8.3	Overstatement of sales; understatement of doubtful debts and financial statement errors	Review of aged trial balance and/or cut off tests and/or detail review
Construction (N=2)	4.1	Omitting disclosure	Review of financial statements
Electricity, Gas and Water Supply (N=1)	2.1	Financial statement errors	Review of financial statements and/or detail review and analysis
Agriculture (N=1)	2.1	Related party	Review of financial statements
Retail Trade (N=1)	2.1	Financial statement errors	Review of financial statements and/or detail review and analysis
Accommodation Cafes and Restaurants (N=1)	2.1	Financial statement errors	Review of financial statements and/or detail review and analysis
Personal and Other Services (N=1)	2.1	Overstatement of sales	Review of financial statements and cut off tests

The auditors surveyed did not state how those errors were committed and whether, for example, they were cut-off errors. Whilst substantive testing was the main procedure signalling these errors in Entwistle and Lindsay's Canadian study, in the present study it was client knowledge and review of financial statements. Summarising the findings, Table 10 shows the relationship between a company having an ineffective system of internal control and lacking a code of conduct and an irregularity having a material impact on the accounts of a company.

Table 10: Type of Irregularity and the Relationship between Ineffective Internal Controls, Without a Code of Conduct and the Irregularity Having a Material Financial Impact on the Accounts

	Without a code of conduct	Material impact on account
Ineffective internal control	Management fraud (p=.000) Employee fraud (p=.000) Error (p=.005)	Management Fraud (p=.000) Employee Fraud (p=.001) Other illegal acts (p=.053) Error (p=.060)
Without a code of conduct		Management fraud (p=.000) Employee fraud (p=.008) Intentional acts (p=.005) Other illegal acts (p=.068) Intentional but not fraudulent or other illegal misstatements (p=.001)

Two of the company characteristics in the ROP model are lack of adequate control procedures that prevent fraud and lack of code of conduct. The ROP model is an integral part of the eclectic fraud detection model proposed. In support of the eclectic fraud detection model, it can be seen that there is a significant probability of companies that have an ineffective internal control system and without a code of conduct, experiencing management and employee fraud and error. Furthermore, in those companies with an ineffective internal control system the management fraud, employee fraud, other illegal acts and errors impacted materially on the accounts. Finally, in those companies lacking a code of corporate conduct, the management fraud, employee fraud, other illegal acts, and other illegal misstatements had a material impact on the accounts.

Table 11: Patterns in Auditors' Detection of Different Irregularities

Type of irregularity	Industry(ies) with high incidence of irregularity	The form(s) it is likely to take	Audit procedure(s) likely to alert auditors to irregularity existence	Statistically significant correlate impacting materially on company's accounts
Manage-ment fraud	Manufacturing Trusts and Fund Management, Construction	Mis-Appropriation of funds; window dressing	Management review and/or tests of controls	Lack of effective internal control system, absence of a code of conduct
Employee fraud	Manufacturing Government Administration and Defence, Finance and Insurance	Expenses recorded incorrectly	Management review and/or tests of controls	Lack of effective internal control system, absence of code of conduct
Other illegal acts	Finance and Insurance, Manufacturing	Non-compliance with accounting standards, breach of security and insurance industry regulations	Substantive testing and/statutory records review	Absence of a code of conduct
Other acts	Trusts and Fund Management, Finance and Insurance	Non-compliance with trust accounts	Review of records	Lack of effective internal control system, absence of a code of conduct
Other illegal Misstate-ments	Trusts and Fund Management, Manufacturing	Accounts did not add up	Review of financial statements and/or review of accounting records	Absence of a code of conduct
Errors	Trusts and Fund Management, Miscellaneous Industry category, Manufacturing	Financial statement errors	Review of financial statements	Lack of effective internal control system, absence of a code of conduct

Table 11 shows the patterns identified in auditors' detection of the six types of irregularities. Irregularity-prone companies are characterised by a lack of an effective internal control system and the absence of a code of conduct. This finding is not surprising when we remember that 76% of the companies where management fraud had occurred had ineffective internal controls and 64% lacked a code of conduct. Similarly, of the companies where employee fraud occurred 71% had ineffective internal controls and 56% lacked a code of conduct. As already indicated, these two company characteristics are significantly correlated. Furthermore, the material impact of these deficiencies on the accounts is pervasive. These findings provide support for the eclectic fraud detection model and attest to the importance of auditors carrying out further tests if they are auditing a company with an ineffective internal control system and lacking a code of conduct. The survey results suggest that these two characteristics point to a higher probability that a material irregularity in the accounts exists. This finding is in agreement with the conclusion reached in the KPMG (1995a) survey that any steps taken by companies to reduce the possibility of an irregularity (including fraud) that will impact materially on the accounts must include improvement in internal control systems and the implementation of a code of conduct.

USEFULNESS OF RED FLAGS

Part II of the survey addressed the usefulness of red flags in detecting material irregularities. Participants were asked to indicate how useful a list of red flags had been to them concerning a material irregularity they had encountered in the last 12 months. More specifically, the respondents were asked whether a red flag had been (1) applicable to the engagement, (2) relevant to the irregularity; and (3) whether it had alerted them during the planning phase. It should be noted here that a small number of respondents indicated that a particular red flag (see below) was relevant to the irregularity but did not also indicate that it was applicable to the engagement, as one would expect. It is for this reason that the figures in the columns 'Relevant...' and 'Applicable...' in a number of Tables below is not consistent. Part II of the questionnaire was completed by 87 participants. As indicated in Chapter 3, and this is borne out by the findings reported below, red flags are of doubtful usefulness if used on their own to detect fraud. Tables 12-19 address the usefulness of eight categories of red flags in alerting auditors during the planning stage to the possible existence of a particular irregularity and, thus, in detecting the irregularities listed in Appendices 1 and 2 of AUS210 (AARF, 1995a) by using aggregate figures and not distinguishing between the different fraud indicator categories.

Table 12: Business Environment

Business Environment	***(Red Flag) Applicable to the engagement*** ***N = 87***	***(Red Flag) Relevant to the irregularity*** ***N = 87***	***(Red Flag) Alerted me during the planning phase*** ***N = 87***
Nature of the business is susceptible to misappropriation	29	24	8
Unduly influential circumstances	14	16	5
Pressure to meet forecasts	13	11	1
Weak management integrity	19	29	6
Ineffective/non-existent regulation by external parties	6	10	2
Survival of company dependant on irregularity(ies)	2	5	3
Ineffective or non-existent code of conduct	15	14	3
Transactions with related parties not at arm's length	7	10	3
Unusual transactions with companies registered in tax havens	1	2	-
Liquidity pressure	10	6	-
Total	116	127	31

Table 12 shows that in the following four business environment fraud indicators feature to a significant degree as both applicable to the engagement and relevant to the irregularity: nature of the business is susceptible to misappropriation; weak management integrity; and unduly influential circumstances; and ineffective or non-existent code of conduct. Despite this, only a minority of those indicators alerted the auditor during the planning stage to the existence of the irregularity.

Table 13: Internal Control

Internal Control Structure	***(Red Flag) Applicable to the engagement*** ***N = 87***	***(Red Flag) Relevant to the irregularity*** ***N = 87***	***(Red Flag) Alerted me during the planning phase*** ***N = 87***
Organisation is decentralised without adequate monitoring	18	24	9
Management override	25	33	13
Ineffective management	17	24	6
Lack of segregation of duties	25	42	13
Weak internal controls	21	32	11
Excessive authority vested in a senior officer	26	32	7
Poor systems	16	23	7
Ineffective internal audit	21	14	4
Total	169	224	70

Auditing standards[12] emphasise the importance of internal controls. However, Table 13 shows that the auditors did not, in fact, pay particular attention to serious weaknesses in internal controls. Consequently, less than half of those indicators alerted them at the planning stage to the existence of an irregularity, despite the fact that they were relevant to the irregularity.

[12] See AUS402 (AARF, 1995b). The criminogenic nature of weak internal controls was confirmed by the successful test of the ROP model in the MFG study.

Table 14: Integrity/Competence of Management

Integrity/Competence of Management	*(Red Flag) Applicable to the engagement* N = 87	*(Red Flag) Relevant to the irregularity* N = 87	*(Red Flag) Alerted me during the planning phase* N = 87
Domineering management	21	23	7
Complex corporate structure	5	2	1
Continuing failure to correct internal control weaknesses	17	17	5
High executive staff turnover	2	5	2
Significant/prolonged under-staffing of the accounting department	8	5	2
Frequent changes of lawyers	-	-	-
The client has engaged in opinion shopping	-	1	2
The auditor's experience with management indicates a degree of dishonesty	7	9	4
Internal audit is improperly staffed	8	8	6
Total	68	70	29

The only two indicators pointing to a concern about the integrity/competence of management were domineering management and continuing failure to correct internal control weaknesses. The auditors' apparent insensitivity to the presence of the other 7 indicators largely explains the finding in Table 14 that they were alerted at the planning stage to the existence of an irregularity to a limited degree. Support of the finding that indicators of management integrity/competence are not effective red flags was reported by Bernardi (1994a). Pincus (1994, 1990), however, reported a contradictory finding on the same issue (see chapter 3).

Table 15: Unusual Pressures Within an Entity

Unusual Pressures within an entity	***(Red Flag) Applicable to the engagement*** ***N=87***	***(Red Flag) Relevant to the Irregularity*** ***N=87***	***(Red Flag) Alerted me during the planning phase*** ***N=87***
Inadequate working capital	10	6	7
Deteriorating quality of earnings	11	11	4
A need for a rising profit	10	8	5
A significant investment in an industry noted for rapid change	6	7	3
Entity heavily dependent on a product or a customer	4	7	2
Management displays an overly aggressive attitude toward financial reporting and forecasts	11	10	5
Pressure exerted on accounting personnel to complete financial reports in unusually short periods	3	3	-
Total	55	52	26

It can be seen in Table 15 that only two out of the seven indicators of unusual pressures within an entity (deteriorating quality of earnings, pressure exerted on accounting personnel to complete financial reports in unusually short periods) were considered applicable to the engagement and relevant to irregularity. It should, also be noted however, that with most of the other indicators there is an average match of 74%, i.e., in most cases they were both applicable and relevant. Surprisingly, however, only half of the indicators listed alerted the auditor at the planning stage to the existence of an irregularity.

Table 16: Unusual Occurrences/Transaction

Unusual Occurrences/Transactions	***(Red Flag) Applicable to the engagement*** ***N = 87***	***(Red Flag) Relevant to the Irregularity*** ***N = 87***	***(Red Flag) Alerted me during the planning phase*** ***N = 87***
Unusual balance date transactions	13	12	2
Payments for services that appear excessive in relation to services provided	4	13	2
Payments for goods which appear to be above/below market price	5	12	3
Evidence of falsified documents	8	31	2
Large cash payments	4	12	2
Payments made to local or overseas officials	2	2	-
Problems with regulatory authorities	-	2	-
Ignored advice by legal adviser	-	2	-
Evidence of unduly lavish styles by officers or employees	4	14	2
Investigations by police	2	2	1
Total	42	102	14

Table 16 shows that, even such crucial information concerning evidence of falsified documents that was relevant to the irregularity, did not alert the auditors to the irregularity concerned at the planning phase. The same is also true, for example, of unusual balance date transactions and evidence of unduly lavish lifestyles by company or employees. The auditors concerned, do not appear to have been aware of the importance of such indicators and/or to have been vigilant about their importance.

Table 17: Unsatisfactory Records/Problems in Obtaining Sufficient Appropriate Audit Evidence

Unsatisfactory Records/Problems in Obtaining Sufficient Appropriate Audit Evidence	***(Red Flag) Applicable to the engagement*** ***N = 87***	***(Red Flag) Relevant to the irregularity*** ***N = 87***	***(Red Flag) Alerted me during the planning phase*** ***N = 87***
Inadequate accounting records	16	19	4
Inadequate documentation	14	29	8
Excessive number of differences between accounting records and third party confirmations	11	18	2
Evasive, unreasonable or unsatisfactory responses by management to inquiries	20	20	7
New client without sufficient information from predecessor auditor	6	4	2
Conflicting audit evidence and inexplicable changes in operating ratios.	7	8	2
Significantly fewer responses to confirmation requests than expected	3	5	2
Total	77	103	27

The auditors' lack of vigilance at the planning stage is further evidenced in Table 17. It can be seen that they failed to be alerted to the irregularity in question by: evasive, unreasonable or unsatisfactory responses by management to their inquiries; inadequate accounting records, inadequate documentation; and excessive number of differences between accounting records and third party confirmations.

Table 18: Market Pressures

Market Pressures	*(Red Flag) Applicable to the engagement N = 87*	*(Red Flag) Relevant to the irregularity N = 87*	*(Red Flag) Alerted me during the planning phase N = 87*
Declining industry	4	3	-
Industry subject to complex legislation	2	1	1
Volatile industry with numerous corporate take-overs	1	2	-
Total	7	6	1

Table 18 shows that evidence of a declining industry was overlooked by the respondents at the planning stage even though such evidence would normally justify an auditor to apply more reasonable care and skill by performing additional tests.

Examination of Table 19 reveals that the respondents were not alerted to the existence of an irregularity at the planning stage by such important features of the EDP environment as lack of clear audit trail and transaction log as well as inadequate computer skills amongst relevant entity staff, despite the fact that they were both applicable to the engagement and relevant to the irregularity.

Table 19: Factors Relevant to an EDP Environment

Factors Relevant to an EDP Environment	*(Red Flag) Applicable to the engagement N = 87*	*(Red Flag) Relevant to the irregularity N = 87*	*(Red Flag) Alerted me during the planning phase N = 87*
Minimal planning for the installation of new hardware	2	1	1
Inadequate computer skills amongst relevant entity staff	7	5	1
Inappropriate hardware or software to perform important functions	3	2	1
Poor physical or logical access controls	1	2	-
Inadequate or inappropriate file access hierarchy	-	1	-
Lack of clear audit trail and transaction log	5	7	-
Hardware failures, including excessive amounts of "down-time" and resultant input backlogs	-	-	-
Software failures	-	-	-
Failure to restrict access to software and documentation to authorised personnel	2	4	-
Program changes that are not documented, approved and tested	4	1	-
Inappropriate data and program storage media	-	-	-
Inadequate detection procedures for system viruses	1	1	-
Inadequate overall balancing of computer transactions and data bases to the financial accounts	1	1	-
Shared or non-specific ownership of data	1	1	1
Total	27	26	4

The findings reported in Tables 12-19 show that the following fraud indicators, provided for in the eclectic fraud detection model, featured to a significant degree both as applicable to the engagement and relevant to the irregularity: no code of conduct; weak management integrity; weak internal controls; financial pressure on management in the form of inadequate working capital (declining industry); lack of clear audit trail; and unduly lavish styles by company officers or employees.

Table 20 summarises Tables 12-19 and shows that only a minority of red flags alerted auditors to the existence of a material irregularity. Out of a total of 561 red flags that were considered applicable to the engagement, only 202 (36%) alerted the auditor during the planning phase. Also, even though a total of 710 red flags were relevant to the irregularity only 202 (28.4%) alerted the auditor at the planning phase. In other words, the auditor was not alerted to the possible existence of the irregularity concerned despite the fact that the majority of the red flags were applicable to the engagement and relevant to the irregularity. Red flags belonging to the unusual pressures within an entity, integrity/competence of management, and internal control categories alerted the auditor to the possible existence of a material irregularity to a greater degree at the planning phase than the other categories.

Taking each of the eight red flag categories separately, Spearman's rank correlation coefficient tests were carried out to examine the relationship, if any, between a red flag being applicable to the engagement, relevant to the irregularity and whether it alerted the auditor during the planning stage. Table 21 shows the results of these tests.

Table 20: Applicability, Relevance and Whether the Auditor was Alerted by Category of Red Flag

Red flag category	Red flag applicable to the engagement	Red flag relevant to the irregularity	Red flag Alerted an auditor during the planning phase
Business environment	116	127	31
Internal control	169	224	70
Integrity/Competence of management	68	70	29
Unusual pressures within an entity	55	52	26
Unusual occurrence/transactions	42	102	14
Unsatisfactory records/ problems in obtaining sufficient appropriate audit evidence	77	103	27
Market pressures	7	6	1
Factors relevant to an EDP environment	27	26	4
Total	561	710	202

Table 21: The Statistical Relationship Between Applicability and Relevance of Red Flags and Whether the Auditor was Alerted by Them

	Relevant	Alerted
AP	Business environment (p=0.001) Integrity/competence of management (p=0.04) Unusual pressures (p=0.04) Unusual occurrence/ transaction (p=0.05) Unsatisfactory records (p=0.03) Internal control NS	Business environment (p=0.008) Integrity/competence of management (p=0.002) Unusual pressures (p=0.01) Unusual occurrence/transaction (p=0.04) Unsatisfactory records (p=0.04) Internal control NS
REL		Business environment (p=0.001) Internal control (p=0.008) Integrity/competence of management (p=0.007) Unusual occurrence/transaction (p=0.03) Unsatisfactory records (p=0.02)

NS= Not statistically significant.

In interpreting the significance of the relationships depicted in Table 21 it should be noted that no test was possible in the case of one red flag category, namely "market pressures" due to N = 1. Also, as far as "factors relevant to an EDP environment" is concerned, only four examples of that particular red flag were reported as having alerted respondents (see Table 19) and, consequently, no correlation test was possible with whether that red flag was applicable to the engagement or relevant to the irregularity. With the exception of internal control (p = .072 i.e., NS), a statistically significant relationship was found between all the remaining five categories of red flags being considered both applicable to the engagement and relevant to the irregularity and alerting the auditor to the existence of an irregularity. However, it needs to be remembered that the respondents provided the data in hindsight. The following conclusions can be drawn from Table 21:

i. Deficiencies in internal control alerted the auditors to the existence of an irregularity if those particular red flags were considered relevant to the irregularity, but did not so if they were considered applicable to the engagement.
ii. The red flags pertaining to unusual pressures only alerted the auditors to the existence of an irregularity if they were deemed applicable to the engagement.

Thus, it appears that the relationship between the applicability and relevance of a red flag and whether the auditor was alerted by it depends on the particular category of red flag.

Finally, a basic premise of the Loebbecke et al. (1989) fraud-risk assessment model is that all its three components must be present for an irregularity to occur. More specifically, they reported that the three components (conditions, motives, and attitudes) were applicable and relevant in 86% of the management fraud cases and 78% were applicable, relevant and alerted. This prediction, however, was not borne out in the present study. In only 22% of the management fraud cases were all three components applicable and relevant and in only 8% of the cases were all three components applicable, relevant, and alerted the auditor.

SURVEY PART II: CORRELATES OF FRAUD PRONENESS

In order to expand the discussion by utilising the data from Part II of the survey, attention will next focus on: (1) identifying fraud-prone industries, audit areas, and audit procedures indicating the presence of material irregularities, and (2) revising the eclectic fraud detection model developed in Chapter 4 so as to incorporate the findings from the survey of auditors and to examine its applicability. To do this, it is imperative that one studies both the irregularity and the offender.

Regarding how the 87 material irregularities were committed, it was found that they involved: theft of cash (52.9%), window dressing (17.3%), errors in financial statement (6.9%), kickbacks (4.6%), stock theft (4.6%), payroll fraud (4.6%), kiting (3.5%), conflict of interest (1.1%), breach of parliamentary rule (1.1%), insurance fraud (1.1%), forging cheques (1.1%), and tax avoidance (1.1%).

As far as the position held by the offender is concerned, it turned out to be: middle management (24.1%), others below management (14.9%), other management in collusion with others (14.9%), directors (13.8%), chief accountant(CA) (8.0%), directors in collusion with others (6.9%), top management (6.9%), chief financial officer (CFO) (5.7%), chief executive officer (CEO) (5.7%), and shareholders (2.4%). This finding is in line with the Ernst and Young (2000:7) survey where it found that almost a third of the frauds committed in the previous 12 months were carried out by management.

It is worth noting that the present survey also found that top management (i.e., CFO, CEO, CA, directors and other top management) were mainly involved in theft of cash. The Chief Accountant and director were also involved in window dressing, either alone or in collusion.

Cross-tabulating the type of material irregularity and the number of accomplices, it was found that theft of cash was usually committed alone (58%) or in collusion with one to two more people (35%). For window dressing, an equal percentage was committed alone (27%) or with one more person (27%). Tax avoidance, forging cheques, breaching parliamentary regulations and kiting were frauds committed without an accomplice. These findings should be considered with the knowledge that in 52% of irregularities detected the perpetrator acted alone, 21% with one accomplice, 13% with two, and 15% with three or more accomplices. For comparison purposes, in the MFG study it was found that the great majority (70%) of the offenders had no accomplices while Loebbecke et al. indicated that in "many" instances there was collusion.. Next, attention is turned to the profiling issue in order to test the applicability of the eclectic fraud detection model of which the ROP model is an integral part.

As would be predicted using the eclectic fraud detection model, it was found that most of the 87 perpetrators encountered by the respondents were males (90.8%), aged 36-45 (60.9%), married (89.7%) , and with post high school education (60.9%). While the picture of the perpetrators painted by the auditors surveyed is no different from that which emerged in the MFG study, the MFG offenders included more members of professional groups such as lawyers. This difference is attributable to the different ways by which the MFG comes to investigate a case of fraud.

Support of the conclusion arrived at Chapter 5 (i.e., that financial pressure due to one cause or another underpins fraud offences by people in positions of financial trust within companies) the following sources of financial pressure on the perpetrators' were discovered by the auditors' survey: lifestyle (40.2%), gambling (13.8%), personal financial problems (12.6%), greed (10.3%), drugs and alcohol (1.2%), and combination of at least two of these sources of financial pressure (21.9%). In other words, the likely fraud perpetrator is characterised by a hedonistic and erratic lifestyle that renders them prone to offending, is in accordance with what one would have predicted on the basis of either Freud's psychoanalytic theory (in terms of a weak superego) or Eysenck's theory of crime and delinquency (in terms of antisocial personality disorder attributes) discussed in Chapter 2 and contained in the ROP model.

The next issue is the industry in which the material irregularities was committed. More than half (56%) of the 87 material irregularities were committed against a public company as opposed to 44% in private companies. As shown in Table 22 most of them occurred in the manufacturing industry. Loebbecke et al. found "significantly more instances of management fraud in Manufacturing, Transportation, High Technology and Communication Companies and fewer in Education and other institutions, which is consistent with their likely ownership character" (p.10). It is worth noting that the KPMG (1999:8) survey found that "Financial Services, Insurance and Government Sectors reported the greatest total financial losses to fraud and that industries in the Business Services, Printing, Publishing and Government Sectors reported the highest average cost of fraud per occurrence". The Ernst and Young (2000) survey however, makes no reference to fraud prone industries.

Table 22: Industry and Status of the Company Where the Material Irregularity was Committed (N=87)

Industry designation	%
Miscellaneous Industry designation	8.0
Agriculture, Forestry and Fishing	6.9
Mining	3.5
Manufacturing	25.2
Electricity, Gas and Water Supply	3.5
Construction	8.0
Wholesale Trade	9.2
Retail Trade	2.3
Accommodation, Cafes, and Restaurants	3.5
Transport and Storage	2.3
Communication Services	2.3
Finance and Insurance	9.2
Government Administration and Defence	3.5
Health and Community Services	8.0
Cultural and Recreation Services	2.3
Personal and Other Services	2.3
	100%

Crosstabulating the type of material irregularity and the industry designation of the company involved, it was found that the types of fraud occurring in manufacturing were mainly: theft of cash (40%), window dressing (27%), errors in financial statements (9%), payroll fraud (9%), whereas in finance and insurance it was theft of cash (63%), window dressing (25%), insurance fraud (12%), Regarding the difference between the types of material irregularity frauds occurring in a public as opposed to a private company, it was found that 58% of cash theft occurred in public companies as opposed to 42% in private companies. Also, private companies had a higher incidence of payroll fraud (75%) whereas forging of cheques, conflict of interest, insurance fraud, and purchase of equipment for self only occurred in private companies.

An interesting question is whether a relationship exists between the type of irregularity and the person detecting it.

Table 23: Who Detected the Irregularity (N=87)

	%
Client	33.3
Auditor:	
Manager	19.5
Senior	19.5
Supervisor	11.5
Partner	8.1
Assistant	4.6
Fraud Auditor	2.3
Whistleblower/ASC/ATO	1.2
	100%

To a large extent, the finding in the present study (see Table 23) that auditors were the ones who detected most of the irregularities reported on reflects the fact that auditors were asked to answer questions about irregularities they themselves had encountered. Crosstabulating the type of material irregularity and the person detecting the fraud, it was found that: the two authorities (ASC and ATO) identified theft of cash and stock but the client was the most successful in identifying theft of cash and kickbacks; the partner and manager were more successful in identifying theft of cash and, finally, seniors appeared to identify more window dressing than partners and managers[13]. Regarding the audit area affected by the irregularity, it was: cash (40.2%), provisions (28.7%),inventories (3.5%), and combination of two-three accounts (27.6%).

Since theft of cash is the most popular type of material irregularity being committed, it follows that cash and provisions were mainly affected. As far as window dressing is concerned, provisions was the account mainly affected. Therefore, auditors need to pay additional attention to these two audit areas because there is a higher audit risk.

Regarding which audit procedure indicated the material irregularity, 33% of the irregularities were not discovered by the auditors. For those that were detected by the auditors it was found that substantive test of details and study of internal controls were the most successful in detecting material irregularities whereas in Loebbecke et al. substantive tests were the most effective type of audit procedure to reveal the irregularity in 50% of the cases.

[13] Bernardi (1994a) found managers more likely to detect fraud and he explained it by saying that managers have higher moral development and are not technically focused like the seniors. Davidson (1994) disagreed with this explanation, maintaining that managers are concerned with fee constraints which have an impact on moral development. However, more research is required to resolve the issue whether managers are indeed characterised by a higher stage of moral development.

Crosstabulating the audit procedure indicating the material irregularity by the type of fraud involved, it was found that for the theft of cash 42% were not detected by the auditor; the remainder were detected by means of substantive tests of details (20%), study of internal control (13%), preliminary analytical procedures (8%) and a combination of procedures for the rest. Substantive audit procedures were useful in identifying window dressing. Errors in financial statements, tax avoidance, insurance frauds and kiting were discovered by the auditor alone, whereas kickbacks and theft of cash were primarily not discovered by the auditor. These findings are in line with Loebbecke et al.'s. The next issue inquired by the survey is the length of time of the client-auditor relationship (i.e., the number of prior audits) when an irregularity was discovered, as well as the duration the irregularity had been committed[14].

Table 24: Relationship Between the Number of Years the Auditing Firm were the Auditors and the Time Period the Irregularity (N=87) was Committed.

Number of prior year-audits of client firm at time of irregularity	**%**
Years	
1	17.2
2	17.2
3	20.7
4	8.1
5	18.4
>5	18.4
	100%
Time Period for which an irregularity was committed	**%**
Years	
<1	36.8
1	23.0
2	21.8
3	8.1
4	3.4
5	3.4
5+	3.4
	100%

Table 24 shows that 55.1% of the irregularities were discovered within the first three years; i.e., a significant proportion of the irregularities were encountered by the respondents when auditing new clients. The fourth year of the

[14] Pincus (1990) and Bernardi (1994a) both reported that fraud detection will increase as an auditor's prior expectations concerning the existence of fraud increase. This was not directly tested by the present research.

auditor-client relationship appears to be a "slack" year as far as auditor-detection of irregularities is concerned. It would not be unreasonable to surmise here that after a spate of successes by the external auditor in detecting irregularities, the culprits "lie low", perhaps perceiving a high risk of being found out. When this deterrent effect of the auditor's successes decreases enough, perpetrators of such illegal acts within companies are back in action! Another argument in the literature is that auditors become comfortable with their clients and start to trust them, possibly too much, so that they don't maintain a proper attitude of professional scepticism and they may under - audit. The present study did not attempt to find how long the employee perpetrators were employed by the company but interestingly enough the Ernst and Young (2000:7) survey found that "nearly half of the employees who defrauded their firms had been with the organisation for over 5 years, of these nearly a quarter had been with the organisation for over 10 years."

REPORTING FRAUD

Given the reporting requirements set out in AUS210 (AARF,1995a) the findings regarding reporting of fraud come as no surprise. Slightly more than half (53%) of frauds detected were reported to the Board of Directors, 21% to the CEO and 2% to the audit committee. Considering that 56% of frauds occurred in public companies, one would have expected more reporting to the audit committee[15]; similarly, one would have expected more reporting to the ASC; in fact, only 2% were reported. Five per cent were reported to the Major Fraud group and the remainder to other authorities. Theft of cash was reported mainly to the Board of Directors (53%)[16], or others (24%), namely financial controller, audit partner and Parliament. Window dressing was reported predominantly to the Board of Directors (57%)[17] and the CEO (36%). Payroll fraud was equally reported to the CEO and Board of Directors. The other bodies to which auditors reported were the partner in charge, anti-corruption branch, in one incident the auditor confronted the perpetrator who admitted to it.

USE OF FRAUD AUDITORS AND FORENSIC ACCOUNTANTS

In view of the difficulty in and importance of detecting fraud, the use made of fraud auditors and forensic accountants is an interesting issue. Forty-five per cent of the respondents stated that their firm provided services by forensic and fraud auditors. Regarding the experience and qualifications held by these specialists, they were: Forensic accountants, mainly: chartered accountants

[15] However not all companies have an audit committee.

[16] This was an alarming finding since, the perpetrators involved in theft of cash were mainly top management, including directors.

[17] As already stated given the perpetrator involved (i.e., directors) in window dressing one would have not expected the auditor to report to the Board of Directors.

(33%), chartered accountants and lawyers (13%), and registered company auditors and chartered accountants (33%). Fraud auditors were: chartered accountants (45%), chartered accountants and registered company auditors (43%) and, finally, some had experience as psychologists or criminologists -5% in each field.

The forensic accountants and fraud auditors who participated were of the opinion that had their services been used, material irregularity could have been prevented or detected earlier. The other respondents, however, did not share that opinion. As for the number of times a fraud auditor had been used in the last 12 months, it ranged from one (40%), to two (33%) whereas for a forensic accountant it was mainly: one (40%), two (10%), three (10%), ten (20%). These findings suggest that fraud auditors and forensic accountants are not used very frequently.

THE ECLECTIC FRAUD DETECTION MODEL REVISITED

The results yielded by the survey of auditors add to the broad range of information-inputs into effective fraud-detection contained in the eclectic fraud detection model (see Figure 4) and show the model's applicability. More specifically, the findings obtained show that:

- used on their own, red flags are not particularly useful in alerting auditors to the existence of material irregularities at the planning stage;
- the different high-risk industries (e.g., manufacturing) where the auditor is likely to encounter different types of irregularities (e.g., management fraud, employee fraud, and error);
- the audit procedure(s) likely to identify a particular type of irregularity;
- the forms (e.g., theft of cash, window dressing) each type of irregularity is likely to take;
- which audit areas (cash and provisions) are high fraud-risk ones; and
- the lack of an effective internal control system and the absence of a code of corporate conduct are significant correlates of an irregularity (including management fraud, employee fraud and errors) impacting materially on the accounts.

In support of Albrecht et al. (1995) and Cressey (1986), the findings also stress the importance of the auditor being alerted to information about individuals within a company who are high risks of perpetrating an irregularity, including fraud, because they face a serious financial problem. The financial problem itself is most often due to a person in a position of trust living beyond their means for one reason or another.

The additional findings obtained and not contained in Figure 2 (i.e., particular high-risk audit areas and patterns in auditors' fraud detection) have been incorporated in Figure 4 (see Chapter 7) so as to make it more comprehensive. The findings provide empirical support for the applicability of the eclectic fraud detection model. They do this by confirming the crucial importance of its various components (the audit firm; the auditor; and fraud-risk information, including the ROP Fraud model in Figure 3 – see Chapter 7) for more effective and efficient fraud-detection performance by auditors.

CONCLUSIONS

The survey was carried out in an attempt to reduce the gap in our knowledge about the nature of material irregularities (including management fraud, employee fraud and error) encountered by auditors in Australia. The 108 relatively experienced auditors who participated in the study reported having encountered a total of 768 irregularities in the last five years. This indicates it is relatively rare for auditors to encounter material irregularities when taking into account an auditor's total number of engagements.

Summing up the findings obtained by the survey, the following industries are prone to the following irregularities: management fraud and employee fraud (manufacturing); employee fraud (manufacturing, government administration and defence); other illegal acts and other acts (finance and insurance); errors (trusts and fund management).

In addition, the six irregularities examined tend to take the following forms:

- management fraud (window dressing);
- employee fraud (wrong expense claims and stealing of cash);
- other illegal acts (non-compliance with accounting standards or legislation);
- other acts (non-compliance with a trust deed);
- other illegal misstatements (accounts not adding up), and
- errors (financial statement errors).

In contrast to what Loebbecke et al. (1989) reported, one of the significant findings obtained in the survey is that red flags are of limited usefulness to auditors in detecting irregularities, including fraud. In only a minority of cases, the auditors were alerted to the existence of an irregularity, by a red flag indication. This is despite the fact that the majority of red flags were both applicable to the engagement and relevant to the irregularity. The relationship between the applicability and relevance of a red flag and whether the auditor was alerted to the irregularity depended on the particular category of red flag indicators. Overall, however, the survey results show that fraud-risk assessment utilising red flags is not effective.

In comparing the findings from the two studies some differences between the auditors who participated in them need to be borne in mind. Loebbecke et al.'s auditors were from one firm only and were partners[18]. Compared to the

[18] As far as fraud detection is concerned Hackenbrack et al. (1993) stated that audit experience and training of auditors in the Big 5 firms differs to that of medium or small size firms. It is also worth noting that partners are not the ones that performing the actual audit work.

auditors in the present study, they were significantly older, a factor that explains the fact that they had twice as much audit experience (in years). The participants in both studies, however, were included in the research because they were experienced in detecting irregularities. Loebbecke et al.'s auditors had an average number of engagements of 3.1 where an irregularity had been encountered and/or had encountered an irregularity in 1.3% of the total number of engagements they had worked on. By comparison, the auditors in the present study who came from various firms across the country and had only been in the position of (predominantly) manager or partner for three years, had an average of 5.2 engagements where an irregularity had been encountered and/or had encountered an irregularity in 19% of their total number of engagements. However, the auditors in the present survey were 4.5 times less likely than their counterparts in the U.S. study to have encountered an irregularity themselves. Often an irregularity would be detected by a combination of audit procedures.

It should be noted at this point that substantive testing was the audit procedure used by the respondents in the present study to detect a material irregularity, encountered within the last 12 months in Part II of the questionnaire. The same finding was also obtained for other illegal acts. Also, management and employee fraud was detected by management review and/or tests of controls

The present study found that more than half of the irregularities were detected during the first three years[19] (and especially in the third year) of an engagement and that auditors were not likely to discover it. The survey highlights the crucial importance of auditors not ceasing to be vigilant however long they have been auditing a company's books. Auditors in the survey reported a material irregularity mainly to the board of directors and did so especially when it involved theft of cash and window dressing.

Finally, the findings reported in this chapter provide empirical support for the eclectic fraud detection model developed in Chapter 4. The survey emphasises that audit experience alone is not sufficient to improve the auditors' fraud-detection performance as they seem to seldom encounter irregularities. In addition, the use of red flags on its own is not enough for effective fraud detection by auditors. By reporting patterns in the kinds of relationship between different industries, different irregularities, different ways that alerted the auditors, and different audit procedures that appear to detect them, the survey of auditors has added new knowledge to fraud risk assessment. The findings generally, support the general profile of fraud offender constructed on the basis of the MFG study, but also emphasise the importance of a person having a vice such as gambling as a good indicator of their being a fraud risk. The *eclectic fraud detection model* was borne out by the findings of the survey. Furthermore, the results of the survey help to revise the model and to make it even more useful to auditors by showing

[19] Loebbecke et al. found that most irregularities occurred in companies that had been audited for 1-10 years.

that fraud-risk assessment has to be multifaceted if it is to achieve its objective. In the light of the evidence, it can be concluded that the fraud detection model proposed in Chapter 7 is more likely to be useful to auditors as it makes good the deficits in Albrecht et al.'s (1995); Cressey's (1986) and Loebbecke et al.'s (1989) models.

The results of the survey challenge Loebbecke et al.'s (1989) assertion that all three of their model's components must be present for fraud to occur. The proposed fraud detection model weaves together features and patterns identified at different levels, namely: the economic environment, the particular industry, the company, particular financial areas within the company and particular individuals holding positions of financial trust where they can effect fraud. Hence, the ROP Fraud aetiology model is an essential component of the revised *eclectic fraud detection model* (see Figure 4, Chapter 7). The fraud-detection model depicted in Figure 4 informs auditors that: particular fraud-prone industries are characterised by five different types of irregularities; that particular kinds of audit procedure are more likely to identify particular kinds of irregularities, as well as what factors alert auditors to different irregularities in the different industries. This additional knowledge enables the model developed in Chapter 4 to be further refined and makes it more useful to auditors in a more practical way, by providing specific guidance on what to look out for and how to approach it in planning their audit and carrying out a fraud risk assessment.

The research findings should benefit auditors as far as fraud indicators are concerned, and assist them to enhance their audit effectiveness. It is also hoped that the research results reported below can be used to identify ways of detecting, preventing and reducing major fraud within companies more effectively and efficiently than at present.

The next chapter describes the refined models of why people commit fraud and of fraud detection and considers in what sense the present thesis can be said to be making an original contribution to knowledge in the fields concerned.

CHAPTER 7

DISCUSSION OF THE ROP FRAUD MODEL AND THE FRAUD DETECTION MODEL

- A comprehensive model of the aetiology of fraud
- Eclectic fraud detection model
- Future research

Fraudulent activity such as management and employee fraud are examples of irregularities that can have a material impact on the financial statements. Such frauds are very costly for both the entities defrauded and society at large and are also significant for the auditing profession. In Australia, the detection and prevention of irregularities rests with management. This book has argued that the ability to detect fraud is vital to auditors, even though auditors in Australia, England, New Zealand, Canada and the U.S do not have a legal duty to detect irregularities, including fraud, but only to audit with reasonable skill and care. This is because of: (1) the legal liability auditors can face when they fail to detect fraud; and (2) the fact that fraud detection is an important component of the expectation gap and audit beneficiaries want an expanded role for the auditor as society's corporate watchdog. Auditors are under increasing pressure to accept responsibility for detecting material fraud.

Since auditors cannot become experts at fraud detection through audit experience alone, they need to utilise the relevant knowledge about why people commit fraud that is available in such other disciplines as psychology, sociology and criminology. The review of relevant theoretical perspectives and available empirical evidence in those disciplines identified a number of fraud correlates regarding the offender's personality attributes, thus making it possible to talk in terms of fraud-prone individuals, i.e., persons possessing certain personality traits and who are motivated to commit fraud. The notion of fraud-proneness has been lacking in various fraud-detection models put forward to assist auditors in assessing the risk of fraud when planning their audit.

Results reported in this book show that the existence of an opportunity for, and financial pressure on, someone to commit fraud are not enough to account for individual differences in who does or does not commit management or employee fraud. The book has also identified and evaluated a significant amount of knowledge regarding specific ways of improving auditors' ability to detect fraud. This includes being aware of company-level and financial-area-level correlates of fraud-proneness, as well as a broad range of approaches to fraud detection put forward in recent years. It needs to be emphasised in this context that different approaches to fraud detection by auditors are best thought of as supplementing one another.

A DESCRIPTIVE MODEL OF THE AETIOLOGY OF FRAUD (ROP FRAUD MODEL)

The study of 50 major fraud cases prosecuted by the MFG, examined the applicability of the proposed ROP model of the aetiology of fraud (see Chapter 5). The results of the study support the basic premise of the model (see Figure 3) that fraud is generally committed as a result of a combination of factors, namely the existence of a crime-prone person with a motive (P), an opportunity (O) and the possession by such a person of rationalisations (R) that make it possible for him/her to commit the crime once or repeatedly (see Figure 3). The MFG study cast serious doubt on the validity of the Loebbecke et al. (1989) model because it fails to take into account one's rationalisations for committing fraud. The ROP model was revised in the light of the results of the study and highlights the importance of both "situational factors" and "company characteristics" in operationally defining the "opportunity" component of ROP. The MFG study results also confirmed that the "person" component of ROP consists of two inseparable parts, namely "motive" and "crime-prone personality". Finally, the findings obtained confirm the crucial importance of "rationalisations" for fraud to occur.

The profile constructed on the basis of the literature discussion and the results of the MFG study comprises information at two levels: firstly, at a general level, the culprit is likely to be a male first offender, aged 31-45, occupying a position of trust, who needs to solve a financial problem (or, simply, is motivated by greed), often acts alone, breaches that trust and commits a spate of deception offences defrauding a number of victims; secondly, the profile incorporates a taxonomy of offenders that comprises a detailed account of twelve offender typologies. The profile is significantly more detailed than what has been reported by other authors and includes a minority of offenders who are professional predators (see the 'motive' component of Figure 3). The offender profile constructed would be useful to auditors if used in conjunction with other relevant knowledge about fraud risk, such as different industries and financial areas. The profile constructed ought to be used in combination with (1) the knowledge concerning the statistically significant inter-relationships found between offence, offender and victim characteristics; and (2) the eclectic fraud-detection model reported in Chapter 6 (see Figure 4).

The findings obtained show that the *modus operandi* (deceptive action) of serious fraud offenders is very much the same whether they operate in Australia or in the U.S. and that the MFG-prosecuted offenders were very prolific.

Additional issues addressed by the two studies and incorporated in the ROP model

Reflecting on the importance of opportunity, most (94%) of the offenders victimised someone they knew. The fact that approximately one-third of the offenders had a criminal record (that was especially the case with managing directors) points to the importance of careful screening of applicants for positions of financial trust, including background checks, in order to reduce the risk of fraud victimisation (see "Company characteristics" in Figure 3).

The finding that about one-third of the offenders had accomplices means that for such offenders the decision to commit fraud follows a group discussion, a very important factor not previously discussed by other authors in this area, a factor catered for in the ROP model (see "Company Characteristics" part of the "Opportunity" component of Figure 3). In a sense, the availability of one or more other crime - prone person(s) can be considered an opportunity to collude in order to perpetrate fraud by, for example, beating the internal control system.

The findings from the survey of auditors support the general profile of a fraud offender constructed on the basis of the MFG study, but also emphasise the importance of a person having a vice/motivation, such as gambling, as an indicator of their being a fraud risk. The results of the survey do not support Loebbecke et al.'s (1989) assertion that all three of their model's components (conditions, motives and attitudes) must be present for management fraud to occur. In the light of the evidence, it can be concluded that the ROP model is more likely to be useful to auditors, as it makes good the deficits in Loebbecke et al.'s model.

Contrary to what Gottfredson and Hirschi's (1990) *General Theory of Crime* predicts, most major fraud offenders were not immersed in crime in the sense of being recidivist career offenders. The offenders surveyed can, however, be said to support Gottfredson and Hirschi's theory to some extent in so far as they evidenced low self-control and exploited opportunities available to them. The MFG study indicates that a diversity of people commit fraud for a variety of reasons and in different circumstances, and who the offenders are is not random. In other words, the offenders studied comprise a number of typologies of major fraud offenders, many of whom experienced situational pressures (e.g., high personal debts, financial losses) and who rationalised their offending to make it acceptable to them, and thus to continue to perceive themselves as successful professionals in their fields. Also, it should not be forgotten that solicitors, accountants and bank managers, to name but a few, operate in an occupational culture that values wealth and corporate success, considers failure quite unacceptable and at the same time provides opportunities for major fraud.

The ROP model sets out the different ways in which fraud becomes possible. These are: when a crime-prone individual under financial pressure or with other motives, perceives at least one opportunity to commit fraud; when the individual has both the knowledge to commit the crime (alone or in collusion) and to conceal the fraud; and, finally, the individual possesses the rationalisations needed to justify to him/herself committing the offence once or repeatedly. The need to locate the three components of ROP in a broader socioeconomic context is emphasised. Rationalisations constitute by far the most vital of the three components that make up the psychological process of information processing and decision making that precedes an act of fraud. The model's eight assumptions listed in Chapter 4 were borne out by the MFG study.

It is acknowledged earlier on in this book that the methodology used in the MFG and the survey of auditors has its limitations. These limitations include the fact that the offenders' rationalisations were studied after the offenders were apprehended by the police and convicted by the courts. It is therefore, not certain whether the same rationalisations existed before the offences in question or whether they could be used to predict fraud. Also the fact that some types of irregularities plagued one type of industry rather than another may well be due to some industries (e.g., manufacturing) having more companies.

Without ignoring the limitations of the two studies, the findings show that it is no longer justifiable to talk about major fraud offenders as a homogeneous population and emphasise the need to desegregate sub-categories of such offenders. The MFG offenders surveyed made many decisions, both about their everyday life, their business activities, about who and how to deceive in order to obtain money and whether to act alone or with one or more accomplices. More specifically, for the majority of them who are not professional conmen, there is the original decision to solve their financial problem by committing fraud, but there is also the decision to continue committing fraud or to desist.

Whether the sentences imposed by the higher courts on such offenders serve the purpose of individual and/or general deterrence is impossible to say on the basis of the studies carried out. However, examination of voluntary statements made to the police by the offenders concerned indicates the following: a term of imprisonment of five years or less is unlikely to be a deterrent because they fancy their chances of not being apprehended; if charged, they believe they "can beat the charges" against them and, even if they are incarcerated, they know they would be unlikely to serve their full sentence. Without a subjective perception by serious fraud offenders that (1) there is a high risk of being detected, prosecuted and convicted; and (2) that the likely penalty upon conviction will be severe enough, deterrence becomes a questionable moral justification at the sentencing stage.

ECLECTIC FRAUD DETECTION MODEL

In support of similar conclusions reached on the basis of the findings from the survey of auditors reported in Chapter 6, the findings obtained in the Major Fraud Group study suggest that auditors played but a rather limited role in the detection of the frauds involved. The fraud detection model, which includes the ROP model as one of its components (see Figure 4), shows how auditors can improve their fraud detection ability. Given that most frauds involve financial pressure on an individual and that factor plays such an important part in contributing to fraud taking place, a simple income-expenditure assessment of professional people in positions of trust should help to identify potential/actual major frauds. Future research should also consider fraud in a variety of officially-known and self-reported offenders in order to identify the factors that best explain their specific nature and prevalence. There is a need to desegregate fraud in order to be able to integrate information about individual offenders, their modus operandi and clues in their "distorted stories", as well as to assist auditors to narrow their search for major fraud offenders and to detect fraud.

It is not claimed that, armed with the criminal profiling results obtained, auditors can identify an offender and significantly increase their fraud-detection efficiency. This is simply because, on the basis of existing knowledge in this area, it is just not possible to predict accurately who in a company will commit or has been committing fraud. What the ROP model can do is to increase an auditor's sensitivity to fraud-risk and focus his/her attention on persons who are potential fraud risks.

The survey of Australian auditors' experience in detecting material irregularities including fraud found that for auditors encountering material irregularities is a rare event and that the use of red flags is not particularly helpful on its own. Therefore, auditors cannot rely on red flags or audit experience alone in their endeavours to improve their fraud detection effectiveness. It is hoped that the eclectic fraud detection model constructed will go some way towards enhancing auditors' fraud-detection ability.

The irregularities about which the respondents answered questions put to them were important, since 39.7% involved management fraud, the kind of fraud most likely to land auditors in costly litigation suits in the courts. The survey of auditors has added a new dimension to fraud-risk assessment by: (1) reporting patterns in statically significant relationships between different industries, different irregularities, different ways auditors were alerted, and different audit procedures that appear to detect such irregularities; and (2) identifying two significant correlates (absence of an effective system of internal control and a code of conduct) of an irregularity having a material impact on the financial accounts of a company. Furthermore, the research reported in Chapter 6 is the first time such issues have been addressed with reference to four kinds of irregularities, namely other illegal acts, other acts, intentional non-fraudulent misstatements and errors.

The eclectic fraud detection model was supported by the findings of the survey. The results of the survey were used to revise the model and make it even more useful to auditors by showing that fraud-risk assessment has to be multifaceted if it is to achieve its objective. As in the cases of the profile of the major fraud offender, the fraud-detection model weaves together features and patterns identified at different levels. These levels are: the economic environment, the particular industry, the company, particular financial areas within the company and particular individuals holding positions of financial trust where they can effect fraud. Hence, the ROP model is an essential component of the fraud detection model. The survey of auditors indicates that, unlike their counterparts in the U.S., auditors in Australia appear to be less vigilant at the planning stage and too often fail to be alerted by one or more red flags to the existence of a material irregularity. The survey findings also highlight the crucial importance of auditors not ceasing to be vigilant however long they have been auditing a company's books.

The fraud detection model constructed also highlights the importance of having a competent, ethically-minded auditor, who is well versed in the aetiology of fraud, in management deception strategies and counter deception strategies, and who enjoys the full support of his/her firm as far as fraud detection is concerned. Additionally, an auditor should: have a good bird's eye view of the company's environment and internal control system, be alert to information about both individuals within the company who are high risks of potential fraud and the company's relationship with outside parties. Finally, the auditor should be aware of and guard against his/her own unintentional biases in carrying out the audit.

Without ignoring its limitations, what the research reported in Chapters 5 and 6 can do is to increase the fraud awareness of auditors. Together with empirically obtained knowledge about other sets of red flags pointing to vulnerable types of industries/companies as well as vulnerable areas within particular types of industries/companies, the red flags inherent in the ROP model provided above can at best be used to alert an auditor to a greater likelihood of fraud and thus negate an auditor's sense of complacency.

FUTURE RESEARCH

Future research should, explore further the patterns identified between offence, offender, victim and criminal justice characteristics with a larger sample of such offenders, including self-reported (as opposed to officially-known) fraud offenders, in order to replicate the two-component criminal profile of a fraud offender reported above. It could also examine the applicability of the two models with a larger and more representative sample of management and employee fraud cases and auditors respectively and test experimentally the use by auditors of red flags contained in the fraud-detection model proposed in Chapter 6. This could help ascertain the actual usefulness of the two proposed models to auditors in detecting fraud. Another approach would be to utilise interviews with fraud offenders to shed some light on the various decisions that are necessary for fraud to occur. Finally, there is a need to replicate the MFG findings by measuring fraud offenders' level of self control using the instrument developed by Grasmick et al. (1993).

No single book can ask all the relevant questions, let alone provide satisfactory answers to them. The author hopes the research contained in this thesis provides some much-needed answers to two basic but important contemporary issues/questions for auditors, namely why people commit management and employee fraud and how auditors can become better at detecting such fraudulent activity.

Figure 3 Level 2: Detailed Account of the Descriptive Model of Fraud Aetiology (ROP Risk Assessment Model)

In addition to the content information in Figure 1 Level 2 outlined in Chapter 4, the following aetiological details have been added in the light of the results reported in Chapter 5

Situational Factors:

- The existence of gullible people willing to trust strangers with their money.

Company Characteristics

- Inadequate screening of applicants for management positions.

Motive(s)

- To restore social identity.
- A professional conman, with or without disguised identity

Crime-Prone Personality

- Authoritarian;
- Inability to postpone gratification; and
- A strong sense of entitlement to whatever one can get by deceiving others.

Rationalisation

- I am entitled to whatever money I can get;
- Deceiving is what I do for a living;
- Others do it too;
- I, too have a right to enjoy my life;
- I just need the money, there is no other way;
- I can get away with it; and
- It is OK to borrow from clients' accounts because they do not really need the money.

Figure 4 Level 2- ***Eclectic Fraud Detection Model***

In addition to the content information in Figure 2 Level 2 outlined in Chapter 4 the following pertinent details have been added in the light of the results in Chapter 6.

Audit Firm

- Utilise forensic accountants and fraud auditors.

Auditor

- Should be on the lookout for fraud indicators throughout the audit.
- Should not lower audit vigilance despite being on the same audit team for the same client for more than three years.

Fraud - risk information

- Difficult to audit transactions.
- In planning the audit and carrying out a fraud-risk assessment to be aware that: different material irregularities are more likely to be encountered in particular industries and audit areas; auditors are alerted in different ways about different irregularities; and different audit procedures are more likely to be detected different irregularities.

BIBLIOGRAPHY

A climate for fraud? (1996). *Charter, 67*(10), 9.

Albrecht, W.S., & Romney, M.B. (1986). Red-flagging management fraud: A validation. *Advances in Accounting, 3*, 323-333.

Albrecht, W.S., Romney, M.B., Cherrington, D.J., Payne, I.R., & Roe, A.J. (1982). *How to Detect and Prevent Business Fraud.* New Jersey: Prentice Hall inc.

Albrecht, W.S., Wernz, G.W., & Williams, T.L. (1995). *Fraud, Bringing Light to the Dark Side of Business*. United States:Richard D. Irwin.

Allsopp, J.F., & Feldman, M.P. (1974). Extraversion, neuroticism, psychoticism and antisocial behavior in schoolgirls. *Social Behavior and Personality, 2*, 184-190.

American Institute of Certified Public Accountants (AICPA) (1987). *Report of the National Commission on Fraudulent Financial Reporting (Treadway Commission)*. New York: AICPA.

American Institute of Certified Public Accountants (AICPA) (1978). *The Commission on Auditors' Responsibilities: Report, Conclusions and Recommendations* (Cohen Commission). New York: AICPA.

American Institute of Certified Public Accountants, Auditing Standards Board (1997). *Statement on Auditing Standards, SAS 82: Consideration of fraud in a financial statement audit*. New York: AICPA

American Institute of Certified Public Accountants, Auditing Standards Board (1988). *Statement of Auditing Standards, No.53: The auditor's responsibility to detect and report errors and irregularities*. New York: AICPA.

Anderson, U., & Marchant, G. (1989). Auditor's assessment of the competence and integrity of auditee personnel. *Auditing: A Journal of Practice and Theory, 8* (Supplement), 1-16.

Aronson, E., & Mettee, D.R. (1968). Dishonest behavior as a function of differential levels of individual self-esteem. *Journal of Personality and Social Psychology, 9*, 121-127.

Arthur A. (1995). Pre-emptive fraud investigations and the audit function. *The Journal of Applied Accounting Research, 2* (II), 21-49.

Ashton, A.H. (1991). Experience and error frequency knowledge as potential determinants of audit expertise. *The Accounting Review*, *66*(2), 218-239.

Association of Certified Fraud Examiners (ACFE) (1994). *Certified Fraud Examiners Manual*, Vol *I,II*, Austin, Texas:ACFE

Auditing Practices Board (1995). *Statement of Auditing Standard, SAS 110: Fraud and error*. London: Institute of Chartered Accountants of England and Wales.

Auditing Practices Board (1992). *The Future Direction of Auditing- A Paper to Promote Public Debate*. Auditing Practices Board, London.

Australian Accounting Research Foundation, Auditing Standards Board (AuSB) (1995a). *Auditing Standard AUS 210: Irregularities, including fraud, other illegal acts and errors*. Caulfield, Vic: Australian Accounting Research Foundation.

Australian Accounting Research Foundation, Auditing Standards Board (AuSB) (1995b). *Auditing Standard AUS 402: Risk assessments and internal controls*. Caufield, Vic: Australian Accounting Research Foundation.

Australian Accounting Research Foundation, Auditing Standards Board (AuSB) (1995c). *Auditing Standard AUS304: Knowledge of the business*. Caulfield, Vic: Australian Accounting Research Foundation.

Australian Accounting Research Foundation, Auditing Standards Board (AuSB) (1993). *Statement of Auditing Practice AUP16: The auditor's responsibility for detecting and reporting irregularities including fraud, other illegal acts and error*. Caulfield, Vic: Australian Accounting Research Foundation.

Australian Bureau of Statistics, (1993), *Australian and New Zealand Standard Industrial Classification*, Canberra: Author.

Australian Society of Certified Practising Accountants and The Institute of Chartered Accountants in Australia, Task Force (1996). *Beyond the Gap*. Sydney: ASCPA/ICAA.

Australian Society of Certified Practising Accountants and The Institute of Chartered Accountants in Australia, Working Party (1994). *A research study on financial reporting and auditing- Bridging the expectation gap*. Sydney: ASCPA / ICAA

Bandura, A. (1989). Human agency in social cognitive theory. *American Psychologist*, *29*, 859-869.

Barnes, H.E., & Teeters, N.K. (1959). *New Horizons in Criminology* (3rd ed.). Englewood Cliffs, N.J: Prentice Hall.

Bartol, C.R., & Bartol, A.M. (1994). *Psychology and Law: Theory and Practice*. Pacific Grove, CA: Brooks/Cole Publishing.

Bartol, C.R, & Holanchock, H.A. (1979). Eysenck's theory of criminality: A test on an American prisoner population. *Criminal Justice and Behavior*, *6*, 245-249.

Beasley, M.S. (1996). An empirical analysis of the relation between the board of director composition and financial statement fraud. *The Accounting Review*, *71*(4), 443-465.

Beccaria, C. (1963). *On crime and Punishments*. New York: Robbs Merrill.

Bell, T.B., Szykowney, S. & Willingham, J.J. (1991). Assessing the likelihood of fraudulent financial reporting: A cascaded logit approach. Paper presented at the *Conference on Decision Making Cognitive Science And Accounting*. Carnegie Mellon University, Pittsburgh, PA.

Benson, M.L., & Moore, E. (1992). Are white-collar and common offenders the same? an empirical and theoretical critique of a recently proposed general theory of crime. *Journal of Research in Crime and Delinquency*, *29*(3), 251-272.

Bernardi, R.A. (1994a). Fraud detection: The effect of client integrity and competence and auditor cognitive style. *Auditing: A Journal of Practice and Theory*, *13*(2), 68-84.

Bernardi, R.A. (1994b). Reply: Fraud detection: The effect of client integrity and competence and auditor cognitive style. *Auditing: A Journal of Practice and Theory, 13*(2), 97-101.

Blackburn, R. (1993). *The Psychology of Criminal Conduct*. Wiley Series in Clinical Psychology. Liverpool, UK: John Wiley & Sons.

Blau, T.H. (1994). Psychological profiling. In T.H. Blau (Ed.). *Psychological Services for Law Enforcement* (pp.261-274). New York: John Wiley and Sons.

Bologna, G.J. (1993). *Handbook on Corporate Fraud, Prevention, Detection, Investigation*. Stoneham, USA: Butterworth- Heinemann.

Bologna, G.J., & Lindquist, R.J. (1987). *Fraud Auditing and Forensic Accounting,New tools and techniques*. Canada: John Wiley and Co.

Bologna, G.J., Lindquist, R.J., & Wells, J.T. (1993). *The accountants's handbook of fraud and commercial crime*. Canada: John Wiley and Co.

Bonner, S.E., & Pennington, N. (1990). Cognitive processes and knowledge as determinants of auditor expertise. *Journal of Accounting Literature, 10*,1-50.

Bottoms, A.B. (1993). Recent criminological and social theory. In D.P. Farrington,R.J. Sampson & P.O. Wilkstrom (Eds.). *Integrating Individual and Ecological Aspects of Crime* (pp.57-108). National Council for Crime Prevention, Stockholm, Sweden.

Box, S. (1981). *Deviance, Reality and Society* (2nd ed.). London:Holt, Rinehart and Winston.

Braithwaite, J. (1989). *Crime, Shame and Reintegration*. Melbourne, Australia: Cambridge University Press.

Buikhuisen, W., & Hemmel, J.J. (1972). Crime and conditioning. *British Journal of Criminology, 12*,147-157.

Cadbury Committee (1992). *Report of the Committee on the Financial Aspects of Corporate Governance*, December, London.

Canadian Institute of Chartered Accountants Auditing Standards Committee (1994). *Auditing Recommendations Section 5135: Auditor's responsibility to detect and communicate misstatements*, Toronto: CICA.

Canadian Institute of Chartered Accountants (1988). *Report of the Commission to Study the Public's Expectations of Audits, (Macdonald Commission)*. Toronto: CICA.

Canter, D. (1995). Psychology of Offender Profiling. In R. Bull & D. Carson (Eds.), *Handbook of Psychology in Legal Contexts* (pp.343-55). Chichester:John Wiley and Sons.

Canter, D. (1994). *Criminal shadows: Inside the mind of the serial killer*. London: Harper Collins.

Carter, L. (2000). And Justice for all – the last word. *Charter, 71*(5): 58-61.

Caspi, A., Moffitt T.E., Silva, P.A., Stouthamer-Loeber, M., Krueger, R.F., & Schmutte P.S. (1994). Are some people crime-prone? replications of the personality-crime relationship across countries, genders, races, and methods. *Criminology*, *32*(2), 163-195.

Chandler, R.A., Edwards, J.R., & Anderson, M. (1993). Changing perceptions of the role of the company auditor, 1840-1940. *Accounting and Business Research*, *23*(92), 443-459.

Clarke, R.V.G., & Mayhew, P. (Eds.). (1980). *Designing Out Crime*. London: HMSO

Clarke, R.V.G. (1980). Situational crime prevention - theory and practice. *British Journal of Criminology*, *20*, 136-147.

Clolery, P. (1993). Fraud investigation: Three CFEs who have cashed in. *The Practical Accountant*, *26*(2), 23.

Cohen, L.E., & Felson, M. (1979). Social change and crime rate trends: A routine activities approach. *American Sociological Review*, *44*,588-608.

Coleman, J.W. (1987). Toward an integrated theory of white-collar crime. *American Journal of Sociology*, *93*(2), 406-439.

Commission on Sponsoring Organizations of the Treadway Commission, COSO (1992). *Internal control: Integrated framework*. Harborside, NJ:AICPA.

Copestake, S. (1994). Shadows people leave. *Forensic Update*, Issue 38,15-17.

Crazy Eddie admits guilt. (1996). *Accountancy*, *118*(1234),17.

Cressey, D.R. (1986). Why managers commit fraud. *Australian and New Zealand Journal of Criminology*, *19*(4),195-209.

Cressey, D.R. (1980). Management fraud, accounting controls, and criminological theory. In R.K. Elliott & J.J. Willingham (Eds.). *Management fraud: Detection and Deterrence* (pp.117-147). Princeton, New York: A Petrocelli Book.

Cressey, D.R. (1953). *A study in the social psychology of embezzlement: Other people's money*. Glencoe, Ill: Free Press.

Davidson, A.S. (1994). Discussion of fraud detection: The effect of client integrity and Competence and auditor cognitive style. *Auditing: A Journal of Practice and Theory*, *13*(2), 85-89.

Deakin University (1994). *Fraud Against Organisations in Victoria, Summary of Findings From a Survey of Medium and Large Organisations in 1994*. Deakin University.

Detection and prevention task force is short-lived. (1994). *The CPA Journal*, *64* (11), 9-11.

Dirkis, M., & Nichol, G. (1996). Corporate and white-collar crime. In Hazlehurst, K. (Ed.). *Crime and Justice: An Australian Textbook in Criminology* (pp. 257-282). Sydney: Law Book Co.

Douglas, J.E. & Burgess, A.E. (1990). Criminal profiling, a viable investigative tool against violent crime. In National Center for the Analysis of Violent Crime (Ed.). *Criminal investigative analysis, sexual homicide* (pp.1-5). U.S. Department of Justice.

Douglas, J.E., Ressler, R.K., Burgess, A.W., & Hartman, C.R. (1986). Criminal profiling from crime scene analysis. *Behavioural Science and Law*,*4*(4),401-421.

Edelhertz, H. (1983). White-collar crime and professional crime. The challenge for the 1980s. *American Behavioral Scientist*, *27*(10), 109-128.

Eisen, M. (1972). Characteristic self-esteem, sex, and resistance to temptation. *Journal of Personality and Social Psychology*, *24*, 68-72.

Elliott, R.K., & Willingham, J.J. (Eds.). (1980). *Management Fraud Detection and Deterrence*. Princeton,New York: A Petrocelli Book.

Entwistle, G., & Lindsay, D. (1994). An archival study of the existence, cause, and discovery of income - affecting financial statement misstatements. *Contemporary Accounting Research*, *11* (1-I), 271-296.

Ernst and Young (2000). Fraud: *The Unmanaged Risk*, Ernst and Young International.

Ernst & Young (1996). *Fraud- the Unmanaged Risk*. Ernst & Young Sydney.

Eyo, I.D. (1981). British delinquets and nondeliquents on seven domains of the self-concept. *Journal of Psychology*, *109*, 37-145.

Eysenck, H.J. (1977). *Crime and personality* (3rd ed.). London:Granada.

Eysenck, S.B.G., & Eysenck, H.J. (1970). Crime and personality: An empirical study of the three-factor theory. *British Journal of Criminology*, *19*, 225-239.

Fama, E.F., & Jensen, M.C. (1983). Separation of ownership and control. *Journal of Law and Economics*, *26* (June), 301-325.

Farrington, D.P. (1993). Have any individual environmental effects been established?. In D.P. Farrington, R.J. Sampson and P.O. Wilkstrom (Eds.). *Integrating Individual and Ecological Aspects of Crime* (pp.7-38). National Council for Crime Prevention, Stockholfm Sweden.

Farrington, D.P. (1979). Environmental stress, delinquent behaviour, and convictions. In I.G. Sarason & C.D. Spielberger (Eds.). *Understanding Stress and Anxiety*, *6* (pp.93-107). Washington: Hemishphere.

Farrington, D.P., Biron, L., & Le Blanc, M. (1982). Personality and delinquencyin London and Montreal. In J. Gumm & D.P. Farrington (Eds.). *Abnormal Offenders, Delinquency, and the Criminal Justice System* (pp.153-203) Chichester, New York: Wiley.

Feldman, P. (1993). *The Psychology of Crime, a Social Science Textbook*. New York: Cambridge University Press.

Fraud Fears. (1997). *Charter*, *68*(3), 13.

Fridson, M.S. (1996) *Financial Statement Analysis*, 2nd edition, New York: John Wiley.

Geis, G. (1991). White-collar crime what is it?. *Current Issues in Criminal Justice, 3*(1), 9-24.

Gibbons D.C. (1975). Offender typologies- two decades later. *British Journal of Criminology*, 15(2), 140-156.

Gill, G.S., & Cosserat, G.W. (1996). *Modern Auditing in Australia* (4th ed.). Queensland: John Wiley & Sons.

Glover, E. (1960). *The Roots of Crime*. London: Imago

Godsell, D. (1990). *Auditors' Legal Duties and Liabilities in Australia,* Monograph 2, Melbourne: AARF.

Gottfredson, M.R., & Hirschi, T. (1990). *A General Theory of Crime*. Stanford, California: Stanford University Press.

Grabosky, P.N. & Smith, R.G. (1996). Fraud: an overview of current and emerging risks. *Australian Institute of Criminology Trends and Issues in Crime and criminal Justice, 62*. Canberra: Australian Institute of Criminology.

Grasmick, H.G., Tittle, C.R., Bursik, R.J. & Arneklev B.J. (1993). Testing the core empirical implications of Gottfredson and Hirschi's general theory of crime. *Journal of Research in Crime and Delinquency, 30*(1), 5-29.

Hackenbrack, K. (1993). The effect of experience with different sized clients on auditor evaluations of fraudulent financial reporting indicators. *Auditing:A Journal of Practice and Theory, 12*(1), 99-109.

Hagaman, J., Wells, G., Blau, T. & Wells, C. (1987). Psychological profile of a family homicide. *The Police Chief, 54*(12), 19-23.

Hare, R.D. (1991). *The Hare Psychopathy Checklist* (revised). Toronto: Multi-Health System.

Hirschi, T.R. (1969). *Causes of Delinquency*, Berkeley: University of California Press.

Hirschi, T.R., & Gottfredson, M. (1988). Towards a general theory of crime. In W. Buikuisen & S.A. Mednick (Eds.). *Explaining Criminal Behaviour* (pp.8-26). Leiden: Brill.

Hough, M., Clarke R.V.G., & Mayhew P. (1980). Introduction. In R.V.G. Clarke & P. Mayhew (Eds.). *Designing out Crime* (pp.1-19). London: HMSO.

Howells, K. (1978). The meaning of poisoning to a person diagnosed as a psychopath. *Medicine, Science and the Law, 18*, 179-184.

Humphrey, C., Turley, W.S., & Moizer, P. (1993). Protecting against detection: The case of auditors and fraud? *Accounting, Auditing and Accountability Journal, 6*(1), 39-62.

Humphrey, C., Moizer, P., & Turley, W.S. (1992). *The Audit Expectations Gap in the United Kingdom*. London: ICAEW.

Huntington, I., & Davies, D. (1995). *Fraud Watch: A Guide for Business*. London: KPMG Accountancy Books.

Institute of Chartered Accountants in England and Wales (1985). *Report of the Working Party on the Future of the Audit* (Benson Report). London: ICAEW.

International Federation of Accountants, Public Sector Committee (2000). Exposure Draft to replace *ISA 240: The auditor's responsibility to consider fraud and error in an audit of financial statements*. New York: IFAC.

International Federation of Accountants, Public Sector Committee (1995). *ISA 240: Fraud and error*. New York: IFAC.

Jackson, J.L. & Bekerian, D.A. (1997). Does offender profiling have a role to play? In (Eds.) Jackson J.L. and Bekerian D.A. *Offender Profiling: Theory, Research and Practice*, (1-7). Winchester: Wiley.

Jamal, K. (1991). *Detecting Framing Effects in Audit Judgement*. Unpublished Doctoral Dissertation, University of Minnesota.

Jamal, K., Johnson, P.E., & Berryman, R.G. (1995). Detecting framing effects in financial statements. *Contemporary Accounting Research*, *12*(1), 85-105.

Johnson, P.E., Grazioli, S., & Jamal, K. (1993). Fraud detection: Intentionality and deception in cognition. *Accounting, Organizations and Society*, *18*(5),467-488.

Johnson, P.E., Grazioli, S., Jamal, K., & Zualkernan, I.A. (1992). Success and failure in expert reasoning. *Organizational Behavior and Human decision Process*, *53*, 173-203.

Johnson, P.E., Jamal, K., & Berryman, R.G. (1991). Effects of framing on auditor decisions. *Organizational Behavior and Human Decision Processes*, *50*, 75-105.

Jones, J.J., & Maher, M.W. (1987). *Characteristics of Companies Investigated by the SEC for Fraudulent Financial Reporting*. Unpublished working paper, University of Michigan, January.

Judd, C.M., Smith, E.R., & Kidder, L.H. (1991). *Research Methods in Social Relations*. Sixth edition. United States of America: Hartcourt Brace Jovanich.

Kahneman, D., & Tversky, A. (1986). Choices, values and frames. In H.R. Arkes, & K.R. Hammond (Eds.). *Judgement and Decision Making: An Interdisciplinary Reader* (pp.194-210). Cambridge: Cambridge University Press.

Kaplan, H.B. (1980). *Deviant Behavior in Defence of self*. New York: Pergamon.

Kaplan, S.E., & Reekers P.M.J. (1984). An empirical examination of auditors' initial planning process. *Auditing: A Journal of Practice and Theory*, *3*(2), 1-19.

Katz, J. (1978). Legality and equality: plea bargaining in the prosecution of white-collar and common crimes. *Law and Society Review*, *13*(2), 431-459.

Knox, J. (1994). Why auditors don't find fraud. *Accountancy*, *113*(1206), 128.

Korn, R.R., & McCorkle, L.W. (1959). *Criminology and Penelogy*. New York: Holt.

KPMG (1999). *Fraud Survey. Sydney, Australia: KPMG Forensic Accounting*

KPMG (1996). *International Fraud Report*. Amsterdam, Netherlands:KPMG International Headquarters.

KPMG (1995a). *Fraud Survey*. Sydney, Australia: KPMG Forensic Accounting.

KPMG (1995b). *Fraud Survey Report Executive Briefing*, May, Toronto, Canada: KPMG CA.

KPMG (1993a). *International Fraud Report*. Toronto, Canada: KPMG Forensic Accounting.

KPMG (1993b). *Fraud Survey Results*. New York: KPMG Peat Marwick.

Krambia-Kapardis M. (2000). Enhancing the Auditor's Fraud Detection Ability: An Interdisciplinary Approach. Unpublished Doctoral Dissertation. Faculty of Business, Edith Cowan University , Western Australia.

Langdale, R. (1990). *Case Studies in Corporate Crime*. Sydney, Australia: NSW Bureau of Crime Statistics and Research.

Levi, M. (1987). *Regulating Fraud, White - Collar Crime and the Criminal Process.* London: Tavistock Publications.

Loebbecke, J.K., Einning, M.M., & Willingham, J.J. (1989). Auditors' experience with material irregularities: Frequency, nature, and detectability. *Auditing: A Journal of Practice and Theory*, *9*(1),1-28.

Loebbecke, J.K., & Willingham, J.J. (1988). Review of SEC Accounting and Auditing Enforcement Releases. Unpublished paper.

Loisel, E.L.D. (1996). *Minimising Employee Theft in Contemporary Victoria, Australia,* Unpublished Master of Arts Dissertation, Department of Criminology, University of Melbourne.

Longshore, D.R., Stein, J.A. & Turner S. (1998). Reliability and Validity of a Self-Control Measure: Rejoinder. *Criminology, 36*(1):175-182.

Maddi, S.R. (1980). *Personality Theories: A Comparative Analysis*. Homewood III, Dorsey Press.

Marshall, B.R., Albrecht, W.S., & Cherrington, D.J. (1980). Red-flagging the white-collar criminal. *Management Accounting, 61*(9), 51-57.

Matsumara, E.M., & Tucker, R.R. (1992). Fraud detection: A theoretical foundation. *The Accounting Review, 67*(4), 753-782.

Matza, D. (1969). *Becoming Deviant*. New Jersey: Prentice Hall.

Mayhew, P., Clarke, R.V.G., & Hough, J.M. (1980). Steering column locks and car theft. In R.V.G. Clarke & P. Mayhew (Eds.). *Designing out crime* (pp.19-31). London: HMSO.

McCord, J. (1979). Some childrearing antecedents of criminal behavior in adult men. *Journal of Personality and Social Psychology, 37*, 1477-1486.

McCullogh, W.M. (1949). Embezzlement, a rising menace. *The California Accountant, 2*, 7-13.

McCusker, M.J. (1990). *Report of Inspector on a Special Investigation into Rothwells, Pursuant to Companies Code (WA)*, Part VII, Part 1. Wembley, WA: Government printer.

Monroe, G.S., Ng, J.K.L., & Woodliff, D.R. (1993). The importance of inherent risk factors. *Australian Accounting Review, 3*(2), 34-46.

Monroe, G.S., & Woodliff, D.R. (1994). Great expectations; Public perceptions of the auditor's role. *Australian Accounting Review*, *4*(2),42-53.

Moses, C.A. & Kalton, G. (1981). *Survey methods in social investigation*. London: Heinemann Educational Books Ltd.

National Companies Securities Commission, NCSC (1988-1989). *Tenth annual report*, Melbourne: NCSC, Government Printers.

National Joint Limitation of Liability Task Force of the Institute of Chartered Accountants in Australia and the Australian Society of Certified Practising Accountants, (1994). *Inquiry into the law of joint and several liability, established by the federal attorney-general and the NSW attorney-general*. Sydney: ICAA

New Zealand Society of Accountants (1986). *Auditing Guideline AG 9: Fraud and error*. New Zealand: NZSA.

Palmrose, Z.V. (1987). Litigation and independent auditors: The role of business failures and management fraud. *Auditing: A Journal of Practice and Theory*, *6*(1): 90-103.

Pheasant, B. (1997, May 8). Quinn jailed four years for fraud. *Australian Financial Review*, pp.1, 8.

Pincus, K.V. (1994). Discussion on fraud detection: The effect of client integrity and competence and auditor cognitive style. *Auditing: A Journal of Practice and Theory*. 13(2), 90-96.

Pincus, K.V. (1990). Auditor individual differences and fairness of presentation judgments. *Auditing: A Journal of Practice and Theory*, *9*(2), 150-166.

Pincus, K.V. (1989). The efficacy of a red flags questionnaire for assessing the possibility of fraud. *Accounting, Organizations and Society*, *14*(1/2), 153-163.

Piquero, A.R. & Rosay, A.B. (1998). The reliability and validity of Grasmick et al. self-control scale: a comment on Longshore et al. *Criminology*, *36*(1):157-173.

Pollak, O. (1950). *The Criminality of Women*. New York: Barnes.

Porter, B.A. (1993). An empirical study of the audit expectation-performance gap, *Accounting and Business Research*, *24*(93), 49-78.

Porter, B.A. (1990, July). *The audit expectation-performance gap- an empirical investigation*, AAANZ Conference. Perth, Australia.

Porter, B.A. (1988). *Towards a theory of the role of the external auditor in society'*, Research Monograph No.1., New Zealand: Accountancy Department, Massey University.

Price Waterhouse. (1985). *Challenge and Opportunity for the Accounting Profession: Strengthening the Public's Confidence*. New York: Author.

Public Oversight Board of the SEC Practice Section, AICPA (1993). *In the Public Interest-Issues Confronting the Accounting profession*. POB Report, Stamford.

Purvis, S.E.C. (1987). *The Impact of Documentation Format on Auditor's Preliminary Evaluation of Internal Accounting Control*, Center for Accounting Research, University of Southern California, Working Paper, January.

Reckless, W.C. (1961). *The Crime Problem* (3rd ed.). New York: Appleton-Century- Crofts.

Reckless, W.C., & Dinitz, S. (1967). Pioneering with self-concept as a vulnerability factor in deliquency. *Journal of Criminal Law, Criminology and Police Science, 58*, 515-523.

Reese, J. (1979, August). Obsessive-compulsive behaviour: The nuisance offender. FBI Law Enforcement Bulletin, 48.

Richman, C., Brown, K., & Clark, M. (1984). The relationship between self-esteem and maladaptive behaviors in high school students. *Social Behavior and Personality, 12*, 77-185.

Robertson, J.C. (1996). *Auditing* (8th ed.). USA: Irwin Book Team

Ross, E.A. (1977). The criminaloid. In G. Geis & R.F. Meir, (Eds.) *White - Collar Crime Offences in Business, Politics, and the Professions* (revised edition), (pp.29-37). London:Collier MacMillan Publishers.

Rothwells fraud pair jailed four years. (1996, December 17). *Australian Financial Review*, p.3.

Rothwells officers guilty of fraud. (1996, November 27). *Australian Financial Review*, p.5.

Royal Commission of *Inquiry into the Activities of the Nugan Hand Group* (June 1985). Parliamentary paper 368/1985 Vols 1 and 2 Final. Canberra: Australian Government Publishing Service.

Sadgrove, K. (1996). *The Complete Guide to Business Risk Management*. Hampshire: Gower.

Schilit, H.M. (1993). Financial Shenanigans. *How to detect accounting gimmicks and fraud in financial reports*. : Boston: McGraw Hill.

Schrag, C.C. (1961). A Preliminary Criminal Typology. *Pacific Sociological Review*, Spring, 11-16.

Sender, J.W., & Moray, N.P. (1991). *Human error: Cause, prediction and reduction*, Hillsdale, NJ: Eribaum.

Settled Claims. (1995, January 2). *The Age*, p.13.

Shaub, M.K. & Lawrence, J.E. (1996). Ethics, Experience, Professional scepticism: a situational analysis. *Behavioral Reasearch in Accounting,8*:124-157.

Sorensen, J.E., & Sorensen, T.L. (1980). Detecting management fraud: Some organizational strategies for the independent auditor. In R.K. Elliott, & J.J. Willingham (Eds.). *Management Fraud: Detection and Deterrence* (pp.195-206). Princeton, New York: Petrocceli Books.

Sorensen, J.E., Grove, H., & Selton F. (1983). Detecting management fraud: An empirical approach. In *Symposium on Auditing Research 1982* (Department of Accountancy, University of Illlinois at Urbana-Champaign.

Spark, J. (1994, June). *Fraud and business $$ everyone's concern*. Institute of Chartered Accountants of Australia, PD Forum, Melbourne.

Sullivan, J. (1993). *The value of audit research to practice: Past, present and future*. Invited paper, University of Southern California Audit Judgement Symposium.

Sutherland, E.H. (1949). *White Collar Crime*. New York: Dryden.

Sutherland, E.H. (1939). *Principles of criminology* (3rd ed). Philadelphia: Lippincott.

Sutherland, E.H., & Cressey, D.R. (1970). *Criminology* (8th ed). New York: Lippincott.

Sykes, T. (1996, February 28). Australia: Connell-gone but not forgotten. *Australian Financial Review*, p.1.

Tajfel, H., & Turner, J. (1986). The social identity theory of intergroup behavior. In S. Worchel & W. Austin (Eds.). *Psychology of Intergroup Relations* (pp.7-24). Chicago: Nelson-Hall.

Taylor, I., Walton, P., & Young, J. (1973). *The New Criminology: For a Social Theory of Deviance*. New York: Harper and Row.

Tetem, H. (1989). Offender profiling. In W. Bailey (Ed.), *The Encyclopedia of Police Science*. New York: Garland Publishing.

Thomas, D. (1979). *Principles of Sentencing*. London: Heinemann.

Thomas, P. (1992). Fraud offenders and psychological treatment. In I. Freckelton, A.Knowles & J. Mulvany (Eds.). *Current Controversies in Psychiatry, Psychology and Law* (pp.123-128). Melbourne.

Thornhill, W.T. (1995). *Forensic Accounting*. United States: Irwin.

Touche Ross (1976). *Management Involvement in Material Transactions* (rev. ed.). United States: Touch Ross.

Turco, R.N. (1990). Psychological profiling. *International Journal of Offender Therapy and Comparative Criminology*, *34*(2), 147-154.

Turner, J.I. (1980). Classifying acts of fraud. In R.K. Elliott & J.J. Willingham, (Eds.). *Management Fraud: Detection and Deterrence* (pp.95-106) Princeton, New York: Petrocelli Books.

Uretsky, M. (1980). An interdisciplianry approach to the study of management fraud, In R.K. Elliott & J.J. Willingham (Eds.). *Management Fraud: Detection and Deterrence* (pp.89-94). Princeton, New York: Petrocelli Books.

Virta, E. (2000). The overlapping fields of white-collar and conventional crime. Paper presented at British society of Criminology Conference. University of Leicester, England 5-7 July 2000.

Vivian, J., & Brown, R. (1995). Prejudice and intergroup conflict. In M. Argyle & A.M. Colman (Eds.). *Social Psychology* (pp.57-77). London: Longman.

Walker, N.D. (1987). *Crime and Criminology: A Critical Introduction*. Oxford: Oxford University Press.

Walker, N.D. (1980). *Punishment, Danger, and Stigma. The morality of Criminal Justice*. Oxford: Blackwell

Walker, N.D. (1977). *Behaviour and Misbehaviour, Explanations and Non-Explanations*. London: Basil Blackwell.

Wallace, W. (1983). Detecting management fraud: An empirical approach - a critique. In *Symposium on Auditing Research* 1982, (Department of Accountancy, University of Illinois at Urbana Champaign).

Watson, D., & Clark, L.A. (1984). Negative affectivity: The dispositon to experience aversive emotional states. *Psychological Bulletin, 96*, 465-490.

Weisburd, D., Chayet, E.F., & Waring, E.J. (1990). White-collar crime and criminal careers: Some preliminary Findings. *Crime and Delinquency, 36*(3), 342-355.

Wells, J.T. (1993). Accountancy and white-collar crime. *ANNALS of the American Academy of Political and Social Science, 525*, 83-94.

Wells, L.E. (1978). Theories of deviance and the self concept. *Social Psychology, 41*, 189-204.

Wheeler, S., Weisburd, D., & Bode, N. (1982). Sentencing the white-collar offender: Rhetoric and reality. *American Sociological Review, 47*(5),641-659).

Wheeler, S., Weisburd, D., Waring, E., & Bode, N. (1988). White collar crimes and criminals. *American Criminal Law Review, 25*, 331-357.

Williams III, F.P & McShane, M.D (2000). Criminological Theory (3rd edition). NJ: Prentice Hall.

Williams, K.S. (1991). *Textbook on Criminology*. London: Blackstone Press.

Worden, A.P. (1993). The attitudes of men and women in policing: Testing conventional and contemporary wisdom. *Criminology, 31*,203-241.

Yamamura, J.H., Frakes, A.H., Sanders, D.L. & Ahn S.K. (1996). A comparison of Japanese and U.S. auditor decision - making behavior. *The International Journal of Accounting, 31*(3), 347-363.

Zietz, D. (1981). *Women who Embezzle or Defraud.* New York: Praeger Publishers.